Administrative Justice

Administrative Justice

ADVOCACY AND CHANGE IN
A GOVERNMENT AGENCY

Philippe Nonet

RUSSELL SAGE FOUNDATION · NEW YORK
1969

RUSSELL SAGE FOUNDATION was established in 1907 for the improvement of social and living conditions in the United States. In carrying out its purpose the Foundation conducts research under the direction of members of the staff or in close collaboration with other institutions, and supports programs designed to improve the utilization of social science knowledge. As an integral part of its operations, the Foundation from time to time publishes books or pamphlets resulting from these activities. Publication under the imprint of the Foundation does not necessarily imply agreement by the Foundation, its Trustees, or its staff with the interpretations or conclusions of the authors.

Library of Congress Catalog Card Number: 68–58126

Printed in the United States of America by
Connecticut Printers, Inc., Hartford, Connecticut

Foreword

IN THIS STUDY of the politics of procedure, Philippe Nonet follows the best tradition of the "case study" in social science. He uses quite specialized materials to help develop a theoretical perspective. For most people, including social scientists, the administration of workmen's compensation is not a salient concern. But Professor Nonet understands that, to a very large extent, justice is done and undone in the shadowed places where administrative decisions are made. And he has brought to his study a sociological awareness that casts light on larger issues of contemporary jurisprudence.

Administrative Justice provides fresh data on matters that are of the keenest concern to students of legal institutions: the place of administrative discretion in a law-governed system; the social and legal significance of the adversary principle; legal and civic competence; the relation of law and politics; the quest for an affiirmative approach to law in a world irrevocably committed to positive government. It approaches these issues from the standpoint of the sociology of law, emphasizing the study of law in action and in context; the interplay of social forces and formal systems; the dependence of law on social support; the social dynamics of legal change.

A special feature of this book is the attention it gives to the organizational context of legal decision. In fact, the study belongs as much to the sociology of organizations as it does to the sociology of law. The pertinent and closely related themes are (1) how the "character" of a government agency is transformed—in self-conception, in distinctive competence, in mission and role; (2) the dynamics of institutionalization, that is, the way a new perspective is built into the operating procedures of the agency; and (3) the fate of values in the course of institutionalization. All this, it is shown, takes place in a larger context of social change, especially the increasing capacity of the trade unions to participate in the legal process as advocates and adversaries.

The treatment of values, adaptation, and institutionalization places this work in a peculiar genre—the sociology of the cop-out. A major theme is the erosion of commitment to welfare ideals; and it is argued that the "new" agency, in its role as a court, has seized upon the symbols of adjudication but has shied away from firm procedural standards. There is more than a hint that bolder and more perceptive administrative leadership might have held the agency closer to its original welfare mission. But there is also a sympathetic recognition that the plight of the agency has been mostly due to forces beyond its control. As is so often true in other settings, the political basis for the agency's moral commitment was weak, and in such circumstances the attenuation of goals, the cop-out, is well-nigh inevitable.

Moreover, Nonet is sensitive to the ironies of institutional history. He recognizes that the legalization of workmen's compensation, though it weakened administration and deflected goals, had a redeeming significance. Legalization brought to the disabled worker a greater civic competence and a less paternalistic, more rights-conscious system of administrative justice. In the longer run, full awareness of a specialized court's potential for legal and policy development might go far to fulfill the original promise.

Before he came to Berkeley, Philippe Nonet was a student of law and social science at Liège. This background may have helped him to sense the voluntarist, pragmatic spirit of American law, and the concomitant blurring of public and private spheres. These attributes have helped establish the fidelity of law to the spirit and character of American institutions; but they have also, as often as not, bespoken a pallid leadership and a muted voice. In Nonet's book, this dilemma is searchingly explored.

University of California
Berkeley
October, 1968

PHILIP SELZNICK
Chairman, Center for the Study of Law and Society

Preface

THIS STUDY WOULD not have been possible without the support the Center for the Study of Law and Society, University of California, Berkeley, has given me over the past five years under a grant from the Russell Sage Foundation. A doctoral dissertation grant from the National Science Foundation helped to cover the expenses of field work. To all I am most grateful for the opportunities they provided me.

The Center has offered more than support for my work; it has been a source of encouragement and an exciting place of learning. My warmest thanks go to all the friends and colleagues I found there, especially Jerome Skolnick and Elliot Studt, who, with or without knowing it, contributed much to the ideas I present in this study. Stewart Macaulay and Arthur L. Stinchcombe read the manuscript and gave me the benefit of their critiques. Jerome Carlin participated in the whole study and made many invaluable suggestions. To Sheldon L. Messinger I owe special thanks; I have relied heavily on his criticism and his unlimited ability to suggest new perspectives. Nothing I could say would account for what I owe to my teacher and friend, Philip Selznick; my debt to him is both too deep and too personal.

Mr. Abe F. Levy first introduced me to the problems of workmen's compensation in California. Mr. Thomas N. Saunders, then a member of the California Industrial Accident Commission, welcomed me at the agency and did much to facilitate my inquiry. Mr. George Lane, Referee, Workmen's Compensation Appeals Board, provided invaluable information on the earlier history of the IAC. Mr. Eli P. Welch, Chief of the Permanent Disability Rating Bureau, Division of Industrial Accidents, helped me to get acquainted with compensation issues in their richest details. To them and to the countless informants, IAC staff members, lawyers, union officers, insurance agents, and injured workers, who gave me so much of their time and patience, I want to express my most sincere gratitude.

The book is dedicated to Anne-Marie, my wife. She and the three children who were born while the study was being done did much to sustain an inspiring climate of creativity; in spite of this chaos, she heroically managed to create a home where all of us would find warmth and freedom. Without her art and understanding, this project would not have been possible.

Contents

I Introduction

THIS IS A STUDY of law, politics, and administration. The inquiry began as an effort to look at law in action by studying the history of a government agency to which important dispute-settling, rights-determining functions had been assigned. A branch of the California Department of Industrial Relations, the Industrial Accident Commission (IAC) was responsible for administering state workmen's compensation laws, that is, the legislation governing the liability of employers for injuries occurring to employees in connection with their work. Neither the IAC nor workmen's compensation has attracted much public or scholarly attention. Yet their creation in the early 1910's marks one of the major innovations of the welfare state, and their history dramatizes problems that have been central concerns of students of law and government.

Briefly, the history of the IAC is a story of the transformation of a welfare agency into a court of law. Designed as an administrative authority, the early commission had a mandate for social action, aimed at improving the welfare of disabled workers by means of relief and rehabilitation. It had broad discretion in making and interpreting its policies, and enjoyed considerable freedom from procedural restraints and judicial review. Fifty years later, the agency has lost most of its early sense of initiative and public mission; it has acquired the outlook of a passive arbitrator, responsible only to those private interests of labor and industry it was originally meant to regulate. The IAC has become a highly self-conscious judicial body, largely removed from the concrete problems of welfare policy and governed by exacting standards of procedure. Its primary function is to hear and decide claims of right under a determinate set of laws.

As the agency changed, its modes of interpreting policy were increasingly legalized. Initially, the workmen's compensation legislation was part of a broad program of social welfare, sharply divorced from the legal context of the employment relation. Although this legislation was developed and implemented by the IAC with considerable energy, it was interpreted in a way that was characteristically unsophisticated and narrow; and it was often enforced with little regard for the rights of affected persons. The history of workmen's compensation is one of growing detachment from public purposes, and progressive incorporation into the private law of employer and employee. Although this legalization revealed a loss of purpose on the part of the IAC, it also reflected an increased responsiveness to the claims of interested constituents and a steady enlargement of their rights. In the process, a set of administrative policies was infused with legal conceptions and took on the character of a body of law.

A striking feature of this evolution was the way it was affected by the changing character and capabilities of those whom workmen's compensation was meant to serve and protect. The early IAC was designed to reach workers who could not be counted upon to act as effective claimants and to bear the burden of promoting their interests. Workmen were then largely unorganized, politically resourceless, and highly vulnerable to the unrestrained power of employers; labor appeared unable to confront industry as an equal adversary. At this early stage, administrative initiative was an alternative to partisan advocacy. Later, with the growth of organized labor, a passive and dependent constituency became an increasingly powerful and active participant. Unions found means of promoting among injured workers a more assertive consciousness of their rights, and developed a system of representation and advocacy that was capable of furthering their interests under the law. With the growing strength of labor, workmen's compensation became a focus of political conflict among organized interest groups, and the administrative process became an arena of continuing legal controversy.

This account brings into focus some important issues of sociological jurisprudence. First, an opportunity is afforded to explore the meaning and institutional foundations of legalization. "Legalization" refers in part to a growth of the relevance of law in practical problem-solving, as well as to the elaboration of legal rules and doctrines that occurs in this process. Such an outcome often depends on the emergence of a system of procedures and modes of reasoning that can serve as vehicles for the use and elaboration of law. The history of the IAC underscores the significance of this procedural aspect of law—law as a distinctive *process* of reaching authoritative decisions. It also invites inquiry into the interplay of the legal process and institutional change.

Second, the IAC suggests that legalization may be more than a simple extension of legal procedures to a setting where they had been unknown; this extension may involve significant changes in the *character* of the legal process, as it is understood and experienced in administrative practice. The evolution of the IAC can be seen as a movement between two contrasting conceptions of the nature and role of law. In its hostility to law, the early agency exhibits a rather conventional approach to law, which identifies the legal process with the particular modes of adjudication embodied in traditional courts. This view stresses the rigidity of legal procedure, and sees its relevance as narrowly limited to the special task of resolving disputes under a framework of acknowledged rules. In its positive use of law to enlarge the rights of parties, the later IAC reflects the emergence of a more generic conception of law, that sees legal procedure as furthering broader values. This conception focuses on the larger contributions the legal process can make to authority and citizenship; it invites a broadening of the role of law in government.

Finally, our analysis suggests how this evolution is linked to a growing involvement of organized constituencies in legal action. Thus understood, the history of the IAC bears on larger problems of the legal order in modern society, especially the enlargement of the meaning and functions of law in government, and the growing significance of legal advocacy as a mode of political participation.

The Role of Law

The architects of the welfare state had a characteristically narrow and negative conception of the role of law in government. To them, law evoked a system of rigid constraints that paralyzed initiative and prevented effective action to solve the problems of society. Government had to be freed from undue legalism, relieved of the burdensome formalism of legal procedure. It needed broader discretion in making and interpreting public policy. The growth of positive government would depend on the development of an alternative machinery, removed from the ambit of law, and free to "administer" policy in the light of public purposes. The informality and flexibility of the administrative process would provide the freedom needed for enlarging public authority.[1]

This conception rested on much experience with legal institutions. Critics of the welfare state had found in law a means of resisting the extension of government. There was an apparent affinity between the historic concerns of constitutional law, with its stress on restraining the uses of power, and the critics' interest in confining the functions of government. Legal ideals could easily be interpreted in a restrictive spirit, as holding that power would best be restrained if law would *limit* governmental authority. This restrictive approach, as it might be called, is exemplified in A. V. Dicey's classic statement of the contrast between French and English conceptions of administration and the "rule of law."[2] Inspired in part by Tocqueville, Dicey had been impressed by the special privileges and extensive powers government enjoyed in the French system, a system that protected administrative decisions from judicial review, and offered avenues of redress only before administrative tribunals and under the special standards of "administrative law." In Dicey's view, the genius of English institutions lay in having made government accountable to law under the same terms and before the same courts as any citizen. A system that gave special recognition to administrative authority would, he thought, destroy all restraints on government and reduce its subjects to subservience.

Dicey saw administration as an awesome affirmation of public authority. The growth of government meant an extension of control and surveillance, diminishing the capacities of citizens and weakening individual powers of self-determination. Only a reduction of government initiative would restore the dignity and freedom of individuals. In this perspective, the legal process appeared as a means of imposing restrictions on the extension of public authority. The emphasis was on law as a set of binding rules that would specify the limits of citizens' obligations and thereby enlarge their freedom. What the state lost in power and freedom, the citizen would gain. For the advocates of limited government, the judicial process offered a welcome model. With its elaborate procedures, and the heavy burdens of accountability it imposed on deciders, adjudication seemed to provide a guarantee of strict adherence to rules in official conduct.

The restrictive approach, still predominant in constitutional law, has had an important influence on administrative law.[3] It pictured the role of law in administration as an *external restraint* imposed by courts on government; the principal issue became that of the relative powers and competence of "courts," which presumably stood for legal control, and "administrative agencies," which were assumed to aim at freeing and enlarging public initiative. Not only did this view obscure opportunities for securing *internal* restraints in government, by building legal control within the administrative process; it also ruled out the possibility that, through the courts from without or through built-in legal processes, law might *positively* contribute to the capacities of government and further the realization of public purposes.

The crucial weakness of the restrictive approach is, paradoxically, that despite its critical impulse it diminishes the scope and import of legal criticism. This follows from its tendency to remove policy issues from the legal process. In a restrictive perspective, the chief concern is to reduce the scope of discretion in the exercise of authority. The legal process is a means of confining officials within the bounds of rules. The rules themselves are taken as given; only fidelity to rules is problematic. Apart from issues of procedural fairness in the assessment of evidence, the only question legal argument can raise is: did government exceed its statutory authority? If it had the requisite authority, it is let alone. If not, its action is forbidden. The potentials of legal argument are thus impoverished in two ways.

First, the narrower the discretion officials enjoy in the implementation of policy, the fewer are the opportunities for interested parties to challenge and influence existing policies. This is quite apparent in the classic picture of adjudication as a mechanical process of applying clear and settled rules to disputed factual situations. The judge is denied discretion, but only to be made a docile executor of policies that are determined outside the judicial forum, and hence beyond the reach of affected persons.

Second, and more important, while focusing on whether government acted within the scope of its authority, legal criticism is diverted away from the substance and import of official determinations. The system allows administrators to develop protected areas where they can exercise discretion without legal scrutiny; once their authority in such areas is legally confirmed, its use is free from further control. This is reflected in the often stated principle that judicial review of administrative determinations should be restricted to questions of jurisdiction, and should not extend to the merits of agency decisions. In either case, whether discretion is reduced or indirectly protected, there is no place in legal argument to challenge official policy. The legal process renounces any role in fashioning the substance or direction of public policy.

This point suggests that the crucial problems of law in administration have less to do with whether and how much discretion officials are granted, than with how that discretion is exercised. As a student of administrative law observes:

> "Public policy" is often barely developed at the time cases come up for administrative adjudication. . . . Necessarily, a vital and on-going process of policy formation is taking place in the form of adjudication. The basic issue may not be informality or no; rather it may be the question whether the adjudicative process is sufficiently broad-gauged to identify and encompass the full range of considerations which should enter the quasi-particularized, quasi-generalized decision in the given case. In short the most vital question—more vital than speed, or expertise, or even fairness—may be *representation*.[4]

This and other recent discussions of the welfare state have brought fresh perspectives to the issue of law and administration.[5] They implicitly suggest an alternative approach, one that affirms the responsibilities of government, but at the same time extends the reach and relevance of legal criticisim.

This approach recognizes a need for public initiative; it expects government to increase opportunities for social and civic participation, and to enhance the freedom of individuals. The weakness it sees in administration lies less in the extension of government per se than in the tendency to let governmental powers be eroded or diverted from their proper ends. What is demanded of law is not a restriction of government authority, but rather assurance that administrative discretion be used in a manner consistent with the aims of public welfare. The problem is to render administration responsive to the individual and larger interests it is meant to serve.

At issue here is the very meaning of legal procedure. Procedure is not primarily a way of confining government within the limits of rules.[6] Instead, it is seen as *a structure of opportunities for participation and criticism,* allowing affected persons to challenge and influence official policy. In this perspective, the function of legal criticism is less to reduce the role of government than to use and develop the resources governmental policy offers for promoting individual and group interests in public welfare. Law can contribute to the growth of public policy in two related ways. First, the legal process can help to assure positive regard for affected interests in administrative policy-making. Such use of law involves in part an enlargement of the meaning of "fairness" in administrative proceedings—beyond the observance of minimum standards of evidence and due process, toward an affirmative search for maximum representation of interested groups and persons. It also involves a creative development of opportunities for gaining recognition of substantive rights in administrative programs. Legal argument offers a strategy for transforming the "favors" of government assistance into vested "rights," thus helping to secure and enlarge the benefits of public welfare. As Charles Reich argues, "Only by making such benefits into rights can the welfare state achieve its goal of providing a secure and minimum basis for individual well-being and dignity. . . ."[7] This latter point suggests a second way in which law can contribute to public policy: Legal argument can transform public purposes into authoritative principles, by which administrators can be criticized and held to affirmative duties. In both ways, law helps insure that the benefits of governmental programs are meaningful and that they effectively reach those for whom they are intended.

The assertion of rights and the affirmation of public purposes are, of course, closely intertwined; indeed, they should not be seen as separate. A characteristic feature of the legal process is precisely the use of self-interest and advocacy as means of exploring the meaning and bringing out the concrete implications of principles and policy. Law implies and fosters a special conception of authority. The restrictive approach assumed that authority is incompatible with individual initiative and self-assertion, thriving on passivity and subservience; law may curb authority, but cannot change its character. But the legal process also offers an alternative model of governance, where authority is seen as nourished by effective criticism, and enlarged by its ability to respond to the demands of a constituency.

Law that provides a vehicle of participation will not rule out the exercise of discretion. Rather its role is to subject decisions to a special discipline, one that opens them to new influences and imparts new orientations to policy. The judicial process may remain a model for administrative authority; but the model cannot be drawn from the more routine and mechanical forms of adjudication, under which judgments are bound by fairly specific and unquestioned rules. Rather the image is that of a creative process, sometimes found in appellate adjudication, in which courts assess policy in the light of a special commitment to hearing and recognizing claims of right.

Legal and Civic Competence

The contrasting perspectives we have discussed rest in part on a basic ambivalence in the legal process. The latter is always torn between the enforcement of binding rules and the creative use of principles in policy. Law can drift into legalism, adjudication into a blind application of unexamined policies. There are similar variations in the administrative process as between agencies that see their responsibility as limited to the implementation of a defined set of regulations and others that pursue the more positive aim of realizing a "program" of action. The problem then is to discover the conditions that will produce one or the other outcome. Of special importance is the relation between advocacy and the pursuit of political interests.

With its emphasis on fidelity to rules, the restrictive approach to administration reaffirmed a traditional view of legal debate as casebound, sensitive to precedent, and geared primarily to factual inquiry. The image of advocacy conjured up a man proceeding individually to demand obedience to law in the handling of his case. In this conception, a sharp line is drawn between law and politics. Law is seen as the realm of the passive subject; only in politics does the citizen acquire an active role, making demands that are meant to influence policy. This dichotomy of citizen and subject is made explicit in a recent study of civic participation,[8] in which the authors distinguish between *political* competence—the ability to participate in policy-making through the use of power, and *administrative* competence—the ability to relate to officials as a subject:

> The competent citizen has a role in the formation of general policy. Furthermore, he plays an *influential* role in this decision-making process. . . . The subject does not participate in making rules, nor does his participation involve the use of political influence. His participation comes at the point where general policy has been made and is being applied. . . . This kind of subject influence, or administrative competence, is more circumscribed, more passive than that of citi-

> zen. . . . It is not a creative act of influence that can affect the content of decisions themselves, except in an indirect way.[9]

The best the legal actor can hope for, in exchange for his own obedience, is to gain the compliance of authority with its rules. Although it regularizes authority, law remains an alien instrument of power. And appeals to law, even if assertive, are primarily defensive; the separation of law and politics empties them of significance as acts of citizenship.

The continuity of law and politics is restored when discretion in the formulation of policy is accepted as a central feature of the legal process. Then emphasis shifts from the problematic case to the problematic rule, and the individual claim comes to be seen as representing a larger class of interests. As a vehicle of participation, legal advocacy offers a unique opportunity—*it provides a forum that is in some degree independent of the power of participants.* In principle, law moderates the role of power in the political community. But as the potential of legal action is extended, advocacy comes to require greater political skill and resources. A politically meaningful legal order can restore the continuity of citizen and subject roles, but only if the subjects can act as citizens.

A competent legal actor needs the knowledge and skill, or the effective representation, to make his way in the legal world. But this is more than passive knowledge of rights and duties. It is an active and searching awareness of the opportunities offered by law for enhancing one's position in society. One might call this "law-consciousness." Another aspect of legal competence is assertiveness. The legal actor transforms his problems into issues of principle, his needs into grounded claims, his aspirations into reasoned arguments. Like the political actor, he wants to influence decisions, but his appeal is less to power, interest, or good will than to the authority of principle. In this perspective, the assertion of a principled claim is the paradigmatic act of *homo juridicus.* Legal participation is not submission to authority but, on the contrary, a way of insisting that authority is problematic, open to criticism, and in need of justification. A new form of authority is envisioned, one that is less preoccupied with stability and acceptance, and that values the unsettling impact of controversy and the participation of an assertive citizenry.

The capabilities that an effective use of law requires are of course highly precarious and unevenly distributed in the social structure. Historically, variations in legal competence have deprived underprivileged groups of meaningful access to legal opportunities. The emergence of the welfare state was in part a response to this weakness of the legal order; administration offered a mode of governmental action that could do away with civic participation. Administrative programs could relieve the incompetent of the burden of legal initiative. But that also freed administration from legal criticism.

This dilemma is resolved by the formation of competent constituencies. The strength of the latter need not depend on the capabilities of individual actors. The organized group can be the agency for building effective constituencies and lending individuals the moral support and political skills needed for competent advocacy. Indeed, the greater the role of groups in sponsoring legal action, the more likely it is that advocacy will serve social interests and be a political instrument.

Hence, although law may provide a mode of participation that is less contingent on power, this ideal is always precarious. If its realization depends on the formation of effective constituencies, the problem of power is never avoided. Here lies a basic dilemma of the legal order—that its ability to further equality is crucially dependent on self-help. There is a risk indeed that those who lack the needed competence may find their failure to gain justice under law more profoundly alienating than even the arbitrariness of paternalistic government. A commitment to law as a mode of governance requires that more thought be given to means of promoting the growth of a competent citizenship, including the possibility that legal institutions might assume more affirmative responsibilities for developing the capacities of their constituents.

The Study

A few words of introduction, but also of caution, should be said about how this research was carried out. Although the contemporary IAC has taken much of our attention, this is primarily a historical study. And it is the historical part of the research that has created the most serious problems of inquiry.

Legislative documents provided one source of information, unfortunately an all too often very poor source. Although the text of legislative bills in their main successive versions are printed and published, and the *Journals* of the state legislature report the actions taken by committees as well as on the floor, there is usually no way of knowing from the legislative documents alone what the proposed measures meant to accomplish, what objections they met, and by what groups they were supported or opposed. This information must therefore be gathered from other less accessible and less systematic sources, such as administrative files and the records of interested private organizations. However, since 1944 the Industrial Accident Commission has been under almost continuous investigation by various committees of the Senate and Assembly. The reports of those inquiries, including abstracts of the testimony presented by interested parties, provide a rich source of information on legal and administrative changes during the last twenty years of IAC history.

In studies of institutional change, administrative documents are perhaps the single most valuable source of data. But here again the historical records of the IAC are scarce and fragmentary. The only published documents are the uninterrupted series of yearly reports of the commission and the Department of Industrial Relations; the successive versions of the IAC *Rules of Practice and Procedure,* published since 1947 as a part of the California Administrative Code; and a few other papers and brochures published by the commission itself. The first ten years of agency history are fortunately well covered by those published sources. The official reports of the IAC were then lengthy and richly informative, qualities they lost in later years; they are supplemented by a variety of published statements of policy, special reports, addresses, and papers. For recent years, the internal files of the commission provide an adequate supply of information, but they do not go back earlier than 1944. For the earlier period, one has to rely on whatever documents were privately kept by members of the staff; fortunately for the historian, some of them have kept fairly rich collections of instructions, minutes of staff meetings, memoranda, and the like, which extend as far back as the early 1920's. The written sources have been supplemented by interviews with the older employees of the commission.

In addition to documentary sources, materials on the contemporary IAC have been drawn from (1) field observations of administrative proceedings and law firm and labor union practices; and (2) interviews with members of the commission and agency employees, practicing lawyers, insurance agents, and union officials. The field work was carried out mainly between April, 1964, and January, 1965, and thereafter intermittently throughout 1965 as the need for additional information became apparent.

Origins of the Agency

Before turning to the details of our story, it may be useful to remind the reader of the legal and historical background from which workmen's compensation and the IAC emerged. Before workmen's compensation was adopted, the law of employers' liability was dominated by the principles of liability for negligence, a legal outgrowth of the idea that each individual is responsible for his faults, and for his faults only.[10] In theory, the injured employee had no special claim against his employer other than the claims any victim of any accident would have had against the author of that harm. The law took no account of the special risks the employee ran in connection with his work. Except for whatever contractual duties the employer assumed, the servant remained a stranger to his master and had only the rights of a stranger.

Even those meager rights had been considerably undermined by some policies of the common law, known as the "common law defenses," that the employer could invoke when his negligence had been established. Those policies included two general rules of the law of torts, which often worked special hardship in the particular context of employment. First, the rule of "contributory negligence" barred recovery, whenever the employee's injury was partly due to his own lack of care. Second, when the employee knew the dangers involved in his work, he was held to have "assumed the risks" of incurring harm, and hence to have voluntarily renounced his right to indemnification. Besides those two general policies, the common law of the early nineteenth century had evolved a special rule for injuries occurring within the framework of the relation of master and servant; although an employer would normally be liable for accidents caused by the negligence of subordinate employees, the "fellow servant" rule exempted him from this responsibility when the victim was one of his own employees, a "fellow" of the negligent servant.

Attempts to reform the common law began toward the end of the nineteenth century. The early efforts did not depart from the fundamental conceptions of the law of negligence; they preserved the principle of liability for fault, but either repealed or restricted the applicability of the "common law defenses." In effect, the "employers' liability laws," as they were called, restored the injured employee to the status other persons enjoyed under the law of torts. By 1910, the federal government and most states, including California, had enacted some legislation along those lines.[11]

Those measures were soon pronounced insufficient, and under the influence of a movement started in Europe, proponents of welfare legislation suggested the adoption of a new principle of liability to replace the law of negligence: Employers would be made responsible for all injuries suffered by their employees "in the course of and arising out of" employment. The rationale was that since industrial work inevitably involved risks for the health and safety of employees, the employer could properly be held to assume responsibility for such risks of his enterprise. He would thus be charged with the "human costs" of production, just as he bore the costs of materials and equipment. At the same time, instead of the common law right to unlimited indemnification of all losses connected to the injury, the new system would entitle the employee only to limited and statutorily specified benefits, consisting mainly of a more or less extensive right to medical treatment and of substitute wages for a length of time varying with the severity of the injury. This kind of legislation became known as "workmen's compensation" law.[12] California was one of the first American states to adopt the compensation system.

The changes workmen's compensation entailed amounted to a quite radical reform. They brushed aside a standard of responsibility that had the support of a solid legal tradition in the common law of torts and was still profoundly embedded in the morality of the times. Only a minor role was left to the idea of fault—that of justifying the imposition of penalties on either employers or employees in case of "serious and willful misconduct" on their part. The change was so radical, indeed, that for a while the constitutionality of workmen's compensation remained in doubt. In 1911, a New York compensation act was found unconstitutional by the highest court of the state. The language of the decision was particularly strong:

> This is a liability unknown to common law and we think that it plainly constitutes a deprivation of liberty and property under the Federal and State constitutions. . . . It authorizes the taking of the employer's property without his consent and without his fault.[13]

This decision came at the very time California was considering the adoption of its own compensation legislation. In order to surmount the constitutional objections raised by the New York court, the California legislature decided to make its first compensation system elective. The Roseberry Act of 1911[14] offered employers a choice of either remaining under the common law of negligence, modified by the elimination of most "common law defenses," or of electing to be covered under the new system. At the same time, it created an Industrial Accident Board with the mission of administering the compensation provisions of the statute. The board had three members, appointed by the governor for revolving terms of four years; it enjoyed exclusive authority to implement the new law, including the responsibility to adjudicate controverted claims; it had the power to appoint the personnel it needed for its task.

While settling for the limited aims of the Roseberry Act, the legislature also voted a constitutional amendment, later adopted in the elections, which would eventually permit the enactment of a compulsory compensation law.[15] This was done at the following session of the legislature. The 1913 Workmen's Compensation, Insurance and Safety Act,[16] known as the Boynton Act, laid the foundations of the present compensation law; continued the Industrial Accident Board under the new name of Industrial Accident Commission; and extended its authority over the regulation of insurance and safety. The constitutionality of the new act was confirmed in 1915 by the California Supreme Court.[17] Still, there were lingering doubts over several aspects of the compensation scheme, including its reliance on administrative control. Three decisions of the United States Supreme Court in 1917[18] and two further amendments to the California Constitution in 1913[19] and 1917[20] were required to establish workmen's compensation on secure legal ground.

In light of those constitutional clarifications, the 1917 legislature decided to reenact and complete the earlier legislation in a new statute. The Workmen's Compensation, Insurance and Safety Act of 1917 left intact the mandate and authority of the IAC.[21]

The study covers the history of the IAC from its inception in 1911, as the Industrial Accident Board, to what may have appeared as its end in early 1966. After a prolonged investigation, the 1965 legislature adopted a plan of reorganization, under which the adjudicative functions of the IAC were entrusted to a "new" board, henceforth to be called the Workmen's Compensation Appeals Board; and some auxiliary administrative services the commission had maintained were placed under the authority of a separate agency, the Division of Industrial Accidents.[22] The reform became effective after completion of the field work for the study, and no attempt was made to analyze its impact.

Chapters II and III deal with the early IAC. The former analyzes the welfare perspective within which the agency defined its mission; the latter is concerned with the means chosen by the IAC to implement its program, and the implications those means had for the authority of the agency. Chapters IV and V trace the growth of initiative and assertiveness among interested parties, especially the organization of labor into an effective constituency, and the emergence of legal advocacy as a mode of participation. Chapter VI argues that the IAC responded to the growth of participation and controversy by withdrawing from administrative responsibilities. Chapters VII and VIII describe the judicialization of the IAC, and assess the significance of this change for the character of the agency. Chapter IX concludes with a general assessment of this institutional transformation, with emphasis on the ambiguities of legalization.

Notes to Chapter I

1. For a broad statement of those issues in jurisprudence, see Roscoe Pound, *Administrative Law* (Pittsburgh: University of Pittsburgh Press, 1942); also Julius Stone, "The Twentieth Century Administrative Explosion," *California Law Review*, LII (1964), 513.

2. A. V. Dicey, *Introduction to the Law of the Constitution*, (10th ed.; London: Macmillan and Co., Ltd., 1961), pp. 328–405.

3. A restrictive perspective underlies most classic discussions of law and administration in American jurisprudence, regardless of whether they favor or fear the growth of the administrative process. See, for instance, James M. Landis, *The Administrative Process* (New Haven: Yale University Press, 1938), and "Crucial Issues in Administrative Law," *Harvard Law Review*, LIII (1940), 1077; "Symposium on Administrative Law," in *Yale Law Journal*, XLVII (1938), 515–674; *Report of the Attorney General's Committee on*

Administrative Procedure (Washington, D.C.: U.S. Department of Justice, 1941), Senate Document No. 8, 77th Congress, 1st sess., 1941.

4. Robert G. Dixon, Jr., Review of Peter Woll, *Administrative Law: The Informal Process*" (Berkeley and Los Angeles: University of California Press, 1963), in *Administrative Science Quarterly*, VIII (1963), 401.

5. See, for instance, Edgar S. Cahn and Jean C. Cahn, "The War on Poverty: A Civilian Perspective," *Yale Law Journal*, LXXIII (1964), 1317–1352; Harry Jones, "The Rule of Law and the Welfare State," *Columbia Law Review*, LVIII (1958), 143; Charles A. Reich, "The New Property," *Yale Law Journal*, LXXIII (1964), pp. 733–787; Jacobus ten Broek, "California's Dual System of Family Law: Its Origin, Development and Present Status," *Stanford Law Review*, XVI (1964), 257–317, 900–981, XVII (1965), 614–682; Jacobus ten Broek and the Editors of the *California Law Review* (eds.), *The Law of the Poor* (San Francisco: Chandler Publishing Co., 1966); *The Extension of Legal Services to the Poor* (Washington, D.C.: U.S. Department of Health, Education, and Welfare, 1964), pp. 23–49.

6. Compare with a recent discussion of the role of purpose and policy, as opposed to rules, in legal decision-making, Graham Hughes, "Rules, Policy and Decision-Making," *Yale Law Journal*, LXXVII (January, 1968), 411–439.

7. Reich, *op. cit.*, p. 786.

8. Gabriel Almond and Sidney Verba, *The Civic Culture: Political Attitudes and Democracy in Five Nations* (Boston: Little, Brown and Co., 1965), pp. 136–185.

9. *Ibid.*, pp. 138, 168–169.

10. On the law of employers' liability, see H. G. Wood, *A Treatise on the Law of Master and Servant* (2nd ed.; San Francisco: Bancroft-Whitney Co., 1886), pp. 670–914.

11. See the Federal Employers' Liability Act, United States, 34 Stat. 252; and California Statutes of 1907, Chap. 97.

12. On workmen's compensation law generally, see Arthur Larson, *The Law of Workmen's Compensation* (New York: Matthew Bender and Co., 1952); Samual B. Horovitz, *Injury and Death under Workmen's Compensation Laws* (Boston: Wright and Potter, 1946); Carl Hookstadt, *Comparison of Workmen's Compensation Insurance and Administration* (Washington, D.C.: U.S. Department of Labor, Bureau of Labor Statistics, 1922), Bull. No. 301; E. H. Downey, *Workmen's Compensation* (New York: The Macmillan Co., 1924); Walter F. Dodd, *The Administration of Workmen's Compensation* (New York: The Commonwealth Fund, 1936); Clarence W. Hobbs, *Workmen's Compensation Insurance* (2nd ed.; New York: McGraw-Hill Book Co., 1939); Marshall Dawson, *Problems of Workmen's Compensation Administration* (Washington, D.C.: U.S. Department of Labor, Bureau of Labor Statistics, 1940), Bull. No. 672; Herman M. Somers and Anne R. Somers, *Workmen's Compensation* (New York: John Wiley & Sons, 1954); Earl F. Cheit, *Injury and Recovery in the Course of Employment* (New York: John Wiley & Sons, 1961).

13. *Ives* v. *South Buffalo Railway Co.*, 201 New York 271, at 294, 298 (1911).

14. California Statutes of 1911, Chap. 399.

15. California Constitution, Art. XX, Sec. 21.

16. California Statutes of 1913, Chap. 176.

17. *Western Indemnity Company* v. *A. J. Pillsbury*, 170 Cal. 686 (1915), at p. 720.

18. *New York Central Railroad* v. *White*, 243 U.S. 188; *Hawkins* v. *Bleaky*, 243 U.S. 210; *Mountain Timber Co.* v. *Washington*, 243 U.S. 219 (1917).

19. California Constitution, Art. XX, Sec. 17 1/2.

20. *Ibid.*, Sec. 21.

21. California Statutes of 1917, Chap. 586. On workmen's compensation law in California, see Douglas A. Campbell, *Workmen's Compensation Insurance: Principles and Practice* (Los Angeles: Parker, Stone and Baird, 1935); Warren L. Hanna, *The Law of Employee Injuries and Workmen's Compensation,* I, *Practice and Procedure,* II, *Principles* (Albany, Calif.: Hanna Legal Publications, 1935); *California Workmen's Compensation Practice,* State Bar of California, Continuing Education of the Bar (n.p.: Sunset Press, 1963).

22. California Statutes of 1965, Chap. 1767.

II The Early IAC
An Agency of Public Welfare

THE BROAD PROBLEMS of industrial accidents that led to the adoption of workmen's compensation may seem fairly easy to understand. What is less obvious is the set of reasons that brought government to choose the specific *means* by which it eventually responded to those problems. Why, in particular, should the handling of compensation issues have been entrusted to an administrative agency? Why not simply pass a new law, and let the courts handle the detailed issues that would later arise in the concrete implementation of legal policies?

To answer this question, we shall have to examine a number of ideas that governed the foundation and development of the early Industrial Accident Commission, and played an important role in shaping its character and the course of its later evolution.

The creation of the IAC was justified in part by the necessity of separating the administration of the new law from established govermental institutions. The policies of workmen's compensation were in many ways radically novel and likely to encounter resistance, especially in the courts. They needed the support of an independent and specialized agency. This function, however, might have been performed by a new court of special jurisdiction as well as by an administrative authority.

A more crucial reason for relying on the administrative process lay in the particular conception the founders of workmen's compensation had of the problems they were dealing with. In their view, industrial accidents were primarily a social problem, calling for expert knowledge and treatment by means of welfare action, rather than an issue of law and justice, requiring a redistribution of rights and duties. Workmen's compensation was a welfare program, a war on poverty; it was not to be seen as defining a legal liability, nor as vesting new rights in the employees.

Given this definition of the problem, law appeared as a potential obstacle to the implementation of the compensation program. The agency in charge of the program had to be free to exercise discretion, to evolve and fashion policies in response to experience, to meet concrete problems and opportunities on their own terms. Any intrusion of law and legal procedure, it was feared, would prevent effective problem-solving and frustrate the aims of the program.

Those ideas must now be explored in some detail. We shall also be concerned with tracing the impact they had on the character and orientations of the early IAC.

A Social-Problem Approach

Fundamental to the character of the Industrial Accident Commission was the doctrine that shaped its conception of the compensation problem and, consequently, of its task. The central idea was that industrial accidents raise a social problem, calling for expertise in social engineering, rather than a legal issue, to be decided on the ground of some principle of justice. To the founders of workmen's compensation, the old common law personal injury trial offered an image of utter waste, both in its complex and seemingly purposeless procedures and in the lengthy and bitter litigation it fostered. What they envisioned for their new program was a simple and frictionless administration, committed to an undisputed common good, unhampered by legal restraints in its efforts to bring under control the social evils of industrial accidents. The problem would no longer be one of just distribution of rights and duties between master and servant; the task would rather consist in mobilizing the necessary resources for the achievement of a better level of public welfare. The law had been responsible for the dreadful social evils of industrial accidents. A remedy could be found only by withdrawing the problem from the legal sphere.

The importance of this idea justifies closer attention, in the hope of sorting out some of its basic dimensions. We shall also examine by what means the IAC hoped to implement this doctrine.

A Problem of Public Welfare. "The problem of compensation is a problem of poverty and poverty is mankind's primal, implacable and unpitying foe. The business of the world is mainly to keep above the poverty line." What looks like a slogan of the War on Poverty is actually quoted from an address written about 1915 by the first chairman of the IAC.[1]

California was not unique in upholding this conception of workmen's compensation. The stage had been set in the numerous national discussions of the problem that had been going on in the early 1900's. Inquiries had been made into the social conditions of injured workers, investigative commissions had been set up in a number of states, and the whole spirit of the debates was one of partly humanitarian and partly aggressive concern with the evils of poverty.[2] This welfare perspective had an especially strong hold on the California commission. The first commissioners saw themselves as waging society's battle against the corrupting influence of poverty. This is made quite clear in the 1915 address of the chairman of the commission, from which we have just quoted:

> Whenever any considerable portion of the population of any country falls definitely below the poverty line life becomes unsafe, property insecure, and the preservation of social order a matter of pure brute force. There comes to be, first, what we call "unrest," then disturbances, "direct action."... As a consequence of unrelieved distress . . . there frequently follows the turning of children loose upon the streets while the mother is earning their keep, or the breaking up of family ties, the putting of children into orphanages or giving them away like surplus puppies or kittens to whoever will take them, all of which experiences are absolutely destructive of the bonds which hold society together. . . .

The commission was quite specific as to the threats it saw in industrial accidents. The following is quoted from another paper, written in 1914 by the same chairman:

> Workmen's compensation is only one of the numerous problems causing our present social unrest . . . approximately 40 percent of the poverty is chargeable to work accidents; and when we have poverty, we have crime, insanity, and all other forms of social evils. . . . It is apparent on the face of it that if these injured people, instead of being unable to bear their burden directly, had been compensated at the time of their injury by industrial compensation . . . so that they could have rehabilitated their earning power and thus kept [themselves] from dropping over into the poverty line, that society would have been richer, private property safer, and our taxes much less.

Criminality was not the only danger. A more immediate concern was to alleviate the burden on public assistance and private charity:

> Compensation is, first of all, founded in that social justice which demands that each industry shall so take care of its own killed and wounded, that they shall not, as a result of industrial accidents, become public charges.[3]

Thus poverty constituted both a *public danger,* in the form of social agitation and criminality, and a *public burden,* by its costs for social assistance. In this perspective, welfare programs tended naturally to adopt a rather aggressive outlook. So it was with workmen's compensation: in protecting the victims of industry, society was fighting a battle for survival. To the chairman of the commission, writing for an address in 1915, compensation "as a system of dealing with the third greatest cause of poverty" was founded on the

> incontrovertible principle that society has the right to protect itself from those influences which tend to force large numbers of persons below the poverty line, thereby making them a menace to social order and social safety. This is why society has said to its industries that they must take care of their own killed and wounded. It is in obedience to the first law of nature, the right of self-defense. . . .

Side by side and subtly mixed with this aggressive outlook there was genuine humanitarian concern for the lot of the injured, and a commitment to better his living conditions and protect his interests. Compensation was not just an act of self-defense on the part of the state and society. It was also as the IAC chairman put it, a "humanizing movement," and even a "forward step made by what we call the proletariat, the working population, against the power-holding class."[4] Thus, the welfare of the injured man was, to a certain extent, seen as an end in itself. Yet, even this concern for injured workers found its justification in an ideal of general public welfare. The early agitation for workmen's compensation did not come from organized labor, as an assertion of the rights or interests of workers; at that time, unions were fighting for the extension of workers' rights under the law of negligence, by adoption of stronger "employers' liability" legislation. Although labor later became the staunchest advocate of workmen's compensation, the original spokesmen and the founders of the program came from intellectuals and politicians of the "progressive movement" who saw this as part of a broader plan of social reform, and were not primarily tied to the interests of the working class.[5] The concern for the welfare of the injured was thus closely bound to a concern for public welfare. Accordingly, the remedy to the condition of industrial victims was not primarily sought in some new or latent principle of right, but rather in a variety of techniques such as "safer conditions for labor, protected machinery, factory and workshop inspection . . . and compensation to the end that they and their families be kept above the poverty line."[6] Emphasis thus remained strongly on welfare measures rather than on giving the injured man what was due him.

Thus, when the Industrial Accident Commission raised the question of "whether workmen's compensation is based on a theory of abstract justice to the worker or whether it is not, in some measure, rather a social expedient for averting poverty,"[7] there was actually no doubt at all about the answer, for two reasons: (1) The general *emphasis on welfare problems*, as they affected both the injured man and the public, tended to divert attention away from issues of law and justice; the focus was on expedient action toward the solution of those problems, rather than on the search for rules and principles for redistributing rights and duties. Even where it was most concerned with the interests of injured employees, the IAC was less interested in granting them rights or enforcing their claims than in offering practical assistance in the solution of their concrete problems, irrespective of what their rights, or lack of rights, might be. (2) In addition, the particularly *aggressive outlook* of this welfare program contributed further to undermine any idea that the compensation law was establishing a new principle of justice and conferring new rights on injured workers. Disabled men were seen as incompetent to solve their own problems and as a threat to the order and welfare of society. They had to be educated and controlled, rather than given additional rights and powers they would be unable to exercise in a responsible manner.

The adoption of this welfare perspective should not be surprising. The shift from liability for fault to compensability without regard to negligence was indeed so drastic a change that it could hardly rest on any other ground but considerations of welfare. There was no way of incorporating the new idea into the law: nothing could be found in the available body of legal ideas and doctrines in terms of which compensation could be rationalized. The law of torts still centered around the concept of fault; the law of master and servant had long degenerated into a mere chapter of the law of contract, which failed to provide any resource for laying the grounds of compensation. The rationale and spirit of the new program thus had to be sought outside the law. They were easily found in social welfare.

Compensation as a Measure of Relief. The welfare perspective had far-reaching implications for the way the commission conceived of the nature of compensation benefits. As the IAC chairman put it in a 1915 address:

> . . . Compensation is not compensation. It does not compensate in any adequate sense of that term. What it is, is insurance. Compensation laws make the employers the limited insurers of their workers, that insurance being limited strictly to what, in the experience of mankind, has been or will be found necessary to tide the injured person and those dependent upon him over their periods of adversity until they can again become self-sustaining. That is all that it is. We have got the right thing but we have got the wrong name for it.

Thus compensation was not to be conceived as damages. It did not purport to indemnify the injured for some loss of value, property, or income he had incurred. Elsewhere the IAC argued that

> [compensation] is not compensation at all . . . but it is relief. It is designed to ameliorate the unsatisfactory and unwholesome conditions of which so much complaint has been made,—to relieve the courts, the employer, the employee and to distribute benefits. . . . "Compensation" is not "damages" nor meant in

> principle to be partial damages. Neither is it based upon the idea of tort, or meant to be a reparation for a wrong.[8]

Indeed, benefits should be low,

> . . . not greater than are needed in order to keep the injured person and his family above the poverty line until a self-sustaining earning power can be developed. In no case will they fully compensate for the loss sustained and the injury inflicted.[9]

The commission even complained about "the great deal of difficulty" it had "in restoring to function individuals who will not try to help themselves, who cannot be detached from the idea that mere pain and discomfort without inability to labor are compensable."[10] The only purpose of compensation was to insure that "the injured person and his family shall be kept above want until they can tide over their period of misfortune."[11] This meant the furnishing of medical treatment; the payment of a certain percentage of earnings (set at 65 percent) for the duration of temporary disability; the payment of a permanent disability benefit designed to support the injured while he was adapting himself to his new condition and seeking and learning a new trade (also set at 65 percent of earnings over a limited period); and providing assistance in his rehabilitation and search for new employment.

Compensation was thus not an indemnity for loss of property, but a form of assistance. In addition, this assistance was not even conceived of as belonging primarily to the injured person; it was not a right under his control, a property for his free and exclusive use. Injured men in distress could not be trusted with such prerogatives. This idea was quite in line with the highly paternalistic and authoritarian welfare perspective that dominated workmen's compensation. As the commission chairman wrote in a paper of 1914:

> These men . . . become floaters, and a floater in general acts as ninety-nine and nine tenths percent loss for society. The other one percent or one tenth is so negligible that it is not worth saving, but yet we must save it because the more the accumulation in numbers the more jeopardized our sacred rights of private property become.

Compensation benefits were not in the interest of the injured only. The commission asserted an active interest in their proper allocation and use, as its secretary did in this letter of 1921 to a claimant who complained of abusive IAC control:

> . . . compensation money does not belong to an injured workman until it becomes due him. . . . The ones who have an interest in that money are the

> injured employee, employer, insurance carrier, if any, *and the State acting through the Industrial Accident Commission.* [Emphasis added.]

The assistance provided by compensation was not designed to support the injured in pursuing his life according to his own plans. Rather, its purpose was to make him a "worthy member of society" again. Policies in allocating benefits had to be

> . . . so framed as to say to the injured man: "True, you have lost an arm, . . . but one-armed men are not necessarily drones, and it is *your duty to become a self-supporting member of society* as soon as you can do so." [12]

Practically this meant, as we read in numerous policy statements of the time, that efforts should be directed at "returning as many men as possible to an efficient working status"; also, the expenditure of benefits should be supervised by the commission so that the money would not "be invested in some ill advised venture or otherwise dissipated and, in half a year, the beneficiary may find himself exactly where he would have been had he received no compensation at all, a pensioner upon public or private charity."[13]

Thus, in accordance with the welfare perspective the commission entertained, compensation benefits had the twofold character of being (1) *measures of relief,* (2) designed primarily to make the injured worker *socially useful* again. In a statement prepared by the Industrial Accident Board in support of the pending Boynton Bill in 1913, we read that

> . . . the paramount purpose of compensation. . . . should be to *get them* [injured men] *back to a self-sustaining status* as soon as possible. It follows, therefore, that the measure of compensation need not be so exactly adapted merely to their ability to live above poverty line from day to day, although it must be adequate to that end also, but that it must primarily be adequate to enable injured persons to readjust themselves to a permanently changed industrial condition.

This conception tended to weaken any idea that they might rightfully belong to the employee as compensation for the losses resulting from the injury. The commission would on the contrary claim discretionary control over their distribution and their use: it would see the granting of benefits as a matter of need or merit, rather than of right and liability, and would strive to maintain effective supervision over their expenditure.

The consequences of these ideas were numerous. The theory served partly as a justification for keeping the benefits at a low level, so that they would not "operate as an inducement to the employee to remain idle or to unnecessarily prolong the period of idleness by malingering."[14] Second, payments would be made by installments in order "to furnish the compensation to the injured person at the same times that the family has been in the habit of receiving support and to insure the payment as needed";[15] the law made it possible for the commission to commute the awards "in the interest of the parties," but the IAC maintained a firm policy to "discourage the commutation of indemnity to lump sums in order to avoid the defeat of the purpose for which compensation is intended and to prevent the dissipation of the indemnity, or the loss of it through the manipulations of designing persons."[16] The agency found it necessary to hire "a welfare worker to ascertain just what is behind an application for a lump sum, see the parties and their references, make sure any money awarded is expended as contemplated, and assist those who venture into business enterprises. This welfare worker can also aid permanently injured workers in their efforts to prepare for new occupations, or guide them toward new work if there is a disinclination to use to advantage the weeks during which there is a fixed income."[17] This latter function would be entrusted to a Department of Rehabilitation, created in 1919 by the IAC, following the adoption by the legislature of an Industrial Rehabilitation Act; its task was "getting the injured persons started again on the road of self-support."[18] Similarly, in the case of death benefits, the commission proposed "careful supervision of each dependent home by a compensation agent, to the end that each family may face the future with the knowledge that the State is a friend and will assist with the problems that relate to living, to education, to health, to planning the future of the children, to finding employment, and to all the other factors that make up a well-rounded home life. . . ."[19] Also, since the commission expected "bad results from allowing the individual to select his own doctor," it gave its support to the policy of giving the choice of physicians and the control of medical care to the employer or insurer, rather than the injured man.[20] In line with the same idea that compensation benefits were not the property of the beneficiary, they were made uninheritable.[21]

The most important consequence of this conception was probably that, in the eyes of the commission, the problem of the injured man's *needs* came to overshadow the issue of his rights or, for that matter, of the employer's liability. Indeed it was expected that, with the new principle of compensability of all injuries arising out of employment, *liability would practically no longer be an issue* and attention could then be focused on meeting the needs of the injured as adequately as possible. Compensation would be "automatic"[22] and it was felt probable that nearly all disabling accidents would be compensated without question or controversy.[23] With this in mind, the IAC devoted the bulk of its energies to finding out what were the "reasonable needs " of the injured, and how to adjust policy to those needs. To this end it needed expertise. One of the first legislative requests of the agency was for legislation empowering it to collect information on accidents and injuries and to create, under its authority, a department of statistics and research. An act was passed to that effect in late 1911.[24] The Boynton Act of 1913 gave the IAC further powers and resources.[25] The act made it possible for the agency to establish a medical department, responsible for assessing medical needs and the quality of medical care; and a Permanent Disability Rating Department, the task of which was to study the effects of injuries on the working and earning capacities of employees, and to develop on that basis a schedule for the rating of permanent disabilities, later to be administered by the same department. Thus much of the early work of the IAC centered on accumulating experience and expertise in dealing with the needs of injured men.

Part of this work had the obvious purpose of enabling the commission to evaluate its policies, propose new legislation, and elaborate administrative programs. More important, the emphasis on needs had a crucial consequence for the day-to-day application of the compensation act: It led the commission to qualify considerations of legal liability by a concern for the "merits" of the parties who appeared before the agency. As will be shown later in more detail, the IAC felt empowered to grant at least partial benefits, even when the employer's liability had not been demonstrated but there was a pressing need to be met; conversely, it would feel free to deny benefits to which the employee was legally entitled, in cases in which it believed they would divert the injured man from "rehabilitating his working capacity," that is, from returning to work. In this way, issues of right and liability were partially set aside for reasons of expediency in meeting presumed requirements of the injured worker's condition.

The legal issues were not only pushed to the background of IAC concerns; the agency deliberately avoided them. The commission was quite self-conscious in deemphasizing the legal significance of compensation issues. In its eyes, law was an obstacle to problem-solving.

Law and Problem-Solving

The attitude of the IAC toward law was of course in part a response to the particular law that the agency had been set up to reform. The new policies of workmen's compensation clashed sharply with the values of traditional doctrine. But quite apart from this specific conflict of policies, the commission was profoundly suspicious of the restraints it saw latent in any kind of legal rule or procedure. Compensation problems were problems of welfare, requiring flexible policies and action responsive to the requirements of concrete situations, not rigid general rules. The need was for rational inquiry and discretion, not legal controversy and restrictive controls.

The Need for Discretion. In the eyes of the early IAC, workmen's compensation was a program of action; the primary test of the value of the law and of the commission's administration lay in the results they would accomplish. The early agency was indeed characterized by a continuing concern for the results of its action. The stress it laid on injured men's needs, as opposed to issues of right and liability, was in effect only one aspect of this more general concern for results. Thus in justifying its action on a petition by the employer to terminate disability indemnities, in a case where a preexisting syphilis was prolonging the normal effects of the injury, the commission explained:

> It appeared, however, that the syphilitic condition *could be cured* by appropriate antisyphilitic treatment. The Commission denied the petition to terminate disability indemnity and ordered treatment for the syphilis. In deciding this case, the commission said: "These disorders are so prevalent that if compensation were denied wherever an injury is complicated by so-called 'specific' disease, a great many worthy people would be without compensation to tide them over their period of adversity, and, in so far, the law *would fail of its purpose to prevent poverty* arising out of injury." [Emphasis supplied.][26]

The substance of the decision is less interesting than the fact it was justified by specific reference to the effects it would have, both on the individual involved—curing him from his disease—and on the overall administration of industrial welfare.

The same concern is evidenced by the many studies conducted by the Statistical Department on the effects of injuries and compensation benefits. The chairman was emphatic on the importance of such evaluations:

> It will, I trust, be the continuous policy of the California Commission to get in touch with, and follow up all families made dependent through industrial injury for in no other way can it be known whether or not the law is rendering a service at once adequate and yet not productive of more mendicancy and industrial helplessness than it has prevented.[27]

This commitment to effective results was not confined to the administration of disability benefits. It extended to all aspects of compensation. When it appeared that permanent disability indemnities would not, by themselves, do the job of returning the injured man to work, the IAC requested and obtained the necessary resources to build a program of rehabilitation; since this itself proved inadequate in making new jobs available to disabled men, the commission proposed the creation under its authority of a department of employment.[28] The same sense of responsibility for results existed in the area of medical treatment:

> The commission feels that the Workmen's Compensation Insurance and Safety Act places an obligation on it that is not specifically defined in the text of the law. That is, it feels responsible for the surgical results to the injured workingman coming under its care. It feels that besides scrutinizing results from the standpoint of indemnities deserved, it should scrutinize them from the standpoint of good surgery. . . .[29]

The state had placed the impoverished injured man "under its care," and provided the means of relief. The IAC now felt accountable for the results of its care.

This result orientation encouraged in the IAC a special conception of the nature of workmen's compensation law. In this view, the *law had an experimental character.* This meant its authority was conditional upon the success it would have in action, as demonstrated in administrative problem-solving. It did not really establish any authoritative principle or lay down any hard and fast set of rules. Rather it proposed a number of policies to be tried and tested in administrative practice and modified as the need would appear. The agency insisted that "most of these laws are made, and naturally must be made, in advance of adequate experience, and may prove defective in certain particulars. Such laws will be amended as may be necessary until perfected."[30] The first ten years of workmen's compensation were marked by intense legislative activity. At every session of the legislature from 1913 to 1919 the IAC came up with new proposals involving major overhauls of the law.[31] In this perspective, it was never assumed that the statute provided a final answer. The experimental approach served the commission in making it freer to change policies its experience had found unsatisfactory, even without waiting for legislative approval. The mandate of the IAC was to make the compensation system workable, and that included the possibility for the agency to experiment with its own rules.

This emphasis on freedom and experimentation in the making of rules extended also to the application of policies in particular cases. Even though existing rules were treated as experimental, they also had to be kept minimal, so as to allow the agency to tailor its decisions and action to the special requirements of each concrete case. The IAC insisted on having maximum opportunities to exercise its expert judgment. The agency felt a need for discretion in problem-solving; rules should never become an obstacle to administrative effectiveness. The IAC was quite sensitive to this problem and sought to keep a proper distance from the law:

> The more one has to do with the administration of a compensation act, the more one becomes impressed with the fact that while it is easy to lay down a general rule, much latitude must be allowed, and much discretion be exercised in the

application of general rules to particular cases; in other words, to a large extent, each case must be decided on the basis of its own particular facts.

Therefore, as the agency argued in support of its legislative proposals in 1913, one had to have a law that could "adjust itself to the needs of the injured with at least a tolerable degree of adaptability." The commission would even have hoped for unrestricted authority in granting and allocating benefits; for example, speaking of the death benefits, its chairman insisted that

> [the] largest latitude obtainable should be allowed the administrative body in apportioning death benefits, to the end that the needs of each [dependent left by the deceased worker] may be met as closely as possible . . . . Of course it would be preferable to treat each individual dependent strictly in accordance with the particular needs of such dependent, but no legislature would be willing to confer upon a board or commission the distribution, at its discretion, of an entire death benefit fund. The most that can be hoped for is that some leeway may be allowed as between dependents of the same family, in order the better to meet their individual requirements.[32]

The law would thus determine the measure of the death benefit as a whole, since this could not be avoided; but the distribution of this benefit among the spouse, children, and other dependents would be left to the discretion of the agency, rather than be a matter of legally predetermined rights.[33] The IAC also reasoned that, as compensation was more an "expedient for averting poverty" than a principle of "abstract justice," it was "under no compulsion to treat all on exactly the same basis": "Our guiding principle will be to apportion the compensation in such a way that it will do the most good. . . . We must give proportionally more to those whose need is greater."[34] Standards of equality under the law, it felt, would unduly hamper it in the task of adapting relief to fluid needs and conditions. This reluctance to be held accountable to general rules is well illustrated in a memorandum written by the chairman of the commission shortly after a series of court decisions in 1915 and 1916 had characterized the IAC as a judicial body:

> It is the purpose of every court in making its decisions to lay down such principles as may be applied to all future cases having similar circumstances. In this way precedents are established and, by the judiciary in general, when established, are regarded as holy and in the nature of divine command, to question the validity of which is little less than blasphemy and certainly anarchistic and having a tendency to overturn civilization and play thunder generally.
>
> An administrative body may, on the contrary, "temper the wind to the shorn land." That is, it may sacrifice consistency in order to do justice in each case.
>
> For instance, . . . an injured employee by failure to use a safety device lost his

> thumb. He himself can be made to bear the consequence of his own act and we might do right in making him bear it, but suppose under similar circumstances failure to use a safety appliance results in death and in throwing upon public or private charity a widow with four or five small children, should we apply the same rigid rule as to wilful misconduct that we would apply in the case of the loss of a finger or thumb? I would be willing to sacrifice consistency in such cases in order to meet the main purpose of the Act, which is to prevent persons [from] becoming public charges through industrial injury, if we could do so legally but I fear that we cannot. Had we been left a commission we could have done justice in such cases at some sacrifice of consistency which so enslaves other courts. Our only escape lies in the adoption of a constitutional amendment giving us fuller judicial powers, but leaving us a commission.[35]

In the same perspective, the commission was careful to specify that its policies were "intended to serve as a guide and cannot be considered as binding in all cases."[36] The commission would feel free to disregard legal liability, or the lack thereof, when the requirements of the case seemed to justify so doing.

In the view of the commission, the compensation acts could never be applied without regard to their purpose and the results that would follow from the decision. To insist on this point was one of the aims of the statutory provision that the act "shall be liberally construed . . . *with the purpose of extending the benefits* of the act for the protection of persons injured in the course of their employment," a provision added in 1917 on the commission's request.[37] To an agency that held itself accountable for results, this kind of discretion appeared essential. Correspondingly, legal restraints quickly took the character of obstacles to effective problem-solving. As stated in Section 1 of the Workmen's Compensation, Insurance and Safety Act of 1917, the mission of the IAC was to see "that the administration of this act shall accomplish substantial justice in all cases expeditiously, inexpensively and *without incumbrance of any character*."[38] The target of this last remark was law itself, with its procrustean rules and reasonings and its paralyzing procedures of decision. In this perspective, law actually meant *legalism*. To the early commission, it conveyed a veneration of rules for their own sake and an utter disregard for consequences; it produced only waste and irresponsibility. The common law system of employers' liability had demonstrated how it was "wasteful, . . . costly to employers and the state, and of small benefit to the victims of accidents."[39] The new remedy would thus have "nothing of the entertaining process of balancing nicely the faults of the employer against the faults of the employee and speculating upon the result, with all the disastrous train of consequences involved."[40] What was true of the substance of the law held all the more strongly for procedure:

> . . . the commission does not propose to make up its mind in relation to controverted issues in accordance with any particular rules laid down in the civil courts of this state, but the commissioners expect to keep their minds open until convinced by such evidence as, in the common and practical affairs of everyday life, would produce conviction in the minds of reasonable men. . . . The commission feels that the success or failure of the whole semi-judicial department of its work depends almost entirely upon its being free to follow the policy above outlined.[41]

In order to be free from the "technicalities" of common law rules of evidence and procedure, it obtained from the legislature in the 1917 act a provision that read in part:

> . . . neither the commission nor any member thereof, nor any referee appointed thereby, shall be bound by the common law or statutory rules of evidence and procedure, but may make inquiry in such manner . . . as is best calculated to ascertain the substantial rights of the parties and carry out justly the spirit and provisions of this act. . . .[42]

Overcoming Adversariness. Closely related to the IAC's views on law and procedure was its determination to overcome the strong element of conflict and adversariness that had dominated the administration of the common law of employers' liability. One of the major objections the agency had against the old system was that, with its highly controversial issues of liability and moral blame, "the operation of the law breeds antagonism between employers and employees,"[43] thus preventing any rational discussion of problems. Financially, it felt, the system amounted to a most irrational waste, since most of the money spent went into litigation costs and attorneys' fees and heavy burdens were put on the court system, with only small benefit to injured employees.[44].

In place of all this "waste and antagonism,"[45] workmen's compensation had established a new system, the purpose of which was to solve problems, not to assign blame or responsibility. The system called for a new way of resolving difficulties: not with the embittered legal battles of the past, but in a spirit of intelligent discussion and collaboration among enlightened men. This would make it possible to "utilize for the benefit of injured employees . . . the vast sums of money wasted under the old system."[46] Rather than fighting costly trials, employer and employee would now sit down together at some conference table and iron out their problems by forthright and rational discussion.

In order to foster this spirit of rational collaboration, the IAC sought to lend the hearings it did hold in disputed cases the character of informal conferences:

> The hearings are conducted informally and in a majority of cases, without the aid of attorneys-at-law. The members of the commission are laymen, and not judges, and the hearings are inquiries and not trials. It is indispensable to the adequate administration of the act that these hearings be informal and simple and direct, as well as summary and inexpensive. The person holding the hearing takes charge of the inquiry, asks most of the questions and feels his way along toward a correct solution of the issues involved, without trying to imitate, to any great extent, judicial procedure. . . . Issues will be decided as similar issues involved in business affairs are decided by practical men of affairs. . . .[47]

In this perspective, the commission saw hardly any need for attorneys or for anything resembling advocacy in its hearings. Now and then certain issues would arise about the constitutionality or the meaning of the act, for which lawyers would be useful. On the whole, however,

> [as] a matter of common experience, it is seldom necessary to have attorneys employed in these cases, and when they are, with now and again an exception, about the only service they can render is to inform the injured person what it will be necessary for him to establish in order to be entitled to compensation, and to advise him how to get his witnesses at the hearing to give their testimony. The person holding the hearing generally does the rest.[48]

With conflict thus overcome and partisan advocacy made pointless, all energies could then be focused on how most effectively to solve the problems of industrial poverty and relief.

Withdrawing the Program from the Legal Order. In line with their desire to protect workmen's compensation from intrusive legal controversy, the founders of the new system intended to withdraw it as much as possible from the ambit of the legal order. Compensation policies had to be insulated from the influence of legal doctrines, concepts, and modes of reasoning, the intrusion of which would have distorted the aims of the program and prevented intelligent administration. The commission therefore sought to sever the new legislation from the context of traditional legal ideas; instead, compensation would find a more favorable setting in the moral and institutional framework of a comprehensive program of public welfare action. This withdrawal of workmen's compensation out of the legal domain expressed itself in two ways: (1) Workmen's compensation was removed from the context of the relation of employer and employee, and responsibility for it was vested in the state; and (2) it was built into a large-scale program of administrative action designed to deal with all aspects of industrial accident problems.

It was quite clear in the minds of the early commissioners that the compensation of injured workers had ceased to be a mere private obligation between employer and employee. The problem had become an issue of public concern. The chairman of the IAC wrote in an address prepared in 1915:

> Compensation is, therefore, not an issue between the employer and his injured employee, but rather an issue between society and its industries, for society has through these compensation laws, said to its industries, "You must take care of your own killed and wounded and those dependent upon them and not throw them upon public or private charity to be cared for. You shall treat this as one of the costs of carrying on your industry and may recoup that cost, if you can, from the consumers of your product, thereby distributing upon society as a whole a portion of the cost of industrial accidents."

Legally, this meant that the employers' liability would no longer be part either of the law of torts or of the law of master and servant. Its foundation would now reside in *public policy;* compensation would be one of those measures the state enacts, on the basis of its police power, for the preservation of the kind of social and economic order it deems essential. "When the State enacts a compensation law, it does so, not primarily to establish justice between an employer and his injured employee,"[49] but for the sake of society and public welfare. The preamble of the 1917 act made this commitment quite clear:

> This act and every part thereof is an expression of the police power. . . ; all of which matters contained in this section are expressly declared to be the social public policy of this state binding upon all departments of the state government.[50]

Insurance would provide the practical mechanism by which this transfer of responsibility to the public would be realized. It would spread the risks of compensation over a large number of employers, who would then be able to absorb a relatively small increase in cost by adding it to the price of their products. Society would thus pay the bill for its own welfare. It was hoped insurance would help to achieve two important objectives. First, compensation would be removed from the adversary context of the relations between employer and employee, and the employer would largely lose any interest in challenging his liability.

> A sticking point with employers is that the compensation system frequently requires them to make compensation even though they are chargeable with no fault of their own. "Why should we pay when we are not to blame?" they demand to know. . . . The employer will not, as a general rule, bear his portion of this cost, but will charge it into the cost of production, and so distribute the burden to the consuming public. . . . Accident insurance is indispensable to the

> employer in that . . . in no other way than by insurance can an employer hope to distribute a loss among ultimate consumers of his product.[51]

Compensation would thus be emptied of both its moral content and its economic significance. Second, since compensation benefits would be drawn out of an insurance fund beyond the immediate control of private interests the power and discretion of the state in allocating this fund would be strengthened. In this perspective, the IAC sought to impose a special liability or tax in substitution for death benefits when a deceased worker left no dependent; this money would then be allocated to a special rehabilitation fund, to be used in the discretion of the agency for the purpose of reeducating disabled men.[52] More generally, the same idea served to broaden the discretion of the agency in awarding benefits on the ground that no immediate right of the employer was at stake.

The founders of compensation sought further moral and institutional support for this welfare approach, by establishing the new legislation as only one part of a wide-ranging program of administrative action, encompassing all aspects of the industrial accident problem from its origins to its consequences, from industrial safety, through the provision of medical care and financial indemnities, to rehabilitation and the readaptation of the family. In this perspective, workmen's compensation would no longer be seen as just an amendment to the law governing the liability of employers; its framework of standards would no longer be the larger order of rules governing the rights and duties of master and servant. Rather, the place the new act occupied in this broad governmental enterprise would underscore its distinctiveness as a welfare program; the standards and the moral impetus for its implementation would come from a special set of programs, attuned to the same goals; compensation policies would gain effectiveness from being flexibly applied in conjunction with other administrative instruments. Discretion would thus be less restrained; also it could be more intelligently exercised with a fuller view of the problems involved, and a broader range of means to cope with them.

> Any comprehensive system of compensation must carry as essential complements a thoroughgoing safety program and provisions for insurance coverage and regulation. The three things are so intimately related and so interwoven aspects of an adequate compensation system as to require intimate knowledge and close contact with all three departments of the work by the same administrative body to bring about the greatest measure of administrative economy and efficiency.[53]

Just as compensation benefits were to take care of all injury-connected problems—medical care, temporary wage loss, permanent disability indemnities, reeducation, reemployment, readaptation of the family—so a complete system of workmen's compensation had to attack the problem of industrial accidents in all its phases, in both its causes and its consequences.

From the beginning, and even though it had not been granted any power in those areas, the agency adopted this comprehensive perspective. In its first publication introducing the Roseberry Act to interested parties, it stressed the need for accident prevention and warned of its determination to find a way of controlling compensation insurance. The Boynton Act of 1913 and the Workmen's Compensation, Insurance and Safety Act of 1917 gave the IAC the enlarged jurisdiction it demanded. The 1917 legislation was accompanied by a constitutional amendment, adopted in 1918, which confirmed this broad authority:

> The Legislature is hereby expressly vested with plenary power. . . to create and enforce a complete system of workmen's compensation. . . . A complete system of workmen's compensation includes adequate provision for the comfort, health and safety and general welfare of any and all workmen and those dependent upon them for support to the extent of relieving from the consequences of any injury or death incurred or sustained by workmen in the course of their employment, irrespective of the fault of any party; also full provision for securing safety in places of employment; full provision for such medical, surgical, hospital and other remedial treatment as is requisite to cure and relieve from the effects of such injury; full provision for adequate insurance coverage against liability to pay or furnish compensation; full provision for regulating such insurance coverage in all its aspects, including the establishment and management of a State Compensation Insurance Fund; full provision for otherwise securing the payment of compensation.[54]

In spite of the obvious interrelation of compensation, insurance, and safety, these responsibilities could very well have been assigned to different agencies. But this is not what the IAC intended:

> The Industrial Accident Board desires a practically exclusive jurisdiction of the whole problem of industrial accidents, and for the reasons following:
> 1. The accident, the injury, disability, compensation, adjudication of controversy, insurance and prevention of similar accidents all constitute practically one problem.
> 2. The functions to be performed are administrative and judicial and inextricably interrelated, and require that something of both powers vest in the same body.[55]

This merging of roles and powers served the important function of multiplying the resources the agency could avail itself in any one of the areas of its jurisdiction. It made it possible to use compensation as an incentive to safety and to securing insurance; insurance premiums as a way of fostering accident prevention; control over insurance as a weapon in liberalizing benefits; safety inspections as a method of investigation for compensation purposes. This broadened the powers of the commission and the range of its discretion. In addition, the sheer fact of placing responsibility for compensation in an agency which, in other areas, enjoyed even wider powers of regulation and supervision, encouraged carrying over to the compensation program the methods and perspectives of these other fields. The social problem approach to workmen's compensation was thus given a definite institutional support.

An Administrative Authority

The welfare perspective had a major implication for the character of the early IAC; the commission conceived of itself not as a court but as an administrative agency. What this meant for the agency was quite complex and seldom clearly articulated. It meant in part that the agency had to be insulated from the established court structure and given special and exclusive jurisdiction over compensation problems. More important, the commission insisted that it needed a kind of power that no judicial body, even an independent court of special jurisdiction, would be competent to exercise.

Separation from the courts was sought first as a mean of protecting the integrity of compensation policy against the potentially subversive influence of received doctrines of liability. Identified as they were with the traditional conceptions of the law of torts, the courts appeared reluctant to accept the full implications of the new legislation. Even after their constitutional objections had been overcome,[56] resistance continued in more subtle forms. Through restrictive interpretations, the courts tended to reintroduce in compensation law ideas of the law of negligence, that weakened its basic principle. The IAC was well aware of this danger.

> While the court decisions have established the statute and so have established the Commission on firm ground in the general administration of the law, this does not mean that other decisions of the Supreme Court have not hampered and restricted the application of the statute, and administration under it, so as to defeat, to an appreciable extent, the beneficiary purposes of the legislation.[57]

There were two major ways in which ideas of fault tended to color judicial interpretations of the new law. The major condition of compensability is that the injury must "arise out of employment," that is, it must be traceable to conditions of the employment situation. In interpreting this rule, the courts were inclined to confuse causation by employment with causation by the *employer*; this they did by construing narrowly what they meant by "employment." Under the prevailing common law theory of employment as a contract, the relation of master and servant was seen as a bare exchange of promised services; in this perspective, the scope of the employer's liability under workmen's compensation tended to be reduced to those injuries only that were strictly related to the performance of the work promised to the master. This view undermined the conceptions of the new law, which sought to cover the full range of losses attendant to the social condition of being an employee. Thus, in an early and important case, the Supreme Court of California established the rule that injuries occuring as a result of playful activities of fellow employees are not compensable.[58] In the award under review, the Industrial Accident Commission had argued that

> [it] is inevitable that when human beings are associated together there will be a certain amount of departure from the work in hand, and certain thoughtless acts of employees, not at all evilly disposed, will result in injury. We think that, up to a certain standard, such risks may properly be regarded as risks of the occupation and a proper charge against the industry.[59]

The court annulled the award, simply stating that it was

> . . . clear that the accident did not arise out of his [the injured worker's] employment. That the act of his fellow servant was but momentary and without malice and not in excess of the usual intercourse between servants makes no difference.[60]

This would be the controlling case until, after repeated efforts of the Industrial Accident Commission, the Supreme Court reversed itself in 1945.[61]

Notions of negligence were also reintroduced by enlarging the scope of a rule, under which the employer's liability for compensation was reduced in case of "serious and willful misconduct" on the part of the injured employee, a sort of civil penalty for gross negligence. The IAC complained the courts were too easy in allowing employers to invoke this rule in their defense.[62]

Given this lack of sympathy on the part of the judiciary, it was felt the compensation program should be located outside the traditional court structure, in a special tribunal that would enjoy relative independence in the making of policy. The IAC stressed the need for maintaining a centralized and uniform administration of the law under its exclusive jurisdiction.[63]

Insulation from the courts performed another function for the commission, besides that of sustaining the doctrinal purity of compensation law. It protected the agency against judicial abridgement of the special powers it had demanded and obtained for the implementation of the law. This brings us to another and more fundamental sense in which the commission objected to being seen as a court. Had autonomy in policy formation been the sole issue, the IAC might have enjoyed it while still being constituted as a judicial institution. But its objections were deeper; they went to the very nature of the powers and resources available to judicial agencies. The task of implementing a welfare law required that the commission be "an administration rather than a judicial body," so that "*methods could be adopted which a court would have neither the power nor the machinery to use.*"[64]

What was this power and machinery? In part, the commission had in mind the development of special procedures designed to expedite the handling of compensation claims. The IAC was quite concerned that, for poor, disabled employees, "justice delayed is justice denied." Delay had been one of the major weaknesses of legal proceedings under the common law of employers' liability; it had to be overcome. However, summary procedures were not unknown to the judiciary; they could easily have been established within a "judicial" commission. The crucial reason why the IAC insisted on its administrative character was the special view it had of its welfare task. The IAC wanted to be free to exercise discretion in awarding benefits, free to supervise recipients, free to control the practices of industry. Therefore the agency wanted power to discount general rules and precedents when desired results so required; to set aside fruitless procedures and pointless advocacy when the need was for rational inquiry and problem-solving; and to retain control of cases which, as *res judicata,* would have escaped its authority.

That is why the IAC thought "the ordinary procedures of courts and rules of evidence will not meet the needs of compensation adjudication."[65] A claim for compensation benefits would thus not be a suit, but an "application for adjustment." The hearings would not be trials, but inquiries:

> Justice cannot be done employer or employee unless the power that determines controversies is at liberty to investigate and search out needed evidence apart from what may be offered by the contending parties. . . . There must also be research and investigation in order that advantage may be taken of what the world knows regarding any issue that may arise.[66]

The commission would be exempted from compliance with the rules of evidence.[67] Informal and pragmatic conferences between reasonable men would replace elaborate and contentious procedures. And the commission would have continuing jurisdiction over its awards for such a time, originally set by law at 245 weeks, as would reasonably enable the agency to test the adequacy of its awards and adapt them if needed.[68] Finally, administrative discretion would be subject only to a limited appellate review: Agency findings were conclusive in factual matters; judicial review could be sought only on grounds of excess of powers, unreasonableness, and fraud in procuring the decision, and then only after a petition for rehearing within the agency had been unsuccessful.[69] Furthermore, a provision was included in the law that directed that "whenever this act, or any part or section thereof, is interpreted by a court, it shall be liberally construed by such court with the purpose of extending the benefits of the act for the protection of persons injured in the course of their employment."[70]

Very quickly, the commission encountered strong opposition to this conception of its character and procedures. The 1913–1914 report of the agency mentions that

> [there] are members of the bar of this state who are unable to reconcile themselves to a procedure wholly different from that which characterizes trials in courts. They feel that unless they are permitted to conduct a case before this commission exactly as they would conduct it before a court, they and their clients are unjustly and tyrannically treated.[71]

In 1915 and 1916, each of three opinions of the Supreme Court of California contained some *dictum* to the effect that the IAC was substantially a judicial body with respect to compensation matters.[72] The commission complained that "the courts have not yielded to exhaustive arguments and authorities to the effect that the Industrial Accident Commission is essentially an administrative body vested with incidental judicial attributes. . . ."[73] Therefore it requested and obtained a constitutional safeguard. The constitutional amendment of 1918 authorizing a "complete system of workmen's compensation" expressly provided that such a system include

> . . . full provision for vesting power, authority and jurisdiction in an administrative body with all the requisite governmental functions to determine any dispute or matter arising under such legislation. . . .[74]

With such authority behind it, the commission could confidently believe its administrative character was securely established. This it was determined to preserve, while "jealously [guarding] procedure against falling into the rut of procrastination. . . ."[75]

Notes to Chapter II

1. Many of the documents from which we shall quote hereafter and throughout the book are unpublished letters, reports, instructions, papers, and addresses, which we have located in the course of our survey of the files kept by the Industrial Accident Commission and by some of the older members of its staff. They are spread over many places, in private homes as well as agency offices, and their filing has not followed any recognizable plan or pattern. In view of this fact, those documents are likely to be inaccessible to most readers, and no system of citation would help any reader to locate them. Rather than footnoting all our quotations from, or references to, such documents, we have

found it preferable to provide the relevant available information in the main text, that is, the nature of the document (letter, report, instruction, address, etc.), its date, by whom it was written, and to whom it was addressed. Published or printed documents will be cited in footnotes in accordance with usual practice.

2. See, for example, Crystal Eastman, *Work Accidents and the Law* (New York: Charities Publication Committee, 1910). An account of the origins of workmen's compensation can be found in E. H. Downey, *Workmen's Compensation* (New York: The Macmillan Co., 1924).

3. *Roseberry Liability and Compensation Law of California* (San Francisco: California Industrial Accident Board, 1911), p. 13.

4. *Proceedings of the 8th Annual Meeting of the International Association of Industrial Accident Boards and Commissions (I.A.I.A.B.C.), September 19–23, 1921* (Washington, D.C.: U.S. Department of Labor, Bureau of Labor Statistics, 1922), Bull. No. 304, p. 63.

5. On the early attitude of organized labor, see Chap. IV, pp. 00–00, and references there cited.

6. *Roseberry Liability and Compensation Law*, p. 9.

7. *Proposed Scale of Workmen's Compensation Benefits* (San Francisco: California Industrial Accident Board, n.d.), p. 4. This report was written while the IAB was preparing its Permanent Disability Rating Schedule in 1913.

8. *Great Western Power Co.* v. *A. J. Pillsbury*, in the Supreme Court of the State of California, Brief for Respondents (1914), pp. 134–135.

9. *Roseberry Liability and Compensation Law*, p. 20.

10. *Report of the Industrial Accident Commission, 1915–1916* (Sacramento: California Legislature, 1916), Appendix to the *Journals of the Senate and Assembly*, Vol. 5, No. 4, p. 24.

11. *Roseberry Liability and Compensation Law*, p. 17.

12. *Proposed Scale of Workmen's Compensation Benefits*, p. 5.

13. *Program for Workmen's Compensation Legislation* (San Francisco: California Industrial Accident Board, n.d.), submitted to the 1913 session of the Legislature, p. 5.

14. *Proposed Scale of Workmen's Compensation Benefits*, p. 5.

15. *Roseberry Liability and Compensation Law*, p. 34.

16. *Report of the Industrial Accident Commission, 1913–1914* (Sacramento: California Legislature, 41st Sess., 1915), Appendix to the *Journals of the Senate and Assembly*, Vol. 1, No. 14, p. 24.

17. *Proceedings of the 4th Annual Meeting of the I.A.I.A.B.C., August 21–25, 9117* (Washington, D.C.: U.S. Department of Labor, Bureau of Labor Statistics, 1919), Bull. No. 248, p. 67.

18. *Report of the Industrial Accident Commission, 1918–1919* (Sacramento: California Legislature, 44th Sess., 1921), Appendix to the *Journals of the Senate and Assembly*, Vol. 2, No. 3, p. 21.

19. *Proceedings of the 9th Annual Meeting of the I.A.I.A.B.C., October 9–13, 1922* (Washington, D.C.: U.S. Department of Labor, Bureau of Labor Statistics, 1923), Bull. No. 333, p. 286.

20. *Proceedings of the 7th Annual Meeting of the I.A.I.A.B.C., September 1920* (Washington, D.C.: U.S. Department of Labor, Bureau of Labor Statistics, 1921), Bull. No. 281; *Roseberry Liability and Compensation Law*, p. 33; A. J. Pillsbury, "Changes in the Compensation Law," *The Recorder* (San Francisco), Vol. XXXIV, Nos. 6–16 (July 9–20, 1917), reprint, pp. 12–13.

21. *Amendments to Workmen's Compensation, Insurance and Safety Act* (San Fran-

cisco: California Industrial Accident Commission, n.d.), suggested by the Industrial Accident Commission to the 1915 session of the Legislature, p. 7.

22. *Sacramento Bee,* February 6, 1911, p. 5.

23. See, for instance, the statement of the agency in *Roseberry Liability and Compensation Law*, p. 20, and *Report of the Industrial Accident Commission, 1913–1914*, p. 6.

24. California Statutes of 1911, Chap. 53.

25. California Statutes of 1913, Chap. 176, Sec. 7.

26. *Proceedings of the 5th Annual Meeting of the I.A.I.A.B.C., September 1918* (Washington, D.C.: U.S. Department of Labor, Bureau of Labor Statistics, 1919), Bull. No. 264, p. 158.

27. *Proceedings of the 7th Annual Meeting of the I.A.I.A.B.C., September 1920,* p. 13.

28. *Report of the Industrial Accident Commission, 1918–1919, pp.* 19–22. An unpublished report of the commission in 1919 further attests to its efforts to create a Department of Employment in addition to the Department of Rehabilitation.

29. *Report of the Industrial Accident Commission, 1915–1916,* p. 21.

30. *Roseberry Liability and Compensation Law*, p. 11

31. They were: California Statutes of 1913, Chap. 176; of 1915, Chap. 642; of 1917, Chap. 586; of 1919, Chap. 183. A further revision of the law was unsuccessfully proposed in 1921. See *Journal of the Senate* (Sacramento: California Legislature, 44th Session, 1921), Senate Bill No. 259.

32. *Proceedings of the 7th Annual Meeting of the I.A.I.A.B.C., September 1920,* pp. 18–19.

33. California Statutes of 1917, Chap. 586, Sec. 14 (2); California Labor Code, Sec. 4704.

34. *Proposed Scale of Workmen's Compensation Benefits*, p. 4.

35. This amendment was soon requested, and was obtained in 1918. See California Constitution, Art. XX, Sec. 21.

36. *Proceedings of the 5th Annual Meeting of the I.A.I.A.B.C.*, pp. 159, 175.

37. California Statutes of 1917, Chap. 586, Sec. 69 (a).

38. California Statutes of 1917, Chap. 586, Sec. 1.

39. *Roseberry Liability and Compensation Law*, p. 2.

40. *Great Western Power Co.* v. *A. J. Pillsbury*, p. 135.

41. *Report of the Industrial Accident Commission, 1913–1914*, p. 9.

42. California Statutes of 1917, Chap. 586, Sec. 60 (a); California Labor Code, Sec. 5708.

43. *Roseberry Liability and Compensation Law*, p. 2. See also *Report of the Industrial Accident Commission, 1913–1914*, p. 20, *1915–1916*, p. 11.

44. This argument is stated in *Roseberry Liability and Compensation Law*, p. 4.

45. *Ibid.*, p. 6.

46. *Ibid.*, p. 2.

47. *Amendments to Workmen's Compensation, Insurance and Safety Act*, p. 14.

48. *Ibid.*, p. 9.

49. *First Report of the Industrial Accident Board, 1911–1912* (Sacramento: California Legislature, 40th Sess., 1913), Appendix to the *Journals of the Senate and Assembly*, Vol. 1, No. 21, p. 5.

50. California Statutes of 1917, Chap. 586, Sec. 1.

51. *Roseberry Liability and Compensation Law*, pp. 11–12.

52. This was the system adopted by the Industrial Rehabilitation Act of 1919 (Statutes of 1919, Chap. 183), which was to be declared unconstitutional by the courts.

53. *Report of the Industrial Accident Commission, 1915–1916*, p. 9.

54. California Constitution, Art. XX, Sec. 21.

55. *Program for Workmen's Compensation Legislation,* p. 11.

56. See Chap. I, pp. 12–13.

57. *Report of the Industrial Accident Commission, 1915–1916,* p. 8.

58. *Coronado Beach Co.* v. *A. J. Pillsbury,* 172 Cal. 682 (1916).

59. Quoted in *ibid.,* p. 683.

60. *Ibid.,* p. 685.

61. *Pacific Employers Insurance Co.* v. *IAC,* 26 Cal. 2d. 286 (1945).

62. *Report of the Industrial Accident Commission, 1915–1916,* p. 9. See also *Great Western Power Co.* v. *A. J. Pillsbury,* 170 Cal. 180 (1915), including the dissenting opinion which seems to indicate that the complaints of the Industrial Accident Commission had some warrant.

63. *Program for Workmen's Compensation Legislation,* p. 11.

64. *Report of the Industrial Accident Commission, 1914–1915* (Sacramento: California Legislature, 42nd Sess., 1917), Appendix to the *Journals of the Senate and Assembly,* Vol. 5, No. 3, p. 11. [Emphasis supplied.]

65. *Program for Workmen's Compensation Legislation,* p. 11.

66. *Ibid.,* pp. 11–12.

67. California Statutes of 1917, Chap. 586, Sec. 60 (a); California Labor Code, Sec. 5708, 5709.

68. California Statutes of 1917, Chap. 586, Sec. 20 (d); California Labor Code, Sec. 5803.

69. California Statutes of 1917, Chap. 586, Sec. 67 (b); California Labor Code, Sec. 5952, 5953.

70. California Statutes of 1917, Chap. 586, Sec. 69 (a). The Boynton Act had a similar but milder provision (Statutes of 1913, Chap. 176, Sec. 86 [a]). On the purpose of this provision, see Pillsbury, *op. cit.,* pp. 11–12.

71. *Report of the Industrial Accident Commission, 1913–1914,* p. 8.

72. *Pacific Coast Gas Co.* v. *Pillsbury* (McCay), 2 IAC 66, 171 Cal. 319, 153 Pac. 24 (1915): *Western Metal Supply Co.* v. *Pillsbury* (Mason), 3 IAC 109, 172 Cal. 407, 156 Pac. 491 (1916); *Carstens* v. *Pillsbury* (Silva), 3 IAC 215, 172 Cal. 572, 158 Pac. 218 (1916).

73. *Report of the Industrial Accident Commission, 1915–1916,* p. 9.

74. California Constitution, Art. XX, Sec. 21. The amendment was also intended to protect the agency against the threat that, if it were held to be a court, the constitutional clause on the separation of powers might be interpreted as preventing it from pursuing its other tasks of regulation and surveillance. With the new constitutional protection the agency could be confident that, even "if the Industrial Accident Commission is held to be a court, it can nevertheless exercise administrative functions as certainly as, being an administrative body, it may, in common with many other administrative bodies, exercise certain judicial functions" (Pillsbury, *op. cit.,* pp. 4–5).

75. Meyer Lissner, "Procedure before the California Industrial Accident Commission," *Southwestern Law Review,* I (January, 1917), 83. Lissner was at that time a member of the commission.

III A Critical Decision
Voluntarism and Positive Government

Committed as it was to a public welfare role, the Industrial Accident Commission was nevertheless profoundly ambivalent as to the means it would choose for implementing its program. Although its aims would seemingly have called for thorough intervention in the management of private interests, the agency was equally strongly committed to a philosophy of government that placed considerable limitations on administrative authority. This philosophy underscored the values of voluntarism and self-government. It saw in consensus the primary foundation of public policy; it invited maximum participation of affected persons in the formation of policies, and encouraged delegating to them an extended role in carrying out governmental programs. The doctrine tended to blur the distinction between state and society and to confuse public interest with the special interests of the governed. It clashed sharply with the view the IAC had of its welfare task, a view that emphasized the public character of the agency's mission and insisted on the need for broad and discretionary jurisdiction. *The history of the IAC is largely a history of the successive accommodations by which it sought to resolve these conflicting perspectives.*

It is therefore important to examine the initial decisions the agency made in selecting its modes of action. Those choices were crucial in shaping the institution and the course of its later transformations. Briefly, they determined the scale of priorities by which the commission would resolve problems of administrative strategy throughout its later history.[1]

The choice initially open to the founders of the IAC presented itself in a concrete form. The welfare perspective saw people as in need of help and unable to secure it. This view went very much against received conceptions of government, which praised the value of self-help and assumed the citizen to be fully competent and able to solve his own problems. The first response to this conflict of approaches can be stated quite simply: employers and employees needed help, but they were capable of helping themselves if given adequate opportunity. A welfare program would thus be created, but it would be *self-administered.* This view underlay the 1911 Roseberry Act.

Failures of the system quickly brought the IAC to redefine its position; the people needed help, and they were potentially capable of self-help, but they had to be helped to help themselves. The 1913 Boynton Act presumed that the job of the commission would be to *make the law self-administering* by actively stimulating initiative and participation in the implementation of the compensation program. Further shortcomings finally brought the IAC to seek more direct *control* over the administration of the statute. The adoption of the last two strategies actually never fully overcame the institutional commitments that had been made at the very beginning. Their order of emergence thus corresponded to their order of importance in the scale of agency priorities; it reflected the basic character and competence of the IAC.

Commitment to a Self-Administered System

The Roseberry Act of 1911 committed the founders of workmen's compensation to a self-administered system. This choice had obvious political foundations. Workmen's compensation was one of the very first steps in the development of the welfare state; it had to overcome considerable moral, legal, and political resistance. The choice of self-administration was a way of managing a transition: it established a new responsibility of the state in the domain of welfare, while abiding by the still solidly anchored conceptions of the passive, liberal state.

Whatever its sources, the choice had critical implications for IAC doctrine. It assumed that the administration of the law would rest on the initiative of the interested parties, employers, insurance carriers, and employees. Compensation law would be self-operating. Interventions on the part of the IAC would be exceptional, called for only when the parties failed to reach a satisfactory solution to their problems. "Not above three cases in the hundred of injuries will ever come to it [the Industrial Accident Board] for determination. The law will be, and continue to be, practically self-operating."[2] More generally, the founders of compensation and the early commissioners were satisfied that the new law would achieve its purposes without any significant change in the structure of industry; it would not be necessary to disturb the status quo by any positive administrative action. The assumption was that compensation acts would spontaneously mobilize such interests as would give impetus and support to the new program. Resting in this way upon existing interests and resources, the success of the law would of necessity be dependent on them. It would, for instance, be conditioned by how much awareness employees would have of the benefits available to them. The commission was fully aware of this risk, but clearly discounted its significance. At any rate it was willing to pay this small cost rather than adopt a system of compulsory social insurance, the extreme opposite to self-administration: "Compulsory insurance, embracing the entire working population, requires an army of officials to execute the laws, and that is contrary to our spirit and genius as manifested in government."[3]

Not only was the commission confident its intervention would seldom be needed; it also had a definite notion of what were the resources upon which it could rely. As we have already pointed out, workmen's compensation was expected to remove the indemnification of industrial injuries from the realm of conflict and controversy. With liability made certain and inescapable, it would be free from legalistic quibblings. The new system would institute a spirit of cooperation and rationality in the administration of the new benefits. Indeed compensation was in the common interest of all—employers, employees, and the public. The public would be free from the threats and burdens of much poverty. To the employee, compensation would provide quick and sure relief. And, owing partly to insurance, the employer would, with hardly any increase in cost, acquire security and protection against potentially threatening damage verdicts, as well as peace with his employees. In a sense, workmen's compensation appeared as a sort of bargain, on the basis of which cooperation would be established between formerly feuding opponents; in exchange for making all injuries compensable, industry obtained assurance that benefits would be so limited as not to increase costs, yet be commensurate with the needs of the injured. Instead of destructive and unreasonable claims and counterclaims under the law of negligence, employers and employees would now have to confront only narrow and specific problems, to be rationally resolved in accordance with their common interests.

This view assumed that the parties were fully competent to understand their common interests, and to solve their problems in this light. The new law was only giving them an opportunity to exercise qualities of intelligence and good faith which had always been latent. This opportunity had only to be recognized for the law to be a success. Whatever resistance the IAC encountered would vanish as the people came to know what the law was:

> At first a great deal of opposition from employers was encountered, but this arose mainly from a dread of the unknown and because of misinformation persistently disseminated, but this condition cleared up as soon as people came to understand what the provisions of the act really were and what the policy of the Commission would be with reference to the enforcement of its provisions.[4]

The administration of workmen's compensation would thus rest upon the intelligent cooperation of employers and employees. There was no doubt as to the ability or willingness of the parties to adopt this approach.

Given this perspective, the IAC naturally looked for a sign of success in the number of controverted cases that came to it for determination. A self-administered law should normally call for little administrative intervention, whatever form the latter may take. But when its self-operating character rests upon cooperation among the parties, a specific kind of administrative action becomes particularly relevant—the resolution of conflicts. To the IAC, a successful compensation law was one that seldom generated controversies; conversely, any increase or decrease in the proportion of disputed cases was for the agency a cause of despair or triumph. Every application an employee would file was an instance of failure. Thus, in 1914,

> [the] number of controversies referred to the Commission was a little more than 10 percent of the compensable injuries. This is a very high average and no doubt constitutes double the percentage of controverted cases that will be encountered when employers and employees have come thoroughly to know their rights and obligations under the act. Any law that is 90 percent self-operative may be regarded as good law and as accepted in good part by those whom it affects as directly as this law affects the employers and employees of California. This Commission hopes within the next two years to reduce the percentage of controversies to 2 percent of the compensable cases, but to reach this goal will require a thorough familiarization on the part of employers and employees with the terms of the act.[5]

In order to make the payment of compensation easily "automatic,"[6] the IAC strove to build the law in such a way as to wipe out all opportunities for controversy. The principle of compensability without regard to fault was, in its eyes, already a step in this direction. The computation of benefits as a percentage of the employees' earnings made another step possible: "earnings" unwittingly came to mean "wages," since "under ordinary circumstances there will be no dispute as to the wage paid."[7] The Medical Bureau of the Commission would provide another facility by making medical information "as nearly incontrovertible as possible,"[8] in case parties would need such help.

Finally, the major hope of the commission lay in the instrument it devised for assessing permanent disabilities: the Permanent Disability Rating Schedule, evolved by the agency from its own research, purported to provide for every injury a corresponding disability rating, that is, a percentage of total disability, taking account of both the age and the occupation of the injured person. The rating tables would indicate, for instance, that the loss of an arm has a "standard rating" of *n* percent (of total disability, defined as total loss of earning power); other tables would then allow adjustment of this rating according to the age of the employee, on the assumption that the older he is, the more difficult it is for him to adapt to his new condition, and thus the more serious his disability; a similar adjustment would be made to take account of the employee's occupation, on the assumption that the same injury may have different disabling effects in occupations that require different skills and physical capacities. Since, by law, the injured employee was normally entitled to four weeks of permanent disability indemnity for each percent of disability, and this indemnity itself was a fixed percentage of the wages (65 percent in principle), it was expected that the precise amount of benefits would thus be easily and unquestionably determined. "It is believed that when these tables are made and in the hands of employers 90 percent or more of cases can be settled satisfactorily, that is, on a basis of real justice, without any appeal to a State Board or Commission."[9]

Thus, an important characteristic of the IAC was its commitment to a self-administered system of compensation. To the agency, this meant (1) a policy of *minimal administrative intervention*: the commission thought it could rely upon the spontaneous mechanisms of control available in the existing industrial structure, and which were felt to provide adequate resources for the implementation of compensation laws; there was thus no need to disturb or change this structure; (2) this policy itself was grounded in a confident belief that *processes of rational cooperation* among interested parties would succeed in solving the problems encountered in compensation administration, thus providing the necessary resources for a spontaneous implementation of the law; in line with this belief, the commission laid emphasis on the common interests of the parties and on the need for pragmatic adjustment of problems; it sought to frame the law so as to minimize the occasions for conflict.

These views had lasting consequences for the structure of the IAC. Three major principles were established by the original Roseberry Act of 1911; the commitments they entailed were to persist throughout the history of the commission.

Compensation by Private Liability. Two major alternatives offered themselves to the founders of workmen's compensation. The first consisted in establishing a system of *accident* insurance, under which the *employee* would be insured against the risks of accident and disease attendant to his occupation; the cost of such insurance could have been borne either by the employees, or by the employers, or by both labor and industry, possibly with some participation of the state. Since accident insurance is intended to benefit the employee directly, it would normally have been carried by agencies independent of the employers and managed either by the state or possibly by labor organizations. This is the system typically followed under "social insurance" plans of workmen's compensation, as for instance under the German law of 1884. The other alternative was to impose a liability on the employer, and to provide for a system of *liability* insurance, which would protect the *employer* against the risks of liabilities incurred for accidents and diseases suffered by men in his employ. Briefly, the choice was between protecting employees against the consequences of their accidents, or insuring employers against the costs of their liability.

Although the former system would seem to accord better with a welfare orientation, concerned with direct relief and rehabilitation rather than with defining rights and duties between employer and employee, it was never seriously considered.[10] The social insurance system was then known mainly for its compulsory features, which apparently overshadowed its distinctive character as an accident insurance plan. Such features were clearly repugnant to the philosophy of limited government that lay behind the preference for self-administration. They were, as the commission put it, "contrary to our spirit and genius as manifested in government." In addition, it was difficult for the founders of compensation fully to free themselves from the notion of liability which had always dominated the relation of employer and employee. The critical differences between accident and liability insurances were thus not fully understood, as shown in some papers of the early IAC:

> *Accident insurance* has been divided into two kinds, "liability for damages" and "*liability* for compensation." Liability for damages insurance meets the principal needs of the employer in that it enables him to distribute the costs of accidents to the ultimate consumer, and if he carries enough of it, it safeguards him against bankruptcy resulting from heavy damage verdicts. . . .
>
> But that form of insurance does not meet the needs of the injured employee. He is only an incident and not a party to the insurance contract. It protects the employer *against the consequences of accidents,* and is, to that extent, opposed to sound public policy. . . . [Emphasis supplied.][11]

The same confusion appears in the commission's assessment of compensation, as well as in its criticism of old forms of "liability for damages" insurance. The following quote is from an address of the chairman in 1915:

> Compensation is not compensation. . . . What it is, is insurance. Compensation laws make the employers the limited insurers of their workers. . . . Compensation is, therefore, insurance and the Workmen's Compensation, Insurance and Safety Act of California makes the employer the limited insurer of his workers but permits him to carry that insurance himself or to hire someone else to carry it for him as he may see fit. That is up to him. In adopting this policy California has followed the English system and not the German, where insurance is compulsory. Englishmen are not readily compellable and neither are Americans. We can be led but not driven.

What the commission was trying to build was a system of accident insurance: the idea of liability simply provided a more readily available means toward that goal. The IAC envisioned that liability would function as an accident insurance carried by the employer for the benefit of employees. Liability would no longer constitute a legal issue as it did between parties in a tort case; this possibility had been removed by the new principle of compensability without respect for fault. The employer would henceforth act as an insurer committed by law and by his well-understood interests to the protection of his client against the consequences of accidents. Liability insurance would only be a way of delegating this task to more expert and more solvent carriers; the latter would be made directly responsible to the employee, by legally requiring inclusion in the insurance policy of a clause to the effect that the carrier "shall be directly and primarily liable to the employee," and thus substituting the carrier for the employer as party to compensation claims.[12]

In this way, liability would at the same time provide an accident insurance, thus satisfying the welfare concerns of the commission, and sweeping aside legal conflicts and technicalities; and leave the solution of compensation problems primarily in the hands of interested parties, thus fulfilling the commitment of the agency and its founders to a self-administered system. The IAC did not perceive the latent strains between its welfare ideals and its insistence on self-administration. By relying on a private liability between employer and employee, the agency ran the *risk of reintroducing in the administration of compensation the very issue it had sought to remove* for the sake of public welfare, one that could potentially become a focus of partisan conflict and a source of "legalistic" developments. This possibility was obscured by the commission's confidence in the capacity of compensation to function as accident insurance and to institute between employers and employees a relation of rational cooperation.

Insurance by Private Carriers. The next choice to be made concerned the way compensation insurance would be carried under the liability system. Would it be left to private companies, responsible only for their interests and those of their clients, the employers? Or would a state fund take over compensation insurance and so remove it from the control of private interests? Would insurance be compulsory or optional for the employer?

The Roseberry Act of 1911 left the whole matter of insurance almost untouched. Since compensation itself was seen as a form of insurance carried by the employer for the benefit of employees, employers kept the option of "self-insuring," that is, carrying it themselves, or of contracting it out to an insurer of their choice. Self-insurance appeared easily feasible. Compensation law made the determination of risks so easy and precise that actuarial methods would quickly estimate their expected cost and allow the employer to set up appropriate reserves. As to the small employer, whose risks might be harder to evaluate or whose solvency might be more doubtful, in the eyes of the chairman writing in 1915, "such employer will be very unwise if he undertakes to carry his compensation insurance himself." His intelligence and self-interest in avoiding bankruptcy would eventually move him to obtain coverage.

Employers were also free to select, by private contract, the insurance company that would best serve their compensation needs. It was expected that under this arrangement the insurer would perform his responsibilities toward employees as the employer himself would otherwise have done. The law provided for this by making insurance policies subject to its compensation provisions, notwithstanding any clause to the contrary,[13] and by rendering the insurer directly liable to the injured employee. In the eyes of the agency, the result of this system was that "the employee is in effect made a party to the contract of insurance, and may enforce, in his own name, the liability of any insurance company which has insured against the compensation risk."[14] In this way, private insurance contracted for the benefit of employers would be made to operate for the benefit of employees. Finally, the solvency of carriers would be guaranteed by requiring approval by the insurance commissioner of companies engaging in compensation insurance.[15] This minimal control had long been imposed on most other branches of the insurance industry. The IAC was not given any power over that matter.

The "Direct Payment" System. Just as the organizational structure of workmen's compensation remained under the control of private industry, so did its day-to-day administration. No provision was made for administrative supervision over the implementation of the law, whether through audit control of cases or through active participation in the adjustment of claims. Instead the law chose to rely on what was called the "direct payment" system; it assumed that the payment of benefits would spontaneously be made by employers or carriers in compliance with legal requirements.[16] If some dispute arose, the parties had the right to compromise their differences by contractual agreement; originally, no administrative control was established over such compromises. The same direct payment method covered medical care as well. Choice of physician and control over treatment were left in the hands of the parties, that is, the employer, since he is "more competent to judge the efficiency of the doctor and to provide proper medical and surgical treatment."[17] The commission was confident that "it is to the interest of the employer to furnish the very best medical and surgical care to minimize the result of the injury, and to secure an early recovery."[18] Once more administrative intervention would be made pointless by the common interests of the parties.

The logic of the system was initially carried well beyond those three prinples. As pointed out earlier, the Roseberry Act made compensation elective. The employer had the choice of remaining under a conventional employers' liability statute or of electing to be subject to the new workmen's compensation system. Although the agency did not consider the elective plan adequate, at least a partial success was certainly expected.[19] Initially, confidence in self-administration extended to matters of accident prevention as well. The Industrial Accident Board trusted the intelligence of the parties to do the work of establishing safety standards. By itself, the compensability of all accidents would "encourage the introduction of preventive devices and preventive discipline, thereby reducing the number of accidents to a minimum."[20] Prevention was indeed "the best and cheapest insurance that can be had."[21] In addition, the law provided penalties on both employers and employees for serious and willful misconduct in disregarding safety standards; fear of these penalties would naturally arouse concern for safety.

Thus, even though the IAC was committed to a broad welfare program, it was equally determined to leave its implementation to the parties directly concerned. In a sense, workmen's compensation was seen as merely creating an *opportunity* for the fulfillment of aspirations and the use of resources that had always been latent in industry. Labor and employers needed help in solving their problems; but, given a chance, they would be capable and willing to help themselves. The program of social reform the new law embodied would thus be entrusted to the very groups that were to be reformed, the assumption being that reason and self-interest would move them toward the desired end.

This commitment to self-administration placed severe limits on the creativity of the agency. Initially at least, it restricted the Industrial Accident Board to the passive role of solving the problems that were brought up by the parties themselves when they had failed to reach a satisfactory adjustment. Although the IAC quickly succeeded in extending its powers, it was never able to overcome the basic limitation that had been imposed by the Roseberry Act. The principle remained that initial responsibility for the implementation of the law would be vested in the interested parties. All programs of action and control the agency would later establish would have to rest on that premise. This meant that the process of day-to-day implementation of the law would remain under the control of private groups and persons, whose special interests might often be alien to the purposes of the agency. The later transformations of the goals and character of the IAC are all traceable to this critical weakness.

The Need for Positive Government

The fact that the Industrial Accident Board had originally been confined to a very limited and passive role did not at first alter its basic character as an administrative body. The commitment of the agency to a self-administered system did not affect its sense of responsibility for the success of the compensation program. The board's belief in self-administration rested upon its confidence that the system was workable and capable of reaching the desired results. It was not long before the system revealed patent inadequacies, and the agency was brought to develop new strategies of administration.

The Failure of Self-Administration. The first major obstacles the Roseberry Act encountered were created by the insurance industry. After one year of experience under its no-intervention policy, the commission concluded that, when private carriers were so "let alone," there developed either "a combination that has been extortionate or a savagery of competition that has resulted in driving hard bargains with injured persons or the solvency of the carriers has been seriously threatened."[22]

Under negligence law, liability insurance had generally been a highly profitable business. The often speculative character of negligence suits made it possible for carriers to charge high premiums while, at the same time, the law let them free to cut down their losses by the variety of pressures they were allowed to bring on the injured victims.[23] Workmen's compensation had been purposely designed to deprive insurers, as well as employers, of much of this unrestricted freedom. Obviously, the mood in the insurance business was not for the "generous cooperation" the founders of the new law had expected. Private carriers sought to discourage employers from adopting the compensation system; this they did by setting the premium rates for compensation insurance at an excessively high level.[24] The number of employers who elected compensation remained very low, and this called for administrative intervention.

Hardly had compensation been made compulsory and insurance available at more reasonable rates, when other problems came up. The Industrial Accident Commission, as we shall see, had relied on competition to bring premium rates down;[25] very quickly this competition became so violent that often rates were depressed to a level where either losses could not be safely covered, or the carriers' solvency was maintained only by illegal maneuvers in the adjustment of claims.[26] This added a second reason for the IAC to become involved in the regulation of insurance.

Employers, too, were failing to live up to what the law expected. The agency had to acknowledge that, under the elective system, "where some employers are under the act and others are not, competitive conditions are unsatisfactory and powerfully dissuade many from electing compensation who would otherwise do so."[27] Only 500 employers out of an estimated 200,000 had elected compensation.[28] In addition, even when under compensation, many employers failed to set up the reserves or contract the insurance necessary to secure the payment of benefits. Compulsory compensation had to be coupled with compulsory insurance, thus making more administrative supervision necessary.

Even so, compliance with the law remained wholly unsatisfactory on the part of both employers and carriers. Instead of the spirit of rational understanding and cooperation it had expected, the IAC discovered that

> . . . adjusters for insurance carriers and employers are inclined to take rather than to give to the injured man the benefit of any marginal doubt which may exist, and sometimes this leads to controversy.[29]

This disturbing amount of controversy was at first the most troubling failure the commission saw; a disappointing adversariness was emerging, thwarting all its plans for smooth and cooperative administration. Partly from its own experience, partly from the results of a survey of compensation cases in New York, the agency soon learned how much more serious the problem was:

> We were lulled into a false sense of security until the investigation in New York got us to prick up our ears. We had felt that the people ought to know their rights pretty well, and if they were not getting them we would hear from them. We took five thousand cases of permanent injuries and went through them, and we found that the people had been cheated out of thousands upon thousands of dollars. . . . You have to look out for these cases all the time and there is something in the nature of the business of adjusting that tends to make a man regard every claimant as his enemy and the man who will gouge him, if he can, and you will have to watch that very, very carefully.[30]

Not only were benefits underpaid, but provisions for medical care of the injured were defeated by insurers and employers who began referring all their cases to physicians they hired to specialize in the mass practice of industrial medicine:

> Many insurance companies have joined together to contract for medical service. This system should be deplored. . . . It has led to dissatisfaction among the injured, to injustice and to misunderstanding. . . . Such "wholesale" medical treatment is good for neither the doctor, the injured, the insurance company, the Workmen's Compensation, Insurance and Safety Act, nor society.[31]
>
> The IAC supports a moral responsibility in this respect . . . and of course desires that the best services shall be accorded the injured working man. . . .

> This is a most deplorable condition since the contracts are frequently made with men of poor equipment and some whose only equipment appears to be a willingness to work for very little money. . . .[32]

This condition carried implications even for the work of the commission itself, since much in its decisions rests on medical evidence. Thus permanent disability ratings were

> based upon reports of attending physicians. Recent investigation of these reports has shown that in many cases the information is entirely inadequate in description, and that often essential contributing factors to the permanent injury are lacking.[33]

Much of this situation might have been corrected more or less spontaneously, had injured employees been powerful and competent enough to protect themselves against these practices; they could have bargained more effectively, or appealed to the IAC, or requested changes of physicians as the law permitted them to do. But the commission had learned it could not count on that:

> There are not a hundred lawyers in California—and California is full of them—who are competent to advise the injured man as to his rights under the compensation law, and that has been going on for ten years. There have been men who have been injured in California who have not heard that there was such a thing as compensation law in the State until after they were injured and somebody asked them what they knew about it. The reason that a large number have not interested themselves in the matter is because they did not expect to be hurt.[34]

Anyway, even when they know, "injured employees are sometimes confronted with the necessity of making choice between the compensation which the law allows them and relinquishing their jobs."[35]

Under such conditions, self-administration was bound to fail, for two major reasons: (1) The *structure of interests* among insurers, employers, and employees was such as to make impossible the system of peaceful and reasonable adjustments in which self-administration was grounded. Whatever costs employers and carriers could pass on to their respective clients and consumers, it remained easier and more profitable for them to cut their losses as much as they could, to the detriment of the injured. (2) Labor *lacked the power and competence* that would have been necessary to protect the injured employees; the latter did not have either the knowledge of their rights or the capacity to assert them, nor even the power to bargain in defense of their interests.

A Committed Agency. Self-administration might have meant that the commission was satisfied to have the compensation law in the books, and would henceforth let everyone take care of his interests under the new rules. But in the eyes of the agency, workmen's compensation was not a matter of private interest to employers and employees. Public welfare was at stake—the new law had established a public policy. Indeed, the goal of the IAC was to withdraw the indemnification of industrial accidents from the private domain of the employment relation. To be sure, compensation had been left in the hands of private parties. But this system assumed that the law would win the support of private interests for what remained essentially a policy of public welfare.

Self-administration was of course in part a concession made to powerful industrial interests in exchange for their acceptance of the new welfare program. And one consequence of the self-administered system had been to make the implementation of compensation law deeply dependent upon the interests of insurers and employers. However, the IAC did not see itself as bound by this dependency. It was not captive of the groups that controlled the operation of the law. To the agency, responsibility for the success of the law remained in its hands, in spite of the many limitations of its powers. At the very beginning of its existence, the Industrial Accident Board felt free to say:

> From the standpoint of public welfare, the existing condition of accident insurance in California is intolerable.
>
> The Industrial Accident Board desires to call attention to the fact that other states and countries have bettered their condition in many ways. . . . However it is done, some way must be found for protecting injured workmen from being pressed, through inexorable necessity, into accepting less than an adequate indemnification for damages sustained where the right to damages is reasonably clear.[36]

The statement continued by threatening such measures as compulsory compensation and insurance, state insurance, and administrative adjustment of all compensation claims. Ten years later, after it had accomplished many of these reforms and gained considerable power, the IAC manifested the same determination:

> Now, the California Commission set up this standard, that it was its business to see that every injured man in the State got the compensation to which the law entitled him, all of it and no more. . . . Now, if we are to get compensation to those who ought to have it, in the measure that they ought to have it, it is going to be only because of eternal vigilance. It can be done in no other way.[37]

Indeed, the fight for workmen's compensation entailed almost of necessity a fight against those groups whose resistance had caused the failure of the early law. What was first a commitment to the success of the law, on the part of a neutral agency responsible to the public, tended easily to become a commitment to the interests of injured workers, against the "power-holding class."[38] This tendency was reflected in and gained strength from a 1917 amendment to the liberal-interpretation clause of the statute, which requested that such interpretation be made in favor of the injured employee, thus changing the character of a clause originally designed only to overcome the common law rule of strict interpretation of statutes.[39] Doubts in legal construction as well as in factual evidence would henceforth benefit the injured worker. The referees would be assigned the task of defending the employee in the disputed cases that came to them for decision, and compromises between adverse parties would be checked in their adequacy for the employee only. Indeed, in all its activities, "this commission takes the position that its primary duty is to see that the injured and the dependents of the killed employees are compensated in accordance with law."[40]

The foundations of this active commitment lay in the welfare approach to compensation the IAC had adopted. The commission held itself accountable for successfully solving the problems of injured workers. This involved a willingness to assume control over insurance and industry should the compensation program be subverted in their hands. Furthermore, the employees themselves invited closer supervision; the agency was concerned that relief be properly used in light of the social purposes of compensation, and did not feel workers could be trusted with such responsibility. The head of the Rating Department wrote to a complaining claimant in 1921:

> Not all men are able to handle an amount of money judiciously. Many of them in fact cannot be trusted to do so. Until such time as it is proven otherwise, the Commission must assume that any one man is no better than any one else.

Thus, given its welfare approach to workmen's compensation, the IAC was bound to try recapturing the reins of administration, for two distinct reasons: (1) A sense of *responsibility for the results* of compensation laws compelled it to respond to the failure of self-administration by more active involvement; (2) the *philosophy of control* over the injured, implicit in some aspects of its welfare perspective, led it further toward administrative supervision.

Strategies of Administration: Participation and Control

Two main strategies were available to the IAC when it decided for positive government. One emphasized participation, the other leaned more heavily on control. Following the latter, the commission would have assumed full regulatory and supervisory authority over all phases of workmen's compensation administration, including safety, insurance, the adjustment of claims, and the supervision of beneficiaries. This approach underscored the distinctively public character of the compensation program; it assumed that the parties would be unable to give any competent and reliable support to the new policies.

The other strategy was for the agency to create and encourage patterns of responsible participation by the parties in the implementation of the law. The IAC would create conditions under which the self-interest of employers and insurers would compel them to assume their new responsibilities. It would strengthen the competence of injured employees to participate effectively in the process of claims adjustment and rehabilitation. This strategy was obviously much more in line with the conceptions and commitments originally developed under the Roseberry Act. The values of self-help and self-government would be preserved; the only role of the commission would be to help the parties to help themselves, to assist them in pursuing their own interests more rationally. Workmen's compensation would remain what it was—an opportunity, rather than a compulsory regulation. But the IAC would actively work to make this opportunity available and see that it was used. In other words, self-administration would no longer be assumed, as it had been; but it would not be rejected either. Rather, it would become a goal to be pursued creatively by positive governmental action.

To the end of making the law self-administering, the IAC first directed its efforts at stimulating whatever interest and support for its program it still believed to be latent and usable.

The Spur of State Competition. Its major weapon in this respect was the State Compensation Insurance Fund, created by the Boynton Act of 1913 on request of the agency, and placed under the authority of the commission acting as board of directors.[41] The purpose of the fund was

> . . . to furnish a standard of fair treatment toward employers and employees, both as to the charging of reasonable rates for insurance and the prompt making of payments that deserve to be made, which other insurance carriers must follow on pain of seeing the business go to the State Fund instead of to themselves.[42]

A model administration would allow the fund to charge the lowest possible premium rates, thereby making insurance available to employers at low costs. In competing with private insurers, it would attract more and more employers to the carrier, which, under the authority of the commission, would also follow the fairest policies in the treatment of injured workers. In this way, private insurance would be compelled to live up to the model set by the state fund.[43]

In the eyes of the IAC, a competitive fund was preferable to a state monopoly of compensation insurance, even though the latter would have permitted greater control.[44] The commission never doubted "this form of competition suffices to secure justice for employer and employee and at practically no cost to the State."[45] And it intended to use this weapon with utmost energy:

> I feel like persisting that we are maintaining a model insurance carrier—model in its treatment of the injured man, model in its treatment of the employer, model as affects its financial integrity—to which the other insurance carriers must accommodate themselves, approximate themselves, or we get the business. The destiny of the stock companies is in their own hands.[46]

Education and Assistance in Problem-Solving. One of the first disappointments of the commission had come from the unexpectedly high number of controverted cases. To the agency, this litigiousness resulted from a failure on the part of all parties to understand the meaning and purposes of the compensation acts. This condition could be remedied by appropriate methods of education and assistance in adjusting claims. In 1913, a special office was created with the task of informing inquiring parties of their rights and obligations and "how to effect adjustments of controversies without requiring formal hearings before the commission."[47] In addition, the commission's secretary became responsible for maintaining a "conciliation" service, available for mediation of troublesome cases, and the referees in charge of the more definitely contested claims were instructed to strive "to bring about a better understanding and leave fewer issues in controversy."

Strengthening the Competence of Injured Persons. The major problem the administration of compensation faced arose from the incapacity of injured employees, through ignorance or lack of protection, to press effectively their claims against employers and carriers. First, assistance to the injured tended almost naturally to become the main function of the information and conciliation services of the agency. After insurance was made compulsory, most employers came to enjoy the services of specialized insurance companies; they were in little need of "education" or "help." The employee became by far the main user of agency services; the information desk provided free legal and administrative counseling, and the conciliation service of the secretary tended to act as a bargaining representative, pressing the claims of injured persons and lending them the authority of the IAC.

However, these services were able to reach only those employees who came to the IAC on their own initiative or were brought to it by some other means. A most important, and at first unintended, instrument for reaching employees and providing them with protection was found in the reports of injuries the commission originally collected for research purposes. As early as 1913, the IAC instructed its Statistical Department to inform all reported injured employees of their rights to compensation and the availability of commission services.[48] The Permanent Disability Rating Department was charged with following up cases where a permanent injury was evident or suspected from the report. In 1918, a specialized Department of Investigations was created to relieve the other departments of this work, which had taken an unexpectedly large share of administrative energies.

Finally, in a paper written by a referee in 1917, we find that the IAC established the policy that in contested cases the employee is "fully entitled to the proper protection of his rights at the hands of the commission itself." The referees were instructed to see to such protection.

This last set of administrative services completed the plans the IAC had for making compensation law self-administering. It may be worth noting at this point that *by so spurring the interests and energies of injured employees, the IAC was potentially threatening the achievement of one of its most important purposes*; while its plan was to build self-administration on processes of cooperative and peaceful adjustment of problems, the active promotion of injured workers' claims tended rather to foster the development of a system based on partisan vindication of rights by contending parties. This would later become a source of major problems for the agency.

Administrative Control

Making the law self-administering still left the agency dependent upon the interests and support it was able to arouse for the realization of its purposes. Reluctantly, the IAC came to find it necessary to assume a more affirmative authority over certain phases of compensation administration. Participation was not forthcoming; control would have to be established.

Control of Insurance. In spite of the availability of insurance at low cost through the state fund, the agency found that many employers failed to secure coverage even when their financial status was quite insecure. In 1917, it was made compulsory for employers either to get insured or to obtain from the IAC a certificate of consent to self-insure, under penalty of criminal and civil sanctions.[49] The Legal Department of the commission was charged with the prosecution of violators. A Department of Self-Insurance was also set up with power to issue and revoke certificates and to require the deposit of bonds or securities as guarantees of solvency.

The IAC also wanted some control over insurance rate-making, in which free competition had pushed some carriers into selling policies at rates that undermined their solvency. In 1913, the IAC proposed that regulatory powers be vested in a State Rate-Making Bureau, placed largely under the control of the commission itself.[50] The bill was rejected. An alternative proposal was adopted in 1915: Uniform premium rates would be established and made compulsory for all insurers; at the same time, insurance policies would be made "participating," that is, the carrier would be allowed to return excess premiums in the form of dividends. However, the IAC was not given any authority over the matter; the insurance commissioner was made responsible for setting rates and the state fund itself was subjected to the official rates.[51]

Control of Claims Adjustment. The Roseberry Act had left claims management in the hands of employers and allowed the parties freely to compromise all their differences. The commission became concerned that under such a system

> . . . abuses will grow up and great pressure will be brought upon injured persons to force them, on pain of losing their jobs, to settle their compensation claims for less than the law entitles them to receive.[52]

Accordingly it requested and obtained a provision in the Boynton Act making the validity of compromises conditional upon agency approval.[53]

The IAC also strove to bring routine claims adjustment under its surveillance. The reports of injury sent by employers, insurers, and physicians to the Statistical Department provided the agency with a ready instrument of surveillance; systematic examination of those reports would cause "those responsible for the payment of compensation to realize there is an ever-watchful eye."[54] Permanent disability cases appeared to need special attention; the functions of the Rating Department, which was initially conceived as an auxiliary service for the determination of contested cases, were enlarged to include supervision of all uncontested cases. The commission gives the following account of this move:

> Our idea when we were forming the [Permanent Disability Rating] Schedule was that we could print such a schedule with directions how to use it so that any employer and any insurance carrier could rate any disability as readily as he could find the time of the arrival or departure of a train in a rail-road time table, doing it as well as we could; but in practice we found that if justice was to be done, all the ratings had to be made in our office, and generally because of inac-

> curate and underestimated description of the nature and extent of the injury. I think it has seldom, or never, happened that the description of the injury upon which the rating was made by an insurance carrier was exaggerated. They never made it out worse than it was, but they so frequently made the condition out so much less serious than it was, that we had to throw over the whole system of self-rating and require that all ratings be made by our permanent disability rating department.[55]

Thus were born what were called the "informal ratings," as contrasted with the "formal ratings" issued in contested cases. Reports of injury indicating signs of permanent disability were turned over to the Rating Department, which would secure additional information from the injured employee himself and issue a rating based on those data. Insurance carriers were expected to comply with such ratings, under the threat of seeing a formal application filed by the employee with the advice and support of the agency.

A similar system enabled the Medical Bureau to review physicians' reports and thereby check on the adequacy of medical treatment and the quality of the medical evidence serving as a basis for the determination of benefits by employers and carriers. In addition, permanently disabled workers were invited to be examined by agency doctors "in order that the report of the company's attending physician might be checked up." The commission expected that this control should "frequently result in change of doctors or exactions of satisfactory treatment by the insurance companies."[56] To this end, the IAC obtained for the employee in 1917 the right to one change of physician, the new one to be selected by the employee from a list of three provided by the employer; and the right to a consulting physician at the cost of the employer. Furthermore, the employee was entitled to request certification by the IAC of the new or consulting physician.[57] These rights, in conjunction with the control and support of the commission, would secure adequate medical treatment. In addition, the 1917 act empowered the IAC to inspect and approve hospital facilities maintained by employers for their injured employees.[58] The agency even considered elaborating "regulations specifying the character of physicians eligible for industrial work,"[59] but this plan was apparently never realized.

However extensive they had become, the commission's *powers of control remained nevertheless quite dependent upon its ability to arouse the interests of the injured man and to support him in pressing his claim.* This often required considerable efforts and resourcefulness. In order to overcome this obstacle, in 1919 the IAC proposed an amendment to the Workmen's Compensation Act that would have empowered the agency "to institute any proceeding to determine rights and liabilities under this act."[60] The amendment was killed in committee.

Control over the Injured. The agency had two major instruments of control over injured workers. First, commutation of benefits from installments into lump sums could not be made without agency approval; the commission used welfare workers, presumably from its Department of Investigations, to assess the competence of the employee and the merits of its plans for using the money; the Rehabilitation Department followed up these cases in order to help prevent "dissipation" of the money. Second, the same Department of Rehabilitation, created by the Industrial Rehabilitation Act of 1919, was conferred extensive powers to reeducate permanently injured employees, place them in new employments, and readjust their families to the new conditions:

> . . . The hurt man will be visited in hospital or home and plans laid for his future. His desire for a new occupation will be ascertained. Undoubtedly the desire will govern, unless all are satisfied of its impracticability. Bedside handicrafts or other useful occupations will be supplied during the hospital period, with an eye single to the end sought to be attained. Workshops will do their part in the re-education. The latest contrivances and inventions to replace lost physical members will be secured. . . .
>
> The time during which compensation is paid will be expended to the best advantage. Technical schools, business colleges, workshops, universities and schools, and all other sources of training and learning will be called upon to do their share. If there is need of more money for tuition, or to keep the family while the hurt man goes away for his re-education, it will be forthcoming. . . . The state will extend the guiding hand. . . . And this is not all. Each re-educated man needs a position. The purpose is to see he gets it. . . . A new day is here for the maimed man. He will be taught when he needs the tuition and he will realize the economic advantages of having each step planned so that his income will be assured and he can step forward unafraid.[61]

The realization of this plan was left in the complete discretion of the IAC.

Control of Safety. Provisions for safety were one of the main points of the reform the agency sought and obtained in the Boynton Act of 1913. The act empowered the IAC to regulate industrial safety and to enforce its regulations through inspection and prosecution of violators.[62] However, the commission kept hoping, as the chairman indicated in a 1915 address, that safety could be realized "through a spirit of cooperation on the part of employers rather than through any effort at compulsion." Education would thus prevail over enforcement:

> The "Star and Club" method of handling inspections has been taboo from the inception of the safety department and a spirit, rather, of cooperation and service has been developed which has won the unqualified support of all concerned.[63]

Here, as elsewhere, the IAC worked along its favored line of combining efforts at making the law self-administering with a moderate use of its powers of initiative and control.

Conclusion: The Seeds of Change

At the apogee of its power and expansion, around 1920, in spite of a determined and impressive deployment of administrative efforts, the IAC had not succeeded in overcoming its initial dependence upon the support and participation of interested parties. However much of its authority was enlarged, its actual powers and instruments of control remained inextricably bound to the original design of a self-administered system. Thus, even though the commission had means of surveillance over claims adjustment, its only practical recourse in case of breach of duty by an employer was to encourage the injured employee to file a claim.

This dependence points to a basic institutional weakness of the early IAC—a source of problems that were to set in motion important processes of change. Briefly, this weakness lay in that the commission had committed itself to means of administration that would become increasingly subversive of its basic mission of public welfare. This inconsistency of aims and means had several aspects.

First, although the IAC was responsible for values of *public* interest, it had nevertheless allowed the development of a system in which interested *private* parties would have primary control over the administration of public policy. The IAC did not fully perceive this inconsistency. In its perspective, the conflict was resolved by *identifying public interest with the common interests of the parties*; once made aware of their joint interests in the compensation program, the parties would give their support to its public ends. This idea performed a crucial function for the early commission; the appeal to common interests served as a way of establishing the authority the agency needed for the pursuit of its public aims. It was a means of creating political consensus. But, built into the very structure of the IAC and the compensation system, the idea tended to make the agency captive of the very groups it was to govern. Practically, this meant that the commission's authority would be weak in the face of dissent, and that private groups would easily be allowed to influence the definition of administrative goals. To the IAC, the exercise of positive control would remain a strategy of last resort, to be sparingly used; control would have low priority in the allocation of administrative resources.

A second inconsistency appears in the fact that, although the IAC based its program on consensus and the common interests of the parties, it actually created a system with built-in conflict. With compensation grounded in a liability of the employer and insurance carried by private insurers, industry had a clear interest in minimizing the amount of benefits it would be charged. Instead of the cooperative understanding the commission hoped to rely upon or create, the agency encountered growing controversy. Indeed in its own efforts to effectuate its program, the IAC itself was bound to arouse rather than reduce controversy; its major administrative weapon was to encourage workers to challenge their employers and assert their rights. By its very action, the agency was inevitably brought to frustrate one of its principal ideals and to undermine the foundation of its authority. Instead of being able to build upon consensus, the commission would be continuously thwarted by dissent and conflict—a situation that, because of its weakly defined authority, it was not prepared to handle creatively.

Finally, as we have pointed out in the preceding chapter, the IAC was firmly committed to promoting a nonlegal view of compensation problems, one that would allow the rational exercise of administrative discretion. Yet the commission had only tenuous control over the manner in which problems would be defined. Self-administration had bound the agency to a system under which the demands of the parties, joint or conflicting, would have critical influence on administrative authority. As long as, through programs of education and assistance, the IAC was able to influence those demands, it was also able to imprint upon them the orientations it deemed appropriate; consensus and cooperation were particularly important in this respect, since they permitted the agency to act more freely in promoting its views. The more conflict would develop, the more the parties would escape the authority of the IAC, the more agency conceptions of the problems and needs to be met would become vulnerable to challenge. Thus, the commission's role as a welfare agency was early placed in jeopardy.

Notes to Chapter III

1. There may be some question whether those decisions involved genuine "choices" on the part of the agency. Although they were in part adaptations to the political circumstances of the time, clearly they were in no way imposed on the agency by outside political forces; the Industrial Accident Commission had the initiative and leadership in the legislative process. Indeed, throughout the first decade, legislation appears hardly distinguishable from administrative policy-making. To say that the IAC chose the path it followed does not mean that the agency had a clear conception of the alternatives that were open; to a large extent, it took for granted that the course adopted was the right one. The decisions were "critical" in their consequences, but they were made rather uncritically.

2. *Program for Workmen's Compensation Legislation* (San Francisco: California Industrial Accident Board, n.d.), submitted to the 1913 session of the Legislature, p. 12.

3. *Ibid.*, p. 6.

4. *Report of the Industrial Accident Commission, 1913–1914* (Sacramento: California Legislature, 41st Sess., 1915), Appendix to the *Journals of the Senate and Assembly,* Vol. 1, No. 14, p. 7.

5. *Ibid.*, p. 6.

6. *Report of the Industrial Accident Commission, 1917–1918* (Sacramento: California Legislature, 43rd Sess., 1919), Appendix to the *Journals of the Senate and Assembly,* Vol. 3, No. 4, p. 11.

7. *Roseberry Liability and Compensation Law of California* (San Francisco: California Industrial Accident Board, 1911), p. 41.

8. *Report of the Industrial Accident Commission, 1913–1914,* p. 16.

9. *Proposed Scale of Workmen's Compensation Benefits* (San Francisco: California Industrial Accident Board, n.d.), p. 12. This report was written while the IAB was preparing its Permanent Disability Rating Schedule in 1913.

10. No American state adopted the social insurance system. There were in part constitutional reasons for this choice; compensation appeared more strongly grounded on a principle of liability than on the bare imposition on employers of a statutory duty to purchase insurance for the benefit of employees. Such a plan might more easily have been struck down as special legislation or unwarranted confiscation of property. Such indeed was the fate of the California Industrial Rehabilitation Act of 1919, which was somewhat more closely inspired from social insurance. It required employers to pay certain amounts into a state rehabilitation fund, from which the Industrial Accident Commission would be able to draw in order to provide rehabilitation benefits to disabled employees. It was found unconstitutional in *Yosemite Lumber Co.* v. *IAC* (Moore), 9 IAC 11, 187 Cal. 774, 204 Pac. 226 (1922).

11. *Roseberry Liability and Compensation Law*, p. 16.

12. Under the Roseberry Law (California Statutes of 1911, Chap. 399, Sec. 24), the employee had the right only to enforce in his own name the obligations contracted by the insurer toward the employer; the Boynton Act (California Statutes of 1913, Chap. 176, Sec. 34 [b, c]) perfected the system by making the insurer liable toward the employee for the full measure of compensation, irrespective of the content of the insurance policy.

13. California Statutes of 1911, Chap. 399, Sec. 25.

14. *Roseberry Liability and Compensation Law,* p. 53. See *above,* pp. 46–47, and n. 12.

15. California Statutes of 1911, Chap. 399, Sec. 25.

16. By contrast with the legislation of some other states, the California law did not even require carriers or employers to secure a formal agreement of the employee as to what benefits he would receive; whatever restraint, if any, this might have imposed on them was not deemed necessary.

17. *Roseberry Liability and Compensation Law*, p. 33.

18. *Ibid.*

19. Thus the agency reported with some assurance that employers "are approaching this movement toward compensation with open minds and in hope of helping to solve, justly and humanly, a perplexing and far-reaching problem." See *Roseberry Liability and Compensation Law*, p. 11.

20. *Ibid.*, p. 2.

21. *Ibid.*, p. 14.

22. *Program for Workmen's Compensation Legislation*, p. 6.

23. As stated in two papers written by the IAC chairman in 1914 and 1915, those were the days of "the unscrupulous liability insurance companies, always looking for the 10%

and 15% profit, championing the employer in his conduct but with the alert eye always on the 10% or 15% profit, and procured by the cold-blooded methods of the ambulance chasing, signing of releases when the unfortunate workman is suffering most with his injury —untrained in his technique of accident litigation and only too glad to get a few dollars so that his wife and family could conduct their bare existence." And, ". . . California was regarded by insurance companies as being a 'good' state. . . . In those good old days the injured man had few rights which employers, insurance companies, courts and juries were bound to respect, and casualty companies prospered."

24. The chairman of the Industrial Accident Commission reported in 1915 that "when the Roseberry Law went into effect it found all the great insurance companies in combination to hold the rates up high and no method of mutual or other insurance available to employers that they might get their insurance at what it ought to cost."

25. See *below,* pp. 55–56.

26. See the complaints expressed by the commission in *Amendments to Workmen's Compensation, Insurance and Safety Act* (San Francisco: California Industrial Accident Commission, n.d.), suggested by the Industrial Accident Commission to the 1915 session of the Legislature, p. 16.

27. *Program for Workmen's Compensation Legislation,* p. 2.

28. *Ibid.*

29. *Proceedings of the 3rd Annual Meeting of the International Association of Industrial Accident Boards and Commissions* (I.A.I.A.B.C.), *September 1916* (Washington, D.C.: U.S. Department of Labor, Bureau of Labor Statistics, 1917), Bull. No. 212.

30. *Proceedings of the 8th Annual Meeting of the I.A.I.A.B.C., September 1921* (Washington, D.C.: U.S. Department of Labor, Bureau of Labor Statistics, 1922), Bull. No. 304, p. 239.

31. *Report of the Industrial Accident Commission, 1915–1916* (Sacramento: California Legislature, 42nd Sess., 1917), Appendix to the *Journals of the Senate and Assembly,* Vol. 5, No. 4, p. 25.

32. *Report of the Industrial Accident Commission, 1916–1917* (Sacramento: California Legislature, 43rd Sess., 1919), Appendix to the *Journals of the Senate and Assembly,* Vol. 3, No. 3, p. 21.

33. *Report of the Industrial Accident Commission, 1918–1919* (Sacramento: California Legislature, 44th Sess., 1921), Appendix to the *Journals of the Senate and Assembly,* Vol. 2, No. 3, p. 15.

34. *Proceedings of the 8th Annual Meeting of the I.A.I.A.B.C., September 1921,* p. 239.

35. *Program for Workmen's Compensation Legislation,* p. 5.

36. *Roseberry Liability and Compensation Law,* pp. 17–18.

37. *Proceedings of the 8th Annual Meeting of the I.A.I.A.B.C., September 1921,* p. 239.

38. *Ibid.,* pp. 62–63.

39. California Statutes of 1917, Chap. 586, Sec. 69 (a); California Labor Code, Sec. 3202.

40. *Report of the Industrial Accident Commission, 1923–1924* (Sacramento: California Legislature, 45th Sess., 1925), Appendix to the *Journals of the Senate and Assembly,* Vol. 4, No. 8, p. 5.

41. California Statutes of 1913, Chap. 176, Sec. 36–48; California Insurance Code, Sec. 11770–11881.

42. A. J. Pillsbury, "Changes in the Compensation Law," *The Recorder* (San Francisco), Vol. XXXIV, Nos. 6–16 (July 9–20, 1917), reprint, p. 23.

43. In addition, the Industrial Accident Commission obtained passage of an act authoriz-

ing the creation by employers of mutual compensation insurance companies. This would provide employers with another opportunity to secure insurance at minimum cost. See California Statutes of 1913, Chap. 177.

44. The Industrial Accident Commission was well aware of the alternative means of control it was forsaking. As the chairman indicated in a 1915 address, "The State . . . might have asserted its power to monopolize that entire field of insurance, but it did not do so. On the contrary, it contented itself with . . . a State Compensation Insurance Fund to do business in competition with other insurance carriers on terms of practical equality."

45. *Program for Workmen's Compensation Legislation*, p. 6.

46. *Proceedings of the 7th Annual Meeting of the I.A.I.A.B.C., September 1920* (Washington, D.C.: U.S. Department of Labor, Bureau of Labor Statistics, 1922), Bull. No. 281, p. 265.

47. *Report of the Industrial Accident Commission, 1913–1914*, p. 7.

48. *Statistical Bulletin* (Sacramento: California Industrial Accident Board, 1913), January 1–June 30, 1913, p. 4.

49. California Statutes of 1917, Chap. 586, Sec. 29; California Labor Code, Sec. 3700–3715.

50. *Program for Workmen's Compensation Legislation*, p. 7.

51. California Statutes of 1915, Chap. 642; California Insurance Code, Sec. 11732–11742.

52. *Amendments to Workmen's Compensation, Insurance and Safety Act*, pp. 8–9.

53. California Statutes of 1913, Chap. 176, Sec. 32.

54. *Proceedings of the 4th Annual Meeting of the I.A.I.A.B.C., August 21–25, 1917* (Washington, D.C.: U.S. Department of Labor, Bureau of Labor Statistics, 1919), Bull. No. 248, p. 65.

55. *Proceedings of the 8th Annual Meeting of the I.A.I.A.B.C., September 1921*, p. 120.

56. *Report of the Industrial Accident Commission, 1916–1917*, p. 21.

57. California Statutes of 1917, Chap. 586, Sec. 9; California Labor Code, Sec. 4601–4605.

58. Approval by the commission would exempt the employer from the provisions regarding the worker's right to a change of physician. See California Statutes of 1917, Chap. 586, Sec. 10; California Labor Code, Sec. 3950–3954.

59. *Report of the Industrial Accident Commission, 1916–1917*, p. 22.

60. *Senate Bills* (Sacramento: California Legislature, 43rd Sess., 1919), No. 581.

61. *Proceedings of the 6th Annual Meeting of the I.A.I.A.B.C., September 1919* (Washington, D.C.: U.S. Department of Labor, Bureau of Labor Statistics, 1920), Bull. No. 273.

62. California Statutes of 1913, Chap. 176, Sec. 51–72.

63. *Proceedings of the 5th Annual Meeting of the I.A.I.A.B.C., September 1918* (Washington, D.C.: U.S. Department of Labor, Bureau of Labor Statistics, 1919), Bull. No. 264, p. 27.

IV The Parties

The Growth of Initiative and Competence

THIS CHAPTER IS concerned with the character and capabilities of the main parties the Industrial Accident Commission deals with —employers, insurers, and employees. As we have seen, the character of the parties had been a major consideration in pushing the agency toward an active role in the administration of compensation law. On the one hand, it had become apparent that insurance and industry could not be trusted with the initiative of distributing benefits; they had to be educated in the new policies, supervised in their day-to-day operations, and often compelled to comply with the law. On the other hand, labor could not be relied upon to manage and protect its interests. In the eyes of the IAC, workers did not have the competence to overcome the many problems associated with industrial injuries; they needed assistance. In addition, control was required to prevent them from diverting compensation relief from its social purposes. Finally, the agency found labor too weak and insecure to press its interests successfully against employers and insurers; workers needed continuing support in the presentation of their claims. Under these conditions, the IAC had to take the initiative.

The later history of workmen's compensation is marked by significant changes in the character and capacities of the parties. One trend was the development of an *adversary* system, in which the parties acquired increasing initiative in defending and promoting their respective interests under the law. Employers and insurers quickly developed a number of powerful organizational instruments that enabled them to affect compensation policies and administration and made IAC control more difficult. Similarly, although later, as labor became more strongly organized, it progressively took over the task of pressing its own interests. The administration of workmen's compensation became increasingly characterized by partisanship and the confrontation of organized groups. Powerful sources of resistance were thus created against attempts by the agency to affirm its authority.

A second major transformation can be described as a growth in the *legal competence* of the parties. The parties became more conscious of their rights and aware of the protections and opportunities the law afforded them; at the same time, as they gained in security, they increased their capacity to assert claims of right and to use the legal process for the promotion of their interests. Of special significance is the role of organized representative groups in prompting this development. This evolution was particularly significant for labor, on which we shall mainly focus. As we shall see, the major result of this process was increasingly to thwart the original IAC plan to preserve its administration free from legal restraints.

The Roots of Adversariness

Quite early the commission had noticed a tendency toward litigiousness in the settlement of compensation claims. The trend, it hoped, would be corrected by educating the parties in the spirit of the new legislation. But the sources of this emerging adversariness were in the law itself; they lay in the very system that had been chosen to finance benefits, and in the structure of interests that had thus been established.

Although workmen's compensation was meant to overcome the litigiousness that had prevailed under common law employers' liability, it actually perpetuated the confrontation of "claimants" and "defendants" it had sought to avoid. This it did mainly by preserving the idea that benefits would be assessed as a personal liability of the employer toward his employee. The system gave the employer an immediate stake in each particular claim any of his employees would make. Each claim involved a threat of new liabilities and therefore invited challenge and resistance.

It was originally envisioned that insurance would overcome this problem. All liability risks would be covered by a fixed insurance premium, thereby enabling the employer to compute the exact cost of compensation and to make it an element in the price of his product. In addition, the employer would be removed from the process of claims adjustment and replaced by the insurer. The latter would in turn be free to set premium rates at whatever level his losses would require. Ultimately, the consumer would bear the whole cost.[1] Those expectations were largely disappointed.

First, insurance was never made fully compulsory. Although the law requires every employer, except public agencies, to "secure the payment of compensation," this can be done by obtaining a "certificate of consent to self-insure" rather than by insuring. The employer who can prove his financial ability to pay compensation and deposits the required surety bonds and securities may be allowed to carry his own insurance.[2] Large employers who have stable and easily predictable risks have often found this alternative less costly than insurance.[3] Without insurance coverage, the employer remains directly responsible for the distribution of compensation benefits; he incurs the liabilities and confronts claimants with immediately adverse interests. Having primary control over claims adjustment, he holds ample opportunities to curtail or deny the payment of benefits.

Second, insurance itself was organized in a way that kept employers sharply exposed to their own liability risks and moved them to take an active role in confronting claimants. This was accomplished by making premium rates closely responsive to variations in the actual losses incurred by each particular employer. The overall level of insurance premiums is of course basically determined by the actual "loss experience" of industry as a whole, that is, the amount of money disbursed in benefit payments. Since this experience in turn depends, among other things, on the policies and practices of insurance carriers in day-to-day claims adjustment, employers share a common interest in keeping some control over those policies and practices. Industry organizations have therefore been concerned with restraining carriers from excessive generosity in the distribution of benefits. The competitive character of compensation insurance provides them with a ready means of bringing pressures on the carriers, namely, by manipulating their clientele.

In addition, an important feature of compensation insurance serves to individualize and sharpen employers' concern with and involvement in insurance claims adjustment. The 1915 act, which authorized the insurance commissioner to determine uniform and compulsory rates for compensation insurance, also established a policy, common to most American states, of using variations in premium rates as an incentive for employers to improve safety conditions in their plants.[4] Premium rates would be made to vary in accordance with the "merit" of each particular employer in reducing accident risks in his firm. Under a system called "experience rating," premiums are raised or reduced, within limits, depending upon how the employer's accident experience deviates from the average of his classification. However, the only workable measure of "accident experience" that has been found is the *loss* experience of the insured, that is, the amount of benefits that are paid on his behalf. Losses, to be sure, are a function of the frequency and seriousness of accidents; but they also vary with other factors, some of which the employer may find easier to influence. Among these are the claims adjustment practices of the insurance carrier. Thus, although it is intended to reward employers for their success in accident prevention, experience rating can only penalize them for the liabilities they incur. Its objective consequence is to limit the spreading of risks that insurance is designed to achieve. As a result, the employer becomes more immediately exposed to the burdens of liability and is encouraged to take an active role in his defense against compensation claims.[5]

That employers are sensitive to the stake they are thus given in the administration of benefits is demonstrated by the way in which they keep insurers under scrutiny and pressure. All carriers have files of letters from policyholders criticizing the conduct of cases by their lawyers or claims adjusters; when benefits are paid in a seemingly doubtful case, when a settlement appears too generous, when too much is spent in possibly unnecessary or too expensive medical care, when an adjuster's investigation or a lawyer's defense looks too "soft," the insurer is likely to be censured and held to account. Besides their eagerness to volunteer information and furnish witnesses, employers will often, in the more serious cases, stay in touch with the carrier during the whole process of adjustment or adjudication. Some will even go as far as sending an observer to commission hearings so as to make sure they are provided with an adequate defense. The ability to withdraw or threaten to withdraw their patronage affords them a powerful leverage against the insurer. Even without confronting the carrier, the employer can influence his losses through the reports of injury he is supposed to send to the carrier. He can avoid reporting the accident, and by refusing to disclose the name of his carrier he can prevent the employee from appealing directly to the insurance company.[6] Quite a few injuries are thus never reported and injury reports are, of course, not always fully complete or accurate.

Although the interests of insurers are by no means identical with those of industry,[7] compensation insurance is a form of liability insurance, in which the client of the carrier is the employer; and the preservation of private competition has made insurers highly accountable to industry and responsive to its demands. The necessity of maintaining his competitive position forces the carrier to minimize his losses. He thus joins the employer in resisting employees' claims.

Thus organized, the system gave employers important stakes in the administration of benefits and entrusted insurance to carriers who were committed to employers' interests. Under such conditions, it should be no surprise that IAC hopes of overcoming adversariness would eventually be frustrated.

Industry: the Organization of Defense

Conflicting interests may be present, yet never seriously confronted. They may remain only dimly perceived, or the parties may lack the power and resources necessary to pursue them. More is needed before anything resembling an adversary structure can emerge; the parties have to become capable of self-help and initiative in the promotion of their interests. Here we are interested not only in their capacities and the means available to them as individuals, but also in the organizational instruments by which they can gather their energies and increase resources for the pursuit of their aims.

To industry and insurance, as might be expected, self-help had never been much of a problem. From the start, the law itself placed the administration of benefits in their hands. Although the IAC later established some measure of control, this "direct payment" system was never abandoned; the adjustment and payment of claims continued to depend upon the initiative of employers and carriers. The latter obviously commanded all social, economic, and political resources necessary to protect themselves effectively.

There can also be little doubt that industry could easily turn to the legal order as a source of defenses. Workmen's compensation was a rare piece of labor legislation in a system that otherwise gave the employer a privileged supremacy. Industry had been accustomed to find in law a powerful ally and rich resources.

It is hardly necessary to mention that, in addition to their individual resources, employers and insurance carriers have long been tightly organized. Employers' groups range from the local trade association, which occasionally brings its protests and requests to a legislator or a member of the commission, to such state and national organizations as the Chamber of Commerce and the Manufacturers' Association, which maintain specialized sections or committees on compensation matters, have standing lobbyists at the state legislature, negotiate with insurance and labor representatives, and keep the IAC under continuous scrutiny—proposing or resisting changes in policy and administrative reforms, following up new lines of cases and suggesting legal interpretations, criticizing IAC staff and seeking to influence commissioners' appointments. To these organizations, the self-insured have added their own Self-Insurers Association, which performs a similar role. Insurance carriers enjoy the same services from a variety of groups, ranging from *ad hoc* committees established to handle a particular problem to such permanent specialized organizations as the Workmen's Compensation Institute and the Association of Casualty and Surety Companies.

The law itself has recognized or even provided for the organization of employers and carriers. When insurance rates were made compulsory in 1915, the state insurance commissioner was empowered to "issue or approve" a system of rating.[8] Actually, the commissioner never "issued" rates on his own initiative. From the start, compensation insurance carriers organized to develop their own rating system and confined the commissioner to the passive role of approving their proposals. A special voluntary association, the California Inspection Rating Bureau, was set up for the purpose of elaborating and applying a common rating system. This organization received formal recognition in 1951; an amendment to the insurance code made it compulsory for all compensation insurers to be members of one "rating organization," and subjected such organizations to licensing and supervision by the insurance commissioner.[9]

The law has also preserved to insurers and employers "the continued right to contract for the issuance of workmen's compensation policies insuring organizations and associations of employers on a group basis." [10] Group insurance, a long-standing practice, was legally recognized in 1941 for farmers' associations[11] and in 1953 for any employers' group.[12] Group insurance has provided the small employer with means that only large corporate employers could muster. Not only has it made insurance more readily available to him; above all it has given him, through trade associations, effective instruments of bargaining and control over the carrier, thus making the latter more responsive to his interests.

The major way in which workmen's compensation law supplies industry with organized power is by the requirement of insurance itself and the substitution of the carrier for the insured as the liable party. When the employer buys insurance, he not only secures financial coverage for his losses, but he also purchases a claims adjustment service and the legal defense he may need. Only the largest employers can adequately develop such services on their own; the self-insured actually come from their ranks. Others find in their carrier a specialized claims administration they would otherwise be unable to avail themselves of. Instead of simply paying whatever liabilities their policyholders have incurred, insurers have taken over the task of determining the very presence and extent of liability. Their claims departments include trained investigators, medical experts, and professional negotiators, who are specialized in the detection of "unwarranted" or "fraudulent" claims and the adjustment of "excessive" demands or "doubtful" cases. The claims service is backed by a legal department or a retained law firm, through which legal advice and advocacy are permanently available. A standard compensation insurance policy provides for the carrier "to serve the insured . . . upon notice of injury, by investigation thereof and by adjustment of any resulting claim in accordance with the law," and "to defend, in the name and on behalf of the insured, claims or suits for compensation or for damages . . . whether groundless or otherwise, which may be instituted against the insured in any legal proceedings . . . all interests accruing after entry of judgment, and all expenses incurred . . . for investigations, negotiations and defense." [13] Thus, to the employer, insurance constitutes much more than a way of spreading individual risks over a large group. One of its major functions is to pool the resources of possibly weak and isolated employers so as to provide them with effective means of self-help and legal defense. Tied to the interests of its clients, insurance comes to serve as a way of organizing industry, supplying it with a capacity for initiative and a legal competence that might otherwise have remained problematic for many individual employers.

Labor: Toward Organized Initiative

Initially the worker's position contrasted sharply with the power and resourcefulness of employers and carriers. The first decades of the century mark the apogee of unrestrained capitalism. Labor, especially the masses of unskilled and semiskilled workmen, shared the usual lot of the underprivileged. A high level of unemployment and a constant oversupply of cheap labor placed the employee under continuous threat of losing his job. Against this insecurity, workers had no defense; the employment contract made hiring and firing a matter for the arbitrary discretion of the employer, and this very vulnerability usually thwarted all attempts by labor to organize for the protection of its interests. To the isolated employee there was no way of voicing his grievances in the firm; nor did he have much part in a political system that had all too often tended to work against him. Ignorance and apathy went along with poverty, making the worker unaware even of the few opportunities that were open to him. Labor was the passive and estranged subject of a social and legal order over which it had little or no control.[14]

To be sure, unions had made some headway in a few trades. But their membership remained very small. In 1909, the Californa State Federation of Labor reported a total dues-paying membership of 25,000; although this number rose quickly to 104,200 in 1929, it stayed around 95,000 during the next decade, reaching a low of 82,100 in 1933.[15] This was also the period of craft unionism, a principle strongly adhered to by the American Federation of Labor and by which the growing masses of unskilled workers were kept outside of organized labor. Even where they were established, unions were paralyzed by their utter lack of security. Antitrust law and the labor injunction, the "open shop" campaign of organized industry, and the soft appeals of "welfare capitalism" were continuously threatening their existence. An even more important weakness resulted from the reluctance and inability of organized labor to carry its cause to the political arena. Partly because of their distrust of an often hostile government, and partly because of their opposition on principle toward protective legislation and other forms of public intervention in labor matters, unions had failed to gain any effective representation in legislative and administrative structures.[16]

This weakness of the labor movement is quite apparent throughout the formative period of workmen's compensation. The new legislation owed its dynamic growth almost entirely to forces outside organized labor: the movement of social reform of the 1910's; the triumph of the Progressive Party in

California; the rise of professional social work; the leadership of liberal intellectuals, especially in the American Association for Labor Legislation, and of state and federal labor administrators; and, finally, the tolerance with which employers accepted the new program in the expectation that it would promote industrial peace at no additional cost. In this latter respect, it is worth noting that workmen's compensation had gained very active support from the National Civic Federation.[17] Actually, although it later changed its policy, organized labor originally opposed the compensation program, just as it objected to any form of social insurance. Its preferences, as evidenced by the legislative program of the state federation in 1907, 1909, and 1911, went to employers' liability laws that would restore the employee to the status other persons enjoyed under the law of torts.[18] When, at the 1911 session of the legislature, the federation turned its support to the compensation bill, later to become the Roseberry Act, this move was taken as a temporary compromise, "the most practical one" under the circumstances.[19] Even so the act made compensation elective and the federation manifested more interest in its liability than its compensation provisions.[20] In 1909, it is true, the American Federation of Labor had declared its support for workmen's compensation and had drafted a model bill;[21] this bill had been endorsed by the California federation at its 1910 convention.[22] But the AFL proposal was actually much more timid than what was advocated by the spokesmen for the compensation movement and by the more progressive state administrations. Not only were its benefits less liberal, but its coverage was restricted to the "extra-hazardous" occupations; for the ordinary worker, organized labor still contemplated a common law liability.[23] Finally, in 1913, the state federation gave its full backing to the Boynton Act and its principle of general and compulsory compensation. Still one finds no indication that it had any role in drafting the statute; this was an administration measure, for which the Industrial Accident Board was primarily responsible.[24] At the next three sessions of the legislature, the most important ones in the development of the IAC, organized labor confined itself to the role of adding its weak and not always wholehearted support to agency-sponsored bills.[25]

From 1921 to the middle thirties, labor stood on the defensive. Yearly reports of the State Federation of Labor repeat some version of the same story of its "successful resistance to attempts at destroying the workmen's compensation law." Every year, its convention passed some four or five resolutions and its officers introduced a few bills. But successes were seldom registered, and then only when the bills were sponsored by the IAC. Throughout the period, one finds no sign of any organized pressure being brought by labor on the IAC, nor of any systematic effort to assist injured workers in the adjustment of their claims, nor even of any campaign against or negotiation with employers or carriers. To be sure, legislative sessions provided occasions to discuss with IAC officials and to confront industry and insurance representatives. And in some of the more lively unions, especially in San Francisco, union agents would sometimes help employees to argue and settle their cases. But none of these activities involved organized effort; they were defensive rather than assertive, they had little momentum and followed no concerted plan. Labor spent the bulk of its energies just striving to survive.

The great depression marked a radical turn in labor history. The New Deal suddenly made support for labor organization and collective bargaining a matter of governmental and legal policy, a policy later strengthened by the need to secure industrial peace for war production. National union membership jumped from three million in 1933 to nine million in 1939 and fifteen million in 1945.[26] Membership reports to the California State Federation of Labor indicate an increase from 82,100 in 1933 to 267,401 in 1939 and 521,356 in 1942.[27] The postwar growth of organized labor was slower. Its estimated membership in California reached 1,354,500 in 1950, a peak of 43 percent of the nonagricultural labor force; it stabilized around 1,750,000 in the late 1950's and early 1960's.[28] The 1930's had infused the labor movement with a new spirit of militancy. The deep social crisis and the split within its ranks between the AFL and the CIO had forced organized labor to reexamine its traditional policies. The transition to industrial unionism had identified it more closely with the interests of working men as a class.[29] Above all, it had learned the many opportunities government opened for the promotion of labor interests, and it could now turn to politics with some assurance of getting a favorable hearing.

Of special interest for our purposes is the new realization by labor of the value of social insurance. With the massive unemployment of the depression, social security had become a crying need. The first official endorsement of unemployment insurance by the AFL came in 1934.[30] The state federation had been pressing for unemployment compensation since 1929;[31] in 1935, California passed its first Unemployment Reserves Act, which became a focus of active and sustained attention by labor.[32] This change of attitude toward social security was dramatically reflected in labor's concern for workmen's compensation. With the beginnings of the depression, workers had become more actively interested in compensation benefits. IAC reports for the years 1929–1930 mention a sudden unexpected increase in cases processed, in spite of the sharp decline in employment,[33] and the insurance literature is full of bitter complaints that workmen's compensation was being transformed into an insurance against unemployment by laid-off workers who fabricated claims in order to make a few dollars.[34] The State Federation of Labor was slow to respond to this new interest of its constituents; except for some increase in the number and vigor of convention resolutions in and after 1935, there was no change in its policies until 1937. The turning point in organized labor's attitude toward workmen's compensation was 1938. That year was marked by two important events: the appointment of a legal counsel to provide specialized advice and services in compensation matters, and the completion of an extensive study by the federation of legislative and administrative problems pertaining to workmen's compensation.[35] These were the beginnings of an organized campaign that would have lasting consequences.

With a larger representation in public office and the support of a more active and competent lobby, labor became capable of effective participation in the legislative process.[36] Controversy at the legislature became suddenly more intense. Since 1943, when a subcommittee of the Assembly Interim Committee on Governmental Economy and Efficiency began a prolonged inquiry into IAC procedures, workmen's compensation has almost uninterruptedly been under legislative investigation.[37]

The campaign of organized labor did not confine itself to legislative demands. With the growing role of labor administrations during the depression and the war, unions had learned the significance of agency practices and policies and acquired experience in dealing with them. The IAC became the target of an endless succession of inquiries and demands affecting all aspects of its operations.[38] The commission was increasingly caught in the middle of a contest among organized groups and subject to the continuing scrutiny and the opposing grievances of each side. In 1955 this situation was recognized in the law by an amendment that provided:

> No rule or regulation of the commission . . . shall be adopted, amended, or rescinded without public hearing at which an opportunity is afforded for interested persons to be heard or to present statements with respect to the proposed rule or regulation, or amendment or rescission thereof. Notice of the rule or regulation proposed to be adopted, amended, or rescinded, of the time and place of the public hearing, and of any action thereon by the commission must be given to such business or labor organizations and firms or individuals who have requested notice thereof.[39]

For the first time the workmen's compensation statute took notice of the existence of labor unions. This provision was further strengthened in 1963 by a requirement that "all meetings of the commission . . . shall be open and public, and all persons shall be permitted to attend any and all such meetings in their entirety, save and except such meeting or portion of a meeting . . . as may be held . . . to judicially determine in a specific case the benefits, if any, to be awarded. . . ." [40] All moves of the IAC thus became conditioned by the adversary confrontation of organized industry and organized labor.

The labor campaign also took the form of direct action against and negotiations with employers and carriers. Private compensation insurance had always aroused bitter complaints from unions, especially because of the partisan control exercised by carriers over medical care and medical testimony. In 1942, the state federation attempted to launch an attack on insurers. It involved a blacklisting of companies whose practices were found abusive, the provision of legal aid to the victims of abuses, and pressures on the IAC to supervise carriers' practices with more energy.[41] Unions also began at that time to set up their own panel of doctors, from which injured employees could select acceptable consultants or treating physicians in case of inadequate services by "company doctors" or favorable witnesses in case of litigation.[42] In 1944 meetings were held with the governor and his administration to present grievances and suggestions concerning the State Compensation Insurance Fund.[43] The federation also succeeded, with the support of the IAC and the California Medical Association, in getting the American College of Surgeons to undertake a survey of medical facilities provided by employers.[44] This was the starting point of an alliance between organized labor and medicine, which was to gain increasing strength in the following years.

Insurance control over industrial medicine rested on two grounds: the right of the employer or carrier to choose the treating physician,[45] and a long-standing policy of the IAC to keep medical fees at a level below usual fees in private practice, on the ground that industrial doctors should not be allowed a higher fee from the employer than they would normally receive from working-class patients.[46] Such low fees made industrial practice profitable only when conducted on a mass basis, and thus made the physician dependent on a regular supply of clients by the insurer or employer. On both these issues of fees and choice of physician, the interests of organized labor converged with those of medical groups. Discussions between the state federation and organizations of industrial medicine began in 1948.[47] Since that year, organized labor has consistently given its support to doctors' petitions for increases in the Medical Fee Schedule of the IAC. In 1950, the federation obtained from insurance representatives a commitment that the schedule would no longer be applied to medical services procured by the employee himself in response to inadequate care by the carrier or employer.[48] Although this had progressively become IAC policy in litigated cases and had been made official by a commission resolution in 1946, the rule had not yet penetrated insurers' adjustment practices. This narrowing of the scope of the Medical Fee Schedule overcame a major obstacle the injured employee met in attempting to secure medical services on his own.

On the issue of choice of doctor, labor efforts focused on getting insurers to spread their cases over larger numbers of practitioners and to allow injured men at least some range of choice. Collective bargaining has also been used to obtain for the worker the right of choice, or to force employers to procure insurance from more liberal carriers. Pressures on the medical profession at first met considerable resistance from groups of industrial practitioners among whom "insurance doctors" were powerfully represented. In contrast with its tough insistence on free choice in other areas of socialized medicine, the California Medical Association kept silent on the issue in workmen's compensation. Finally, in 1964, under pressure from labor and on the occasion of a state study of compensation problems, the CMA was led to undertake a survey of professional opinion on compensation medicine. The results of the survey demonstrated the overwhelming preference of practitioners for free choice by the employee; the CMA had to make a public declaration of its support for labor demands.[49] Once again organized medicine had been brought on the side of organized labor.

The scope of bargaining between labor and insurance and industry has extended beyond medical problems. Collective agreements have often made it possible to gain under private welfare plans supplementary benefits that could not be secured from the legislature. In 1954, an important series of negotiations, concerning the procedures and operation of the IAC, brought together representatives of the State Federation of Labor and the State Chamber of Commerce. Their outcome was a "Joint Statement of Principles with Respect to the Operation of the Division of Industrial Accidents." A bill embodying the conclusions of the agreement was submitted to and passed by the 1955 legislature, and a major revision of IAC regulations was initiated. The significance of the statement and the reforms that followed it lies in the enduring consequences they had for the relations between the parties and the IAC. Their main thrust was to open the agency to fuller control and scrutiny by the organized representatives of the parties. Proposed changes in rules would have to be submitted to business and labor groups,[50] all operations would have to be codified in an administrative manual, provisions of the manual not contained in the compensation law would have to appear in the formal Rules of Practice and Procedure of the commission, the manual would include an organization chart and a complete description of jobs and responsibilities. All facets of the agency would thus become a subject for official consultation with interested groups. More importantly, the history of the Statement of Principles had established a pattern for the future relations between the agency and organized groups. The IAC would no longer be permitted to rule as an independent authority on the conflicting interests and grievances of labor and industry. The parties would rather confine it to the role of endorsing whatever understandings they had reached among themselves and outside its purview. The same pattern would prevail at the legislature. Wide areas of conflict remained between labor and business on which no agreement could be reached, and administrative or political decisions had to be sought. Yet since the middle 1950's no significant statutory or administrative change has been made that did not have the joint and previous assent of both groups.[51]

Through collective bargaining and the grievance machinery, through organized representation in relations with private groups, through more effective channels of access to the administrative process and more vigorous means of political advocacy, labor had come to command considerable initiative in the elaboration and administration of compensation policies. Organization had made it possible for the worker to overcome the precariousness of his social and political position. As we shall see presently, in the course of those and other transformations labor had acquired more than means of bargaining for political action; it had also developed its competence to promote the worker's rights through the legal process.

Labor: Conditions of Legal Competence

We shall now attempt to identify some of the special conditions that have helped labor to gain the skills and energies that made it capable of developing its legal interests under compensation law. Of special interest is the way the injured worker has derived competence from the organizational capacities of the labor movement.

Legal Competence and Civic Competence. One of the more fundamental aspirations of the legal order, and indeed a persistent feature of its imagery, is that all men should be able to appeal to the law, irrespective of their power or their social position or the political leverage they command. Obviously this ideal is often frustrated, for the legal system does not work in a social vacuum. It is of course frustrated when a tribunal is corrupt, subject to illegitimate influence, or captive of a political machine; decisions may then have to be bought or won through pressures on those who own the system. Even where, as in the case of the IAC, the integrity of legal officials cannot on the whole be seriously questioned, equal access to the law is impaired by the sheer financial burdens involved in initiating legal action, such as the cost and length of proceedings and the expensiveness of legal services. And of course ignorance acts as a similar obstacle. Such obstacles, however, seem to fade away as the administration of justice assumes greater initiative in meeting needs and processing demands. A lesser burden is put on the means and resourcefulness of the citizen. When the IAC in its early days assumed the responsibility of notifying the injured worker of his rights, of filing his application for him, of guiding him in all procedural steps, when its medical bureau checked the accuracy of his medical record and its referees conducted his case at the hearing, the injured employee was able to obtain his benefits at almost no cost and with minimal demands on his intelligence and capacities. Even today, in spite of many changes, the theory still is that an applicant can secure free advice if he calls at the commission, that he can get a free medical examination if he cannot afford a private doctor, that he can go through the procedures and hearings without legal assistance. In this sense, the IAC was, and still claims to be, a "poor man's court" through which the pauperized injured employee may participate in the legal process.

But participation may be open, and yet remain so impoverished as to be meaningless. An effective use of law requires more than the sheer accessibility of tribunals and legal services. The critical issues appear when we consider the kind and quality of participation the system allows, and the conditions under which they vary. This leads us to a more important aspect of the relations between political resourcefulness and legal competence. Insofar as the IAC aimed merely to open its doors to the poor man, it could very well dispense with the initiative of injured employees and seek and treat their cases on its own. And its doors were wide open indeed. At the same time, however, the only voice the agency heard in the making of its policies was that of organized industry, the only sure pressures on legislative and budgetary determinations came from the employers' lobby, industrial medicine was the captive of private insurance, and the daily administration of the law by carriers practically escaped all controls. Under these conditions, the worker's participation was likely to resemble more a passive submission than an affirmative use of legal opportunities. He could hardly hope to achieve much effectiveness as long as he did not have positive means of influencing the operation of the law and the working of the commission. These means, as we have seen, he did not acquire before organized labor gave him an active and articulate representation, with bargaining power and political leverage.

However distinctive it is in other respects, an appeal to law is in the first place an *appeal to authority*. As such, its effectiveness depends to some extent upon much the same conditions as affect political action in general. For law is more than a blind and mechanical application of rules to social life; it is also a means of answering needs and fulfilling aspirations, even though it can do so only through and within the confines of its own authoritative standards. The perfection and growth of law will therefore depend upon *how effectively legal authorities are sensitized and made responsive* to the problems and demands of their constituency. In this the citizen's initiative and his political alertness perform a critical role. As his channels of advocacy and his resources for social action develop, as his ties to the political order become closer and his appeals to authority more potent, the law also can more readily take notice of his condition and give recognition to his claims. Thus a prerequisite of legal competence is the development of citizenship and civic competence. Some may derive this competence from the political and social advantages they enjoy by virtue of their established position in the social structure. Others, however, whose position is precarious, may find it only in the concerted action of organized groups, which articulate interests and provide the power and means of promoting them.

Competence, civic or legal, is of course always relative to the political or legal system appealed to. The more passive the posture of governmental and legal authorities, the more burdens they place on the initiative of the citizenry, the greater the resourcefulness that will be required for achieving civic and legal competence. Conversely, the function of some administrative agencies may be conceived as an attempt to overcome the passivity of ordinary tribunals and the lack of resources of certain classes of citizens. The original mission of the IAC was in part programmatic; it consisted in identifying the problems of the injured and framing policies that would answer their needs. To that extent the commission was, in a sense, compensating for the worker's weakness and making him more competent. An agency may even directly attempt to foster the civic capacities of the governed; through it, the legal order assumes then a positive role in the development of citizenship. Although the IAC never sought to build up this kind of strength among workers, it did have a general idea that part of its role was to stimulate the assertiveness of injured employees. Thus one answer to the problem of competence may be the creation of a dynamic administration, committed to the interests and strength of the citizen. Even so, however, much will continue to hinge upon the latter's own capacities. For commitment and dynamism are not simple products of administrative determinations; they emerge from and find their support in the social organization of the system, that is, the character and perspectives of administrative personnel, the recruitment of leadership, and the structure of groups and interests under which the agency operates. In order to preserve the positive orientations of an agency and to keep it in its active role, a group must be capable of influencing the outlook of administrators, of gaining representation in policy-making boards, of making its pressure felt when decisions are made.[52] And this already presupposes a considerable degree of civic competence.

Organization is thus a powerful vehicle of civic competence, in that it provides active representation through which governmental policies and perspectives can be influenced.[53] Here we recognize an important potential function of group conflict in administration, which is to preserve the responsiveness and dynamism of public authorities. In its early years, the IAC derived most of its energies from forces outside organized labor, mainly from the powerful thrust of the Progressive movement. When the latter vanished in the early 1920's, the agency was left alone to confront the determined opposition of insurance and industry. For the next fifteen years, as we shall see, it would become increasingly paralyzed until, in the late 1930's, the rise of labor gave it some new vigor. A special kind of adversary system, resting upon the confrontation of organized groups, was thus set up. It prevented capture of the agency by the single interests of insurance and industry, sharpened the policy issues that faced the agency, and created forces from which the agency could gain support in furthering its aims—or which, indeed, could effectively press it toward action.

Adversariness may, however, be a double-edged weapon. As an agency becomes more dependent on the initiative of the parties, and especially when these are powerful political groups, it may lose all independent authority and be forced to retreat from action into passivity. We shall later examine the conditions which led the IAC into this path; at the same time as labor acquired the strength to face its opposing interests, the IAC was progressively stripped of its powers and transformed by organized groups into a tame and pliable servant.[54] It is worth noting at this point that, by so exercising its growing capacities, labor was actually dispensing with the services of the commission and thus making its competence to deal with the agency and use compensation law increasingly dependent on its own private initiative and resources. Of course it was then in a better position to afford this cost than ever before.

Legal Competence and Conceptions of Law. However necessary it is, civic competence is not in itself a sufficient condition of legal competence. Social resources and political initiative can be used in a variety of ways, and other conditions must be met before they become focused on exploiting the rights and opportunities provided by the legal order. One such requisite is the development of positive orientations toward law.

To labor, law had first been an endless succession of *obstacles* and restraints on its activities.[55] The first three decades of the century were a period of relentless legal harassment; the labor injunction, antitrust law, the doctrine of illegal conspiracy, the use of constitutional law to strike welfare legislation, the free employment contract unable to confer any right on the worker, all combined to prevent labor from achieving status and pursuing its aims. Legal action almost never meant more than attempting to overcome a restriction; court appearances were uniformly for the purpose of defending against adverse suits, and to seek legal change consisted in demanding removal of legal obstacles. The only end labor had in law was to free itself from legal tyranny and gain the liberty it needed for its economic struggle.

Law was not only a restraint on labor's freedom, it was also its *enemy*. Legal restrictions had become the most powerful weapon in the hands of industry; it could break strikes, prevent organization and picketing, and deprive unions of any security. This hostility of the legal order did not lie simply in the substance of its provisions; the whole machinery of the administration of justice appeared to have been captured by labor's foes. From the local courts and police to the federal judiciary, legal officials were recruited, or otherwise controlled, by a political system in which working people had practically no representation. The legal order was the property of the few, and labor had no share in it.

Even in areas of law and public administration where labor had gained some advantages, the system appeared incapable of meeting worker's needs. Statutes lay on the books, often unenforced; administrations were understaffed, timid in their efforts, and paralyzed by the organized resistance they encountered. At least this is what unions maintained:

> The theory often advanced is that all that is needed are good laws, labor laws. Now the fact is, that the statute books of the land are bursting with "labor laws." If one half of these laws were enforced, the condition of the wage-earners would be fairly good; but this, unfortunately, is not the case . . . these laws . . . remain dead letters. . . .
>
> Why is this? Because they keep the minds of the workers off the main task of building their unions and only through their unions can the workers gain improvements in their conditions. These measures turn the workers' eyes away from the economic struggle, from which alone help can come.[56]

Thus even where the laws were good, they only worked as a way of lulling labor into submission. Labor's problems were beyond the capacities of the legal order.

This alienation from law was in large part a response to experience. The law was indeed restrictive, hostile, and impotent. However, this does not fully account for the near apathy of the labor movement toward the problems of its legal condition. Until the late 1930's, and except for an aborted attempt in 1918 to create a legal department,[57] one can see no sign of any serious effort by the California Federation of Labor to examine or exploit available legal opportunities. It had no permanent counsel, no legal adviser in its legislative acitivities, no program of legal education for its membership, and its participation in the promotion of labor legislation was as passive as everywhere in the country. Besides the yearly report on its lobby and the voting record of legislators, its proceedings and the reports of its officers hardly refer to the legal process, except to relate injunction defeats, deprecate the judiciary, complain of the ineffectiveness of labor administrators, and indict the "legal trickeries" of its opponents. And yet opportunities and rights did exist in such matters as compensation, safety, working hours, wages, and woman and child labor, and efforts could have been made to implement them, even with the weak available resources. But labor's alienation from the legal and political order was not just a response to their hostility; rather it had expanded into a doctrine of what the law could be used for. This doctrine did not differentiate between good and bad, hostile and favorable, effective or impotent laws. It addressed itself to the law as a whole and held that

> . . . [organized labor] does not depend on legislation. It asks no special privileges, nor favors from the state. It wants to be let alone and to be allowed to exercise its rights and use its great economic power. . . . In fine, organized labor must depend on its own worth and superiority for continued progress.[58]

Law was not viewed as a means to be used positively for furthering the workers' aims. Labor saw in it an instrument of the state, and thus an interference that could always be weakening or even oppressive and had to be avoided as much as possible. Labor would thus not seek in law the authority or the moral support for its demands; it would rather find this authority in its own private power on the private scene of economic struggles. Although this doctrine undoubtedly drew much of its strength from a generalized perception of law as hostile to labor, it also had clear affinities with widely held cultural notions of the time—the laissez-faire philosophy, its theory of the passive state, its identification of state and law, and its idea of law as protecting freedom through restraint.

With the advent of the New Deal, the legal order suddenly turned from an obstacle and an enemy into a friend and a positive support. The National Labor Relations Act had laid new foundations for labor law[59] and the judiciary had reversed its stand on the constitutionality of government interventions in the economy.[60] All accepted conceptions of the proper roles of law and government had also been shaken up by the social crisis of the depression. The active state was emerging and a new idea of law, already embodied in the flowering legal realism, was now presenting it as an active instrument of political and social change. Organized labor did not immediately respond to these transformations of law and legal conceptions, and throughout the New Deal period it retained much of its apathy toward the legal order.[61] But changes became manifest toward the end of the 1930's. In 1938 the secretary of the California State Federation of Labor concluded his report by strongly stressing the need for workers to learn the laws in their favor and to use and develop them.[62] That same year, the state federation retained two lawyers, one as a general legal counsel, the other as an expert on workmen's compensation and NLRB practice.[63] In 1940 a third attorney was hired to take care of unemployment insurance matters.[64] The secretary's reports for the following years attest to an increasing demand for their services by union locals and individual members, and a growing appreciation of the significance of legal problems as well, including discussions of cases fought and of new legal points won; beginning in 1942, each counsel reported separately on his work and achievements of the year. The legal department and the union lawyer were becoming an established institution of union government. The 1940's also saw a sudden burgeoning of programs to educate union members, stewards, and business agents in their rights and opportunities under the law. In 1943, the United Automobile Workers issued a brochure on the California Workmen's Compensation Law for distribution to its members; it would replace the booklet the IAC provided, and which was considered too tame and inadequate in the advice it gave.[65] With the growth of collective agreements and grievance procedures, legal experience became more salient and meaningful to the employee. The steward was expected to perform as a first-line adviser on legal questions. In case of accident: "When you have a specific problem about which you are doubtful, CONSULT YOUR STEWARD . . . KNOW YOUR RIGHTS. Do not accept your employer's decision as to whether or not you are or are not entitled to compensation. CONSULT YOUR UNION."[66] The law was no longer the employer's law, nor a hopeless obstacle on labor's road to economic success. Labor law had finally become labor's law. In spite of deficiencies and past failures, the law offered labor a source of rights and strength. Rudimentary as the law was, from labor's point of view, it was now accepted as worthy of sustained attention and positive effort.

Legal Competence and Orientations to Authority. Although an appeal to law is basically an appeal to authority, not all appeals to authority have legal significance. Some may not involve more than a compliant request for a favor; other demands are only part of the process of bargaining and compromise between government and the governed. The distinguishing feature of appeals to law is that they hold authority accountable to rules, and found demands upon reasons derived from rules. Thus an important aspect of legal competence is the capacity for independent criticism of authority on the basis of reason and law.

This capacity is closely related to the character of authority relations and the established conceptions of authority and legitimacy among the governed. When the ruler is accepted as the only competent judge of his acts, when his authority rests upon the personal loyalty of the subject, when it is strongly protected by awe or unconditional respect, legal competence can be severely undermined. Even where such conditions do not result in submissiveness among the governed, even where they allow considerable initiative on the part of the citizen and rich reciprocal exchanges between subject and ruler, they nevertheless remain a serious obstacle to the assertion of rights. For whatever advantages are claimed or gained tend to be perceived as flowing from concession, or good will or favor, rather than as obligations that are due as a matter of right.

An important step in labor's progress toward legal competence has been the shift from welfare capitalism and its paternalistic outlook to bureaucratic management and modern conceptions of the employer's authority under the collective contract.[67] Workmen's compensation was deeply involved in this historical transformation. The original compensation program was to some extent a child of welfare capitalism. Both shared a very similar perspective on the relations between workers and authority; both had the same humanitarian concerns combined with a desire to neutralize labor protest; both saw the worker at the same time as a helpless child in need of care and guidance and as a threat to industrial and social peace who had to be controlled; both looked to the state and the employer as providing relief out of good will and generosity and expecting docility and compliance in return; both rejected notions of right and accountability to the employee. We have described how this perspective was embodied in the early IAC; we have also pointed to the support employers gave to workmen's compensation, mainly through the National Civic Federation, one of the main spokesmen for welfare capitalism.[68] The California compensation statute itself served to strengthen the notion that compensation benefits were dispensed out of the generosity of the employer; the direct-payment system rested on the assumption that carriers and employers would spontaneously and under no compulsion be the liberal and fatherly providers of the injured employee.[69] The system tended to convey an image of discretionary good will and to discount the idea that the employer was acting under legal obligation.[70] The same is true of employers' control over medical treatment.

This paternalism received added strength when employers developed their own private welfare plans; in this case the administration of workmen's compensation benefits became inextricably mixed with the distribution of company-sponsored benefits. The injured man got his medical care at the same hospital and from the same personnel from which he and his family would also obtain free medical services in other circumstances; in the first days of disability, his wages were continued, at a much higher rate than statutory compensation rates, just as they were in other cases of illness; and there were also private pensions. Actually these private benefits usually amounted to much less than what the law provided for industrial disabilities. Furthermore, they never conferred rights on the employee, but their distribution always remained a matter of discretion, depending upon what management felt opportune and how good a showing of loyalty the employee made. In this confusion of private and legal benefits, the distinction between rights and company welfare tended to be blurred; compensation took the color of a gratuity, or at least there was always a latent intimation that protest and insistence on legal rights would result in costly losses of free advantages.

Paternalism and the merging of rights and charities came to an end when company welfare plans became a subject for collective bargaining, a change fostered by the rise of union power and the restrictions on wage increases under the war administration.[71] As a result, both private and public welfare became governed by definite legal obligations. Whatever advantage the employee was using, he was no longer asking for a privilege in exchange for his cooperation; he was invoking a rule and claiming a right. In addition, as organized labor was gaining some control over medical care and using its power to influence employers' and carriers' practices in the payment of benefits, the direct-payment system was being stripped of its past connotations; it appeared more clearly as the performance of a duty, which the employer would do spontaneously or the employee would see that the rules were observed. At the same time, the growth of bureaucracy in personnel management, of collective contracts and grievance procedures, were imposing greater restraints on managerial discretion. Authority relations in the firm were thus increasingly placed under the governance of rules, giving the employee more independence and dignity and a greater capacity to invoke the protection of law for his rights. These transformations were reflected in the perspectives and policies of the IAC. How the IAC drifted away from the paternalism of its early conceptions and came to allow and expect independent assertions of right from the injured employee is a theme of the following chapter.

Autonomy and Commitment. When we think of a law suit, the image is often suggested of a person freeing himself from and acting against the weight of social pressures, standing alone on his right and invoking the justice of the sovereign on his behalf. The legal man is thus presented as unbound and uncompromising, free to pursue his moral commitment to legal principles. And correspondingly an often celebrated virtue of the legal order it its capacity to lend authority to the individual against the power of groups and society. Although this imagery can hardly be accepted as an accurate description of how the legal process operates, it nevertheless turns our attention to an important condition of the capacity to use law effectively. Legal competence requires a certain degree of autonomy, a detachment of the person from the system of social relations that determine his position and interests. The more dependent a person is on his ties to others, the more he is involved in some going concern he needs to preserve, the less capable he is of assuming the principled posture legal action requires. Dependency makes the person insecure and captive of his social situation; it encourages passive acceptance and accommodating compromises, rather than moral assertion. What we have said about authority relations in the preceding section may be reinterpreted in this light as a special way in which the lack of autonomy impinges upon legal competence; certain kinds of structures and conceptions of authority undermine this independence of thought and action upon which assertions of right are founded. Here, we are interested in identifying some of the general dimensions and social conditions of moral autonomy. When we speak of an autonomous person, we do not refer only to this free, unbound individual the legal imagery often suggests. This person may of course be a group as well as an individual. More importantly, an individual may have to seek in a group the security and support he needs for developing moral autonomy and asserting his rights.

One element of autonomy is *security*—being free from the fear or threat of losses and reprisals. Persons depend on others for their economic welfare, their social status, and their sense of worth and dignity. The assertion of a right may upset those social relations in which a man has invested his self and his interests, thus exposing him to risks or threats he cannot bear. Few people could have been more vulnerable than the injured worker in this respect. To claim compensation when it had been denied, or to protest an underpayment of benefits, meant getting into trouble with an employer who had discretionary control over hiring, discharge, wages, welfare benefits, and career. Employment, his most important source of income and status, was also his most fragile and least legally protected asset; the contract at will gave no guarantee and the labor market often promised only long unemployment.[72]

As it brought managerial authority under the rule of law, collective bargaining gave the employee increasing security in his job. Hiring, firing, and other job conditions, including welfare benefits, have become subject to collective agreements and the jurisprudence of grievances and arbitration. It is now an abuse of authority for the employer to penalize an employee for legal action against him; it violates the collective contract's requirement of "just cause" for discipline and discharge. As private welfare plans are made objects of collective bargaining, they become sources of legally protected contractual rights; no longer can the threat of withdrawing benefits, or of refusing to rehire a handicapped employee, arbitrarily be used as a means of influence.[73] Even where the contract is silent, the employee is no longer resourceless in the face of company pressure; the union can affect company policies in such areas as welfare and programs of training and employment of the disabled, and see to their fair enforcement. The easiest means of coercion—interrupting compensation payments when a formal application is filed—has become increasingly less effective. One of the major gains of organized labor in its continuing negotiations with insurers and employers has been to secure for the injured man advances on his future benefits, when regular payments are discontinued pending a formal IAC ruling on the claim. Advances are now almost routinely granted by the larger carriers and self-insurers, and even when they are refused, the employee can sometimes get relief directly from his attorney or the union treasury. A major obstacle to legal action—the worker's dependence on continuing wages—has thus been at least partially removed.

The law also has performed a significant role in giving more security to the employee and thus increasing his legal competence. In 1941, organized labor obtained passage of an amendment to the compensation law, which made it a misdemeanor for the employer to "discharge, or threaten to discharge, or in any other manner discriminate against any employee because the latter has filed or made known his intention to file an application or complaint with the commission, or because the employee has testified or made known an intention to testify in any investigation or proceeding held by the commission."[74] Although prosecution under this section is extremely difficult and seldom undertaken in view of the problems of proof and the requirement of a preliminary hearing and positive recommendation by the IAC, it nevertheless always stands as a latent threat. Another important change had been made in 1933 by a decision of the California Supreme Court holding that the continuing payment of wages to a disabled employee, like the payment of compensation, prevents the running of the statute of limitation; the injured man would no longer find himself barred from claiming his right, after having been lured into inaction by the continuation of his wages.[75] However, the major protections of the employee did not come from workmen's compensation law or from the IAC, which did little in this respect beyond adding its pressure to employees' requests for advances on future benefits. The more effective protections came from social security.

Unemployment insurance has of course diminished the threat of joblessness, directly by the benefits it offers and in a more subtle way by its experience rating system, which penalizes the employer for unjustified discharges.[76] But the workmen's compensation claimant has found a much stronger support for his rights in disability insurance. The unemployment compensation disability (UCD) program was adopted by the California legislature in 1946 and entrusted to the Department of Employment.[77] Its purpose was to insure employees against unemployment as a result of illnesses or injuries unrelated to their job, and thus not covered by workmen's compensation. Benefits include a weekly allowance to compensate for loss of wages and an additional daily allowance for days spent under hospital care. Those payments are financed by employees themselves through contributions withheld from their wages. When an injured worker is denied compensation by his employer, he can turn to the Department of Employment and draw his UCD benefits. It would seem that employers and carriers are thus given a golden opportunity to divert their disabled men away from compensation to this public insurance program, the cost of which is borne exclusively by the employees.

Two factors have actually made disability insurance one of the most powerful prompters of compensation claims. First, compensation benefits are on the whole more lasting and extensive than those provided by disability insurance, which expire after a maximum of twenty-six weeks and include no medical care. Although an employee is eligible for UCD as long as there is uncertainty as to whether his case is covered by workmen's compensation or disability insurance, he often preserves an incentive to press his compensation rights. In this way, UCD comes to work as an expedient for giving employees the temporary means of subsistence that make it possible for them to demand and obtain their compensation benefits without being forced by need into a quick and poor settlement. This service has been extended by a 1957 amendment to those injured employees who receive compensation in amount inferior to disability benefit rates; they became eligible for UCD benefits equal to the difference between the full disability allowance and the cash compensation benefits they received.[78]

This incidental effect of disability insurance was reinforced by another factor—the legal policy of preventing duplication of coverage by workmen's compensation and UCD,[79] a policy that received considerable impetus out of the Department of Employment's concern for the solvency of its disability fund. Except for those cases of uncertainty and inferior compensation payments we have just described, an industrially injured employee was normally not eligible for UCD benefits. In order to implement this policy, the Department of Employment had the right to recover all overpayments made to industrially compensated employees;[80] in 1947 it was in addition granted a lien on all workmen's compensation benefits awarded by the IAC to workers who had received UCD benefits pending final determination of their compensation rights.[81] This made it possible for the department to recover overpayments directly from the employer or carrier without having to collect them from the injured. The department soon set up a procedure designed to exploit this opportunity fully—applications for UCD benefits were screened in order to identify those cases that might be industrially compensable or where compensation might not have been fully paid. When such cases were found, the claimant was required, as a condition for receiving UCD, to show proof that he had filed an application with the IAC. The Department of Employment was then in a position to file a claim of lien on the case, and to replenish its fund of the monies that should have been paid from workmen's compensation. Employees were thus not only encouraged but also adminstratively compelled to assert their compensation rights.

Since UCD compensates for any disability that results in unemployment, it does not distinguish between temporary and permanent disability, as does workmen's compensation. Benefits were thus paid to both temporarily and permanently disabled men, and the department enjoyed a lien on both temporary and permanent disability benefits awarded by the IAC. Consequently, permanent disability benefits that are supposed to compensate for permanent loss of working capacity irrespective of loss of wages were often at least partly absorbed by the lien for UCD benefits, which are intended to cover only the loss of wages over a limited period. In order to correct this situation, a series of amendments in 1957 have exempted permanent disability awards from the UCD lien; the lien now applies only to disability insurance benefits covering days for which the employee has been awarded cash payments for temporary disability.[82] The right to claim overpayment beyond the lien was disallowed at the same time.[83] The effect of these amendments was to make permanently disabled workers fully eligible for UCD even though they might be entitled to compensation. For those employees, UCD had become a direct and irrecoverable subsidy for the pursuit of compensation rights. At the same time the Department of Employment kept an interest in filing a lien claim in the hope that, given the unclear line that separates temporary from permanent disability, it would recover some of its disbursements on whatever portion of the compensation award would be attributed to temporary disability.[84]

Social insurance, legal protections, and the collective agreement have thus made the employee much less dependent on his job and his wages and have considerably enhanced his security and his capacity to assert rights against the employer. There is, however, more to autonomy than sheer security. Submissiveness may reflect normative conceptions of the nature of authority, shared by ruler and ruled, having the effect of perpetuating the dependency of the subject. Similarly, one may be *morally captive* of one's social situation, unable to dissociate oneself from common values and perspectives even when they harm one's interests and aspirations. Moral captivity has been recognized in a variety of settings, perhaps most extremely when the inmate of a concentration camp comes to identify himself with the aims of his guards, when the Negro shares the racial conceptions of his white master, when workers adopt the ideology of industry, or when the recipient of public aid approves the violations of his privacy by welfare agencies. In a more subtle way, the same sort of captivity develops wherever the uncritical acceptance of group perspectives transforms the person into a docile performer of social routines. Whether it is a direct response to oppression, insecurity, or group needs, or a more immediate reflection of established value orientations, whether a product of culture or society, this captivity prevents persons from rationally assessing their special interests and developing distinct moral aspirations. Hence it bears critically on the capacity to invoke law. For *the assertion of a right is a form of moral criticism: besides the expression of a demand, it involves an appeal to the authority of principles in support of one's claims.* To assume this posture requires one to take distance from the social world so as to redefine and criticize it in terms of authoritative standards. Legal competence thus rests upon the same moral autonomy in which man finds the ability to set himself apart from the group and to evolve his own moral commitments as a discrete person.

We are interested here in the role of representative organizations as a source of moral autonomy. While all groups, including these organizations, are potential vehicles of moral identification and can thus be conducive to dependence, a special function of the representative group is to free its members from other groups that seek to capture their moral loyalties. Organized representation enables similarly situated persons to recognize the distinct interests they hold in common, and to articulate them in the framework of appropriate notions of justice. Alternative group and value commitments are thus built, which detach members from the setting in which they were caught. The more persons are insecure and morally dependent, the more they need such organized moral support in order to achieve legal competence.

Labor's intellectual and radical critics have long stressed how, before the 1930's, labor had been a prisoner of managerial ideology and the entrepreneurial culture of capitalist society.[85] The middle-class aspirations of the wage-earner, the popular cult of the self-made industrialist, the inability of craft unions to identify with workers as a class, the support given to management's drive for productivity and the lack of concern for the unemployed, the refusal to engage labor in politics on its own, and the "business" conception of the labor struggle as purely private and economic, all these have been pointed out as symptoms of this moral dependence. Looking back at labor's reluctance to rely on law and state intervention, and particularly at its hostility to social insurance, it is worth mentioning how close its justification for these policies was to the arguments industry made against government control:

> Compulsory sickness insurance for workers is based upon the theory they are unable to look after their own interests and the state must interpose its authority and wisdom and assume the relation of parent or guardian.
>
> There is something in the very suggestion of this relationship and this policy that is repugnant to freeborn citizens. Because it is at variance with our concepts of voluntary institutions and freedom for individuals, Labor questions its wisdom.[86]

Labor was drawing its standards from the very model of the free, self-reliant, and thriving individual that its opponents were presenting. Its early hostility to workmen's compensation and preference for liability, its later docile acceptance of a compensation system the structure of which consistently worked against workers' interests, point to the same moral subservience. The 1930's did much to free labor from this dependence. Irving Bernstein argues that "the most significant long-term effect of the Great Depression upon the labor movement was to cause it to re-examine its basic philosophy of voluntarism, the concept of self-reliant trade union that did not depend upon the state."[87] And we have seen labor acquire new means of political action, develop a new orientation to law, and become a powerful advocate of workmen's compensation as well as a persistent critic of its structure. In the course of this change, organized labor increased its competence to represent the injured worker and sustain his moral autonomy.

This work of representation has become a continuing task of labor officials in serving injured employees. Encounters between injured men and union stewards or agents are thus characterized by a recurrent and patterned exchange, which is designed to arouse in the employee a firm insistence on his rights and determination to use legal action if needed. The scene typically involves variations on three major points. One of them seeks to dispel any latent sense of insecurity:

> You know you have a right and nobody can do anything against you for claiming it. If they do, we are here to protect you. And when they stop sending your benefit checks, tell us and we'll find a way of helping you.[88]

This is, usually at least, the easy part of the game. The second point goes more directly to the problem of moral autonomy and attempts to detach the employee from the images of the law and statements of his rights he has been presented by the employer or the carrier:

> Never believe your boss or the insurance company when they talk about your rights. Never take the doctor's word for it: he is not your doctor, he is the company's doctor. You have to look out for yourself and ask questions, and when you have problems, come and see us or call a lawyer. Remember, insurers are not there to help you, but to screw you whenever they can.[89]

Distrust of the employer and his agents is thus built up as a resource for overcoming dependent attitudes. Emphasis is put on the inherent conflict between the injured man and the adverse interests that manage his welfare; the worker is thus led to assume a critical stance, from which he can better guard the integrity of his distinct interests against others' interpretations of what is best for him.[90] The union representative thus builds on this acute and open adversariness, which, as we have seen, has come to characterize the administration of workmen's compensation in the relations among interest groups. He implants an adversary perspective in the day-to-day dealings between discrete employees and insurers, using it as a lever for restoring the injured worker to his moral independence—a lever he would lack if compensation had developed as the program of a friendly or neutral government.

The third message of the union agent to injured employees is an attempt to transform their individual interest in compensation benefits into a moral interest in justice. Autonomy involves more than simply being free from imprisoning moral orientations; it is above all a capacity to pursue one's own aspirations freely and positively. Hence to make a person autonomous also requires the creation of distinct moral commitments. Similarly, legal competence entails more than being free and unbound in the pursuit of one's interests; it presupposes a sensitivity to the legal implications of one's problems and to the ways in which interests are corroded when the standards and principles that protect them are undermined and attenuated. Here is where the role of the representative group acquires its full significance. The creation of moral commitment in the injured worker is often a critical problem. We can understand it from this account by a deputy commissioner from the IAC Los Angeles office of his experience in controlling compromise agreements between employees and carriers; it was written in 1935, at a time when Los Angeles was still weakly unionized and the commission was still concerned about its role in building up the capacity of the injured man to protect his rights.

> Our toughest problem is to convince the applicant that he is not receiving an adequate adjustment. . . . What are we to do, when, after all of our explanation and advice, the applicant still says, "I want to settle." Theoretically his case may be worth $1,000, but practically he is unwilling to make a fight. . . . This is the practical problem connected with the actual handling of compromises and releases within my experience. Roughly speaking, I would say that 50 per cent of

> the people who pass before me with settlements in which it is pointed out that the settlement is inadequate do not appreciate the advice and are absolutely hostile, and many times refuse point-blank to file an application or even request a permanent disability rating. Only this week an injured employee of the Water Department of the City of Los Angeles came in with a settlement of $275.00. His attitude in the beginning is that it was none of our business as to how badly he was hurt or as to why he wanted to take $275.00. In short he was the most outstanding advocate of rugged individualism that I have bumped into in many a day. *I tried to point out to him that if he settled his case for half what it was worth, that in turn meant that every succeeding applicant would be requested and expected to settle on the same basis. All he could see was his individual problem.* Bluntly he did not give a "tinker's dam" for anybody but himself. . . . I have often wondered just what the attitude of the San Francisco region is as compared to the Los Angeles setup. San Francisco is rated as a union town. Los Angeles, on the other hand, openly brags of being an open-shop town, and this attitude is not only one taken by the employers but by a large number of employees. I suppose that this independent attitude is commendable in most things, but I confess to a feeling that in handling the compensation setup I have always felt that the lone-wolf attitude, the refusal to cooperate, the unwillingness to indulge in team play, is much more characteristic of the industrial setup we have in Southern California than it is in other sections where I worked. [Emphasis added.]

This indictment of "rugged individualism" actually addressed itself to the propensity of unrepresented employees to deny the moral relevance of their compensation rights. The representative is specially competent to overcome this denial, because of his ability to present individual cases as instances of a class involving the group as a whole. Thereby he can appeal to group loyalties as a way of generating a moral commitment.

> This is not only your problem, it is our problem. You are not the only one involved; if you don't fight this case, they will keep treating all of us like you have been treated. And, who knows, you may be hurt again, and it will be the same story all over again. You have to make it clear to them we won't let this happen again.[91]

What was the special trouble of an isolated worker becomes the illustration of a systematic practice affecting the whole shop or local: "They are always late in their payments." "They always cut temporary disability before you can really work." "They always send you to this company doctor." An individual demand is then transformed into an occasion for an exemplary case. By insisting on the general implications of single cases, the representative prepares the latter for subsumption under legal rules; the problem thus becomes an issue of principle, while at the same time the individual's commitment to the group is used as a resource for generating a principled posture. In this process, an individual claim for some private money is changed into a group-supported grievance for violation of common rights. As we shall see in the following chapter, the union compensation lawyer also shares in this function of the representative group toward the claimant; just as the union agent seeks to transform individual cases into *exemplary cases,* the lawyer is not infrequently concerned with transforming cases into *precedents.* In doing this, his strategy is much the same as that of the union agent, except its purpose is legal growth and potential rights rather than compliance with existing law and established rights, and its outcome is an even fuller measure of legal competence for the employee—the capacity to promote law rather than simply to exploit it.

As we have argued, the achievement of autonomy is marked by freedom from social pressures, the capacity to transcend limiting group perspectives, and the development of positive moral aspirations. Hence, autonomy is enhanced by the emergence of new group loyalties. The result is necessarily some attenuation of commitment to the group against which claims are made and action is taken. Autonomy may therefore eventually evolve into what has been called "fanaticism"—a posture in which appeals are persistently made to moral or ideological principles, regardless of their consequences for the integrity of the group.[92] This occurs when external loyalties outweigh commitments to the group, and thus permit "irresponsible" advocacy. Fanaticism has its counterpart in certain ways of using law; legal competence may then become a vehicle of legalism. We are accustomed to recognizing legalism in lawyers and administrators when a rigid insistence on rules impairs their ability to solve problems and make needed adaptations. But legalism is also met in the litigious claimant who requests compliance with rules even where this would upset the very order they are intended to preserve; a contracting party who has lost interest in the agreement may begin invoking formal clauses that threaten the successful outcome of the contract; an alienated litigant may exploit procedural rules in a way that thwarts the normal functioning of the judicial process. Legalism in such cases appears as an irresponsible use of law, encouraged by alienation from the social setting in which legal action is taken. What distinguishes legal competence from legalism or fanaticism is that it allows principled criticism while at the same time preserving loyalty to the institution. This is done by transforming the character of loyalty—from adherence to specific persons and modes of social life into a commitment to the order of the group and to law as a way of preserving that order. The autonomy appropriate to legal competence is that of the responsible citizen who, in his attachment to his country, remains free and determined to criticize the government; his loyalty goes to the institutions of government rather than to those who embody them at any particular time. The role of representative organizations in the creation of moral autonomy and legal competence should be understood in this light. The mission of the representative is not to sever group loyalties; it is rather to free the person from dependence upon the special, and always limiting ways in which group life is conceived and organized. In doing so, of course, the representative organization exploits an external loyalty—in this case, the employee's commitment to the union and his fellow employees—as the vehicle for a change of moral identification; he may thus easily foster a process of alienation. Whether alienation and legalism will actually develop depends largely upon the character of the representative organizations; the stronger their commitment to the social order in which they operate, the more positive their orientation to law as a way of protecting and shaping this order, the more they can contribute to genuine legal competence. But the balance of detachment and loyalty may also be upset in the opposite way, if the representative himself becomes a captive of the forum before which the constituency is represented. Insofar as he becomes subservient to received notions of order, he loses his capacity to support the moral autonomy essential to a competent citizenry.

Conclusion

We have seen how the injured employee acquired the security and moral independence he needed for adopting a principled approach to his compensation problems; we have seen him develop the appropriate orientations to authority that permitted him to take a more critical and assertive stance toward his employer and the IAC; we have seen how labor came to recognize law as a positive means of pursuing its moral aspirations, and how it developed the social and political resources that allowed it to participate meaningfully in the legal order. Briefly, we have shown how labor acquired the moral and material energies by which it could confront its powerful and well-equipped opponents in the workmen's compensation system, and do so through legal advocacy within the framework of the legal order.

But in spite of this growth of initiative and competence, it still remains that over 60 percent of nonagricultural laborers are unorganized; that farm labor is just beginning to unionize and has hardly been reached by the developments of protective legislation. It remains also that many existing unions are weak, vulnerable, and in hidden ways captive of adverse interests. Many appear ill equipped for action beyond the narrow shop problems, or cling to the comfortable notion that the IAC is there to care for their interests and will do so, even though hostile groups are forcefully represented before the agency. Above all, it has become increasingly true in recent years that even powerful segments of the labor movement were losing much of their dynamism, and that unions felt at best very dimly this sense of mission and this responsibility for the unorganized workers that had marked them for a while after the 1930's. There are still those *braceros*, migrant workers, and farm laborers, which a recent survey by the California Division of Labor Law Enforcement found being routinely denied their compensation claims, underpaid in whatever benefits they received, given only elementary medical care, fired and moved back to their country when their case appeared too serious, and cut from benefits when they had left on their own. This happens while the most competent unions comfortably enjoy the benefits of their strength.

As we shall see, even while turning to the state and law in a more active and positive way, organized labor has carried over to the legal and political arenas much of its long-standing emphasis on self-help and voluntarism. The unorganized are paying the costs of this strategy.

Notes to Chapter IV

1. See Chap. II, pp. 29–32.
2. California Labor Code, Sec. 3700–3705.
3. A significant portion of the gross insurance premium covers the carrier's anticipated underwriting and administrative expenses; in California, the carrier's profit and premium taxes represent more than one half of the "expense loading" as opposed to "pure premium." Self-insurance makes it possible to avoid these expenses. See *Report of the Workmen's Compensation Study Commission* (Sacramento: State of California, April, 1965), p. 49.
4. California Statutes of 1915, Chap. 642; California Insurance Code, Sec. 11732. The policy had already been introduced in 1913, when the SCIF was created (California Statutes of 1913, Chap. 176, Sec. 40 [a]; California Insurance Code, Sec. 11821).
5. For an introductory discussion of "merit rating" in compensation insurance, see Herman M. Somers and Anne R. Somers, *Workmen's Compensation* (New York: John Wiley & Sons, 1954), pp. 106–109, 228–230. A similar technique has been used in unemployment compensation, in which "experience rating" was adopted as a means of providing "an economic incentive to employers to stabilize employment in their establishments" (*Unemployment Insurance in California* [Sacramento: California Legislature, Assembly, Interim Committee on Finance and Insurance, 1955], p. 76). The contributions of each employer are made to vary with the amount of benefits that are paid to former employees of his plant. Here also the system encourages employers to contest the benefit claims of unemployed workers. Indeed, it is explicitly used for that purpose; experience rating is expected "to create an incentive among employers to aid in reducing the amount of improper payments by informing the administration of cases in which claimants had

disqualified themselves (*ibid.*; see also *Report of the Senate Interim Committee on Unemployment Insurance* [Sacramento: California Legislature, Senate, 1945], p. 82).

6. The frequency of those practices is indicated by the large number of cases in which the information offices of the Industrial Accident Commission at San Francisco and Los Angeles are called upon to find for inquiring injured men the name of their employers' insurers; in those cases, the IAC usually reminds the employer of his duty to post notice of the name and address of his carrier (California Labor Code, Sec. 3713), but in practice this obligation is never enforced.

7. Since much of their profit is derived from investment operations rather than directly from underwriting, insurers would normally be at least as interested in maximizing premium rates as in cutting down benefit payments. Thus they are not likely to oppose an increase in the legal schedule of benefits, provided premium rates are correspondingly raised. Similarly, they have struggled to maintain the expense loading in official rates at as high a level as possible.

8. California Statutes of 1915, Chap. 642; California Insurance Code, Sec. 11732.

9. California Statutes of 1951, Chap. 1123; California Insurance Code, Sec. 11750–11758.

10. California Statutes of 1953, Chap. 889, Sec. 1.

11. California Insurance Code, Sec. 11656.5.

12. *Ibid.*, Sec. 11656.6, 11656.7.

13. Workmen's Compensation Policy, Pol. Form No. E. (California State Compensation Insurance Fund).

14. On the condition of labor before the Great Depression, see Irving Bernstein, *The Lean Years* (Cambridge, Mass.: The Riverside Press, 1960); on labor in California, see Ira B. Cross, *A History of the Labor Movement in California* (Berkeley: University of California Press, 1935).

15. *Proceedings of the 56th Annual Meeting of the California State Federation of Labor, 1958*, pp. 128–129. Those figures do not show the full extent of unionization in California, but they provide an adequate indication of trends. They closely parallel the national experience: estimates of total American union labor indicate an increase from about 2 to 5 million between 1910 and 1920, followed by a decline to about 3.5 million in the 1920's and not quite 3 million in 1933. See Leo Wolman, *Ebb and Flow in Trade Unionism* (New York: National Bureau of Economic Research, 1936).

16. On these points, see Bernstein, *op. cit.*, pp. 83–143.

17. See, for instance, *Proceedings of the Department on Compensation for Industrial Accidents* (New York: National Civic Federation, 1911). On the formative period of workmen's compensation legislation, see Isaac M. Rubinow, *Social Insurance* (New York: Henry Holt and Co., 1916), pp. 155–168. On the character and role of the National Civic Federation, see Philip S. Foner, *History of the Labor Movement in the United States* (New York: International Publishers, 1964), III, 61–77; Philip Taft, *The American Federation of Labor in the Time of Samuel Gompers* (New York: Harper & Brothers, 1957), pp. 225–232; Marguerite Green, *The National Civic Federation and the American Labor Movement* (Washington, D.C.: Catholic University of America Press, 1956).

18. *Proceedings of the 8th Annual Meeting of the California State Federation of Labor, 1908*, p. 94; *Proceedings . . . 10th Annual Meeting . . . , 1909*, p. 58; *Proceedings . . . 12th Annual Meeting . . . , 1911*, p. 94. This early opposition was acknowledged by a representative of the federation in 1913: "In going to our State Legislature two years ago, I felt that labor should ask for the elimination of the common law defenses rather than compensation laws . . ." (*Workmen's Compensation: Report upon Operation of State Laws*, an Investi-

gation by the American Federation of Labor and the National Civic Federation [Washington, D.C.: U.S. Congress, 63rd Congress, 2d. sess., 1914], Senate Document No. 419, p. 21). On labor's opposition to workmen's compensation, see Rubinow, *op. cit.*, pp. 157, 163, 190, 199; *Medical Problems under Workmen's Compensation* (rev. ed.; Chicago: American Medical Association, Bureau of Medical Economics, 1935), pp. 14–18.

19. *Proceedings of the 12th Annual Meeting of the California State Federation of Labor, 1911*, p. 94.

20. *Ibid.*

21. Rubinow, *op. cit.*, p. 199.

22. *Proceedings of the 11th Annual Meeting of the California State Federation of Labor, 1910*, p. 28.

23. Rubinow, *op. cit.*, p. 199.

24. *Proceedings of the 14th Annual Meeting of the California State Federation of Labor, 1913*, p. 93.

25. See *Proceedings of the 16th Annual Meeting of the California State Federation of Labor, 1915*, p. 103; *Proceedings . . . 18th Annual Meeting . . . , 1917*, p. 96; *Proceedings . . . 20th Annual Meeting . . . , 1919*, pp. 114–116, 124. This weak participation is reflected in the surprisingly small representation labor had in contemporary discussions of compensation problems. It is reported that at the 1916 Conference on Social Insurance organized by the International Association of Industrial Accident Boards and Commissions, out of 198 delegates whose affiliation could be identified, only 4 represented labor interests, as against 55 state and federal officials, 33 intellectuals and social workers, and 92 representatives of insurance and industry (*Medical Problems under Workmen's Compensation*, p. 17). Administrators and intellectuals were equally dominant at the National Conference on Workmen's Compensation in 1910. See *Proceedings of the National Conference on Workmen's Compensation for Industrial Accidents, 1910* (Princeton: Princeton University Press, 1910); more generally, see Robert Hunter, *Labor in Politics* (Chicago: The Socialist Party, 1915), especially pp. 102–106.

26. On the evolution of union membership in the United States, see Irving Bernstein, "The Growth of American Unions," *American Economic Review*, XLIV (1954), pp. 301–318. On patterns of union growth under the New Deal, see Milton Derber, "Growth and Expansion," in Milton Derber and Edwin Young (eds.), *Labor and the New Deal* (Madison: University of Wisconsin Press, 1957), pp. 1–44.

27. *Proceedings of the 56th Annual Meeting of the California State Federation of Labor, 1958*, pp. 128–129. A 1939 survey of union labor by the State of California Division of Labor Statistics found that, out of the 1,222 locals that were contacted, 105 indicated that they had been chartered before 1900, 203 beween 1901 and 1910, 163 between 1911 and 1920, only 98 between 1921 and 1930, but 559 between 1931 and 1939; in this latter group, the year 1937, in which the U.S. Supreme Court upheld the constitutionality of the Wagner Act, saw the foundation of 237 locals (*Union Labor in California, June 1939* [San Francisco: California Department of Industrial Relations, 1940], p. 9). State labor statistics indicate that the 1,068 locals that reported their membership both in 1940 and in 1943 had in the meantime grown from 350,402 to 748,836 (*Union Labor in California* [San Francisco: California Department of Industrial Relations, 1943]).

28. For these figures see annual issues of *Union Labor in California*.

29. On the crisis of the labor movement in the 1930's, see James O. Morris, *Conflict within the A.F.L.: A Study of Craft versus Industrial Unionism, 1901–1938* (Ithaca: New York State School of Industrial and Labor Relations, 1958); Philip Taft, *The A.F. of L. from the Death of Gompers to the Merger* (New York: Harper & Brothers, 1959); Walter

Galenson, *The C.I.O. Challenge to the A.F.L.: A History of the American Labor Movement, 1935–1941* (Cambridge, Mass.: Harvard University Press, 1960); Edwin Young, "The Split in the Labor Movement," in Derber and Young (eds.), *op. cit.* pp. 45–76.

30. On the change of labor's attitude toward social insurance, see Edwin E. Witte, "Organized Labor and Social Security," in Derber and Young (eds.), *op. cit.*, pp. 239–274, especially pp. 249–250.

31. *Proceedings of the 30th Annual Meeting of the California State Federation of Labor, 1929*, pp. 13–14.

32. California Statutes of 1935, Chap. 352.

33. *First Biennial Report of the Department of Industrial Relations, 1927–1930* (Sacramento: California Legislature, 49th Sess., 1931), Appendix to the *Journals of the Senate and Assembly*, Vol. 5, No. 13, pp. 28–29.

34. See, for instance, F. Robertson Jones, "Ominous Abuses Threatening the Insurability of Workmen's Compensation," address delivered at the Annual Convention of the International Association of Insurance Counsel, September, 1932.

35. *Proceedings of the 39th Annual Meeting of the California State Federation of Labor, 1938*, pp. 27, 33.

36. At the 1939 session of the legislature, the labor lobby was enlarged and reorganized; its capacities were further enhanced by the creation in 1942 of the S.F. of L. Research Department. See *Proceedings of the 40th Annual Meeting of the California State Federation of Labor, 1939*, pp. 35–36; *Proceedings . . . 43rd Annual Meeting . . . , 1942*, p. 19.

37. See *Investigation of Procedure of the Industrial Accident Commission* (Sacramento: California Legislature, Subcommittee of the Assembly Interim Committee on Governmental Efficiency and Economy, 1945); *Report of the Senate Interim Committee on Workmen's Compensation Benefits* (Sacramento: California Legislature, 1947, 1951); *Partial Report of the Senate Interim Committee on Workmen's Compensation Benefits* (Sacramento: California Legislature, 1953); *Final Report of the Senate Interim Committee on Workmen's Compensation Benefits* (Sacramento: California Legislature, 1953); *Report of the Senate Committee on Labor* (Sacramento: California Legislature, 1955); *Report of the Assembly Interim Committee on the Judiciary* (Sacramento: California Legislature, 1963); *Report of the Workmen's Compensation Study Commission* (Sacramento: State of California, April, 1965).

38. The procedure for permanent disability rating in 1938 and again in 1942 and 1953, the termination of temporary disability payments in 1940, the recruitment of medical experts in 1941, the reorganization of the Department of Industrial Relations in 1943–1945, the revision of the rating schedule in the late 1940's, the development of the Medical Bureau in 1947, agency policies in the commutation of awards in 1948, the problem of medical fees in 1948, 1950, and 1954, the creation of branch offices in the early 1950's, and a complete revision of IAC rules and procedures in 1954–1958 were the more important targets of successive drives by the State Federation. Evidence for these points is drawn from an analysis of the *Proceedings of the California State Federation of Labor*, and from the files and documents of the agency.

39. California Statutes of 1955, Chap. 1822, Sec. 2; California Labor Code, Sec. 5307.

40. California Statutes of 1963, Chap. 1767, Sec. 1; California Labor Code, Sec. 114.

41. *Proceedings of the 43rd Annual Meeting of the California State Federation of Labor, 1942*, p. 46.

42. *Ibid.*, p. 38.

43. *Reports of Officers of the California State Federation of Labor, 1944*, p. 57.

44. *Ibid.*, p. 45.

45. California Labor Code, Sec. 4600.

46. *Report of the Industrial Accident Commission, 1913–1914* (Sacramento: California Legislature, 41st Sess., 1915), Appendix to the *Journals of the Senate and Assembly,* Vol. 1, No. 14, p. 17.

47. *Proceedings of the 46th Annual Meeting of the California State Federation of Labor, 1948*, p. 78.

48. *Proceedings of the 48th Annual Meeting of the California State Federation of Labor, 1950*, p. 83.

49. *Report of the Workmen's Compensation Study Commission*, p. 103.

50. California Statutes of 1955, Chapter 1822, required notice to and hearing of industry and labor organizations on any proposed change in agency regulations. The act was followed by a complete revision of IAC rules, which dragged on for about two years before being finally adopted in 1958.

51. See Chap. VI, pp. 139–159.

52. Organized political action may even be necessary to *curb* the activity of government when this activity tends to hold down the capacities of the governed for independent pursuit of their interests. On this point, see Edgar S. Cahn and Jean C. Cahn, "The War on Poverty: A Civilian Perspective," *Yale Law Journal,* LXXIII (1964), 1317–1352.

53. This point is developed in S. M. Miller, "Poverty, Race and Politics," in Irving L. Horowitz (ed.), *The New Sociology: Essays on Social Values and Social Theory in Honor of C. Wright Mills* (New York: Oxford University Press, 1964).

54. See Chap. VI, pp. 139–159.

55. On organized labor's attitude toward law, see Mollie Ray Carroll, *Labor and Politics: The Attitudes of the A.F. of L. toward Legislation and Politics* (Boston: Houghton Mifflin Co., 1923), pp. 141–169; Bernstein, *op. cit.*, pp. 190–243; Foner, *op. cit.*, Vol. 3, pp. 282–366; Marc Karson, *American Labor Unions and Politics* (Carbondale: Southern Illinois University Press, 1958), pp. 117–149; Elizabeth Brandeis, "Organized Labor and Protective Labor Legislation," in Derber and Young (eds.), *op. cit.*, pp. 195–237; Witte, *op. cit.*, pp. 241–274. On the history of labor law until the New Deal, see Don D. Lescohier, *1896–1932, Working Conditions,* and Elizabeth Brandeis, *Labor Legislation,* in John R. Commons (ed.), *History of Labor in the United States,* Vol. 3 (New York: The Macmillan Co., 1935).

56. Quoted in Foner, *op. cit.*, pp. 284–285.

57. *Proceedings of the 19th Annual Meeting of the California State Federation of Labor, 1918*, p. 19.

58. Samuel Gompers, in *American Federationist* (September, 1900), p. 284, quoted in Foner, *op. cit.*, p. 285. The point is treated more generally in Hunter *op. cit.*; Selig Perlman, "The Basic Philosophy of the American Labor Movement," *Annals of the American Academy of Political and Social Science,* CCLXXIV (March, 1951); Louis S. Read, *The Labor Philosophy of Samuel Gompers* (New York: Columbia University Press, 1930).

59. United States, 49 Stat. 450 (1935), 29 U.S.C. 152 (1946).

60. *NLRB* v. *Jones and Laughlin Steel Corp.*, 301 U.S. 1 (1937); *West Coast Hotel Co.* v. *Parrish,* 300 U.S. 379 (1937).

61. See Brandeis, "Organized Labor and Protective Labor Legislation," and Witte, *op. cit.*

62. *Proceedings of the 39th Annual Meeting of the California State Federation of Labor, 1938*, p. 38.

63. *Ibid.*, pp. 27, 33.

64. *Proceedings of the 41st Annual Meeting of the California State Federation of Labor, 1940*, p. 31.

65. *The California Workmen's Compensation Law* (International Union, United Automobile, Aircraft and Agricultural Implement Workers of America, July 1943). The UAW has remained one of the most alert and active unions in legal matters; it has quite dynamic programs of legal education for its membership and its officials.

66. *Ibid.*, pp. vi, ix.

67. On welfare capitalism and its impact on employees and organized labor, see Bernstein, *op. cit.*, 170–189; Selig Perlman and Philip Taft, *Labor Movements*, in Commons (ed.), *op. cit.*, Vol. 4, pp. 580–602. For a similar critique of managerial ideology in welfare capitalism, see Reinhard Bendix and Lloyd H. Fisher, "The Perspectives of Elton Mayo," *Review of Economics and Statistics*, XXXI (1949), 312–319. On the bureaucratization of managerial authority, see Reinhard Bendix, *Work and Authority in Industry* (New York: Harper & Row, 1963).

68. See *above*, p. 73, and footnote 17; and Chap. II, pp. 17–24.

69. See Chap. III, pp. 48–49.

70. A voluntary system based on payment after agreement with the injured, as practiced in some other states, would perhaps not have secured better compliance with the law, but it would possibly have implanted an idea of accountability of the employer to the employee.

71. On this point, see Abraham Weiss, "Union Welfare Plans," in J. B. S. Hardman and Maurice F. Neufeld (eds.), *The House of Labor* (New York: Prentice-Hall, 1951), pp. 276–289.

72. On the significance of the contract at will, see Philip Selznick in collaboration with Philippe Nonet and Howard Vollmer, *Law, Society and Industrial Justice* (New York: Russell Sage Foundation, in press). That this made a difference for the ability of employees to assert compensation claims is suggested by the fact that layoffs and growing unemployment are typically followed by a rise in the number of claims filed at the Industrial Accident Commission; the unemployed no longer has anything to lose by demanding his due.

73. On the role of collective contract in "constituting" managerial authority under the rule of law, see *ibid.*

74. California Statutes of 1941, Chap. 401, Sec. 1; California Labor Code, Sec. 132a. This would prohibit such practices as requiring employees to ask permission of their supervisor before filing a claim with the Industrial Accident Committee; this was the rule, not long ago, in the fire department of a large California city.

76. See Stanley Rector, "The Frailty of the 'Fallacy' of Experience Rating," *Labor Law Journal*, Vol. II (1951), 338–349; P. L. Rainwater, "The Fallacy of Experience Rating," *Labor Laws Journal*, Vol. II (1951), 95–104; Philip Eden, "The Case against Experience Rating," *Labor Law Journal*, Vol. XI, (1960), 347–366, 423–424.

77. California Statutes of 1946, 1st Extraordinary Sess., Chap. 81; California Unemployment Insurance Code, Sec. 2601 ff.

78. California Statutes of 1957, Chap. 1977, Sec. 6; California Unemployment Insurance Code, Sec. 2629.

79. California Unemployment Insurance Code, Sec. 2629.

80. *Ibid.*, Sections 2735–2741.

81. California Statutes of 1947, Chap. 833, Sec. 1; California Labor Code, Sec. 4903 (f).

82. California Statutes of 1957, Chap. 1977, Sec. 2 and 6; California Labor Code, Sec. 4904; California Unemployment Insurance Code, Sec. 2629.

83. California Statutes of 1957, Chap. 1977, Sec. 4; California Unemployment Insurance Code, Sec. 2735.5.

84. Other lien claimants, that is, creditors of the injured employee who have a right to recover directly from the benefits awarded under workmen's compensation, as, for instance, doctors and attorneys who have performed services for the employee, also contribute to press the industrial victims to assert their rights. However, their influence is much less systematic and less felt than that of the Department of Employment.

85. For a radical statement of that point of view, see Foner, *op. cit.*

86. Samuel Gompers, in *American Federationist* (April, 1916), p. 270, quoted in Florence Calbert Thorne, *Samuel Gompers, American Statesman* (New York: Philosophical Library, 1957), p. 136; see also pp. 90–107, 136–139.

87. Bernstein, *op. cit.*, p. 345.

88. Reproduced from field notes.

89. Reproduced from field notes.

90. This point is developed in Georg Simmel, *Conflict*, trans. Kurt H. Wolff (Glencoe Ill.: The Free Press, 1955), pp. 39 ff; and Lewis Coser, *The Functions of Social Conflict* (New York: The Free Press of Glencoe, 1964), pp. 87–119.

91. Reproduced from field notes.

92. Philip Selznick, *TVA and the Grass Roots* (Berkeley: University of California Press, 1953), pp. 210–213.

V The Legal Profession
Organizational Advocacy

THE AVAILABILITY OF professional legal services is often a prerequisite for the full accomplishment of legal competence. This is, of course, true in the obvious sense that lawyers are the main, if not the only, source of the technical knowledge and skills legal action requires. But the lawyer can bring more to his client than technical expertise. He may have command of social and political resources that are unavailable to ordinary citizens. More importantly, he comes to the layman with a professional commitment to law as the way of ordering social life. A critical aspect of the lawyer's work is his ability to fashion a legal perspective on social problems and to impress it upon his clients. In so interpreting law to the layman, the lawyer can transform received images of the legal order and create new orientations to it, and so encourage its positive use and support fidelity to its principles. Above all, he can define for the aggrieved citizen a posture of independent criticism and assertiveness, which we have seen at the root of legal competence. For the lawyer is a specialist in challenging authority and holding it accountable to rules and reason; this is indeed his distinctive ability, in line with his unique commitment to the rule of law.[1] The legal profession is thus not merely a specialized instrument for already competent persons to realize their potential capacities. It also has a positive role in moving persons and groups toward legal competence by infusing them with this legal perspective through which social needs are transformed into justified grievances.

To industry, legal representation has never been much of a problem. Before labor could obtain similar services, employers had, by themselves and through their organizations, long been the main users of the legal profession; and the latter's concerns had become closely identified with business interests. In workmen's compensation, as we have seen, the law itself had indirectly provided employers with fully organized legal services. By substituting the carrier for the employer as the party to compensation claims, the law had made insurance the defender of its clients.[2] The use of lawyers by insurance and industry, in workmen's compensation as in other areas, increased sharply through the 1920's with the emergence of large law firms and corporate legal departments. But this change was quick and basically unproblematic; the needed resources and organizational instruments were available from the beginning.[3]

Injured employees enjoyed none of those advantages. Critical obstacles prevented their access to legal services; some of those obstacles pertained to the structure of the legal profession, others lay in the policies of the IAC itself. This chapter tells the story of how labor progressively overcame those obstacles, and developed through unions an effective system of organized legal representation.

As a result of those changes, a new pattern of legal advocacy has emerged in workmen's compensation. Its major feature is that the assertion and presentation of claims is systematically sponsored and promoted by organized groups and their legal representatives. We shall look at some of the consequences organizational advocacy has for the character of the adversary system, and for the relation between the legal process, political aspirations, and group interests.

The IAC and the Representation of Claimants

In line with its initial orientations, the Industrial Accident Commission was vehemently hostile to any legal representation of compensation claimants. As we have shown, this hostility rested in part on a belief that the presence of lawyers would introduce undue "legal" formality into compensation administration: the IAC had to be protected against an invasion of law. In addition, it was feared that lawyers' fees might excessively raise the cost of compensation to employers and absorb too high a portion of benefit awards to employees. Although this aversion went to both defense and applicants' attorneys, the commission actually had little means of influencing the use of lawyers by insurers and employers. Furthermore, the conception the agency had of disabled men as incompetent persons, in need of assistance and control, gave special strength to the idea that lawyers had no proper place in the presentation of their claims. The employers did have some rights and interests to protect; but the "applicants" were less "plaintiffs," asserting a right to damages, then "recipients" of welfare, to be given what the agency felt they needed. Their role before the agency was purely passive.

The IAC had a powerful instrument for preventing access by employees to legal services. The workmen's compensation statute of 1917 provided that "No claim or agreement for legal services . . . in excess of a reasonable amount, shall be valid or binding in any respect, and it shall be competent for the commission to determine what constitutes such reasonable amount."[4] Attorneys' fees would thus in all cases be determined by the IAC, which chose to fix them at an extremely low level, around 1 percent to 3 percent of the meager cash benefits awarded; it would even deny any fee when it felt no useful service had been rendered, that is, when it found the applicant did not "need" legal representation. This would effectively deter lawyers from taking compensation cases. In addition, in the advice it gave injured employees on their rights, the commission took care to warn them against needlessly hiring an attorney, and its policy was never to recommend legal representation. In cases of clear necessity, the agency staff would take responsibility for the applicant's case. Injured employees were thus systematically diverted from legal services.

These early policies of the IAC were progressively undermined by two main factors. One was the increasing intervention of defense counsel in IAC proceedings; by the late 1920's, insurance adjusters had to a large extent been replaced by lawyers as representatives of the carriers. This brought considerable imbalance in the respective positions of applicants and defendants, and placed a heavier burden on agency referees in their task of protecting the rights of the unrepresented employee. Protest also came from labor against the failure of the agency to provide adequate legal help.[5] The commission began softening its policy of discouraging the hiring of attorneys; it would more easily recognize the need for counsel in particular cases and, by 1928, it began occasionally referring indigent applicants to legal aid organizations.[6] The agency also decided to be more liberal in the fees it allowed applicants' attorneys.

These changes were fostered by another development in the early 1930's. Apparently under the impact of the depression a number of lawyers became actively interested in developing the as yet untapped area of practice offered by workmen's compensation. The IAC became the target of growing criticism from the bar for its toleration of lay representatives and its discriminating policies against the legal profession. In 1932, the state bar convention was moved to organize an investigation of IAC practices with respect to matters of interest to the organized profession. The report of the investigating committee recommended that lawyers be given a monopoly of compensation practice; argued that IAC control over fees applied only to the lienable portion of the fees; proposed the adoption of a maximum fee schedule by which fees were considerably raised and placed under the control of the bar; and requested the IAC to advise employees of their need for expert representation.[7] A milder version of this report was adopted at the 1934 convention.[8] It suggested that only attorneys should be allowed to represent applicants for a fee, that fees be increased and charged to the employer or carrier, that appellate courts decide on fees in cases appealed to them, and that all practices hostile to professional counseling be discontinued.

In the meantime, the commission had already partly responded to the pressures of the bar. In order to reduce the threat of legislation that would strip the agency of its control of legal fees,[9] the IAC chose to go along, as far as it could, with bar demands. In a letter to the investigating committee of the bar, the commission attorney assured that the commission was willing to deny fees to all nonlawyers, that it would instruct referees to inquire carefully about the lawyer's work in each case and to be fair in determining the fee, that it would instruct lay members of its staff to refrain from giving legal advice to applicants, and that it would no longer tell employees they could prepare their cases without the help of an attorney. In exchange, the commission's authority to determine fees would be preserved and the bar would renounce adopting a fee schedule of its own.[10]

The Emergence of Organized Representation

Although IAC doors would henceforth be more widely open to applicants' attorneys, the legal profession was not yet equipped to serve injured employees effectively. This can best be understood by contrast with the kind of services that were available to employers. The latter never had to search for a lawyer; whatever legal assistance they needed was almost automatically provided by insurance companies. These services came from specialized insurance law firms and legal departments, the only firms in which, at that time, compensation experts could be found. Above all, the services went to the carrier rather than to his individual clients; that is to say, they went to an organization through which employers' claims could be articulated in light of their common interests as a group. The defense of employers' rights was thus free from dependence on individual problems and disputes and capable of focusing more systematically on the structure of compensation law and administrative policies.

But the only services available to injured employees were those of lawyers in personal injury or general practice, who found in workmen's compensation a small supplementary source of income and clientele, were often weakly committed to their clients' cause, and seldom sought more than some immediate short-term remedy for his individual problem. The specialized compensation bar was dominated by insurance attorneys. And except for "ambulance chasing," the abuses of which were the object of bitter complaints by the IAC, there was no established channel through which the worker could readily get a lawyer. These conditions were not peculiar to the compensation field; whenever labor had recourse to legal services, it had to rely on lawyers whose interest in labor law was either scant or inevitably colored by the perspectives of their main client—industry. Just as the law was alien to labor, so was the legal profession; when it was not overtly hostile, it was unable to offer more than fragmentary, marginal, and sometimes corrupt representation.

The middle 1930's saw some critical changes in the structure of the labor law bar. Lawyers and bar associations began taking steps to improve their relations with organized labor.[11] The growth of labor law and administrative law under the New Deal and the sharpened awareness of labor's problems and legal needs helped orient lawyers' interests in this direction. More important, a new specialization was emerging—a growing number of lawyers was developing a labor law practice on labor's side of the controversy. Specialized business lawyers, who sometimes argued a union case, would henceforth increasingly have their counterpart in specialized labor lawyers, who would seldom if ever stand on the employer's side. The labor law bar was thus progressively evolving a group structure that mirrored the division of its clientele.[12] A class of lawyers emerged on which labor could count as reliable defenders of its legal interests. This pro-labor bar, committed to a systematic promotion of labor's legal interests, was in a unique position to shape labor's orientation to the legal order.

The foundations were thus laid for a new pattern of legal assistance, in which unions would extend their role as representative organizations and assume the task of organizing legal services for their constituents. One of the two lawyers retained by the State Federation of Labor in 1938 for its new legal department was a specialist in workmen's compensation practice.[13] Although his main function was to advise the federation itself in legislative and administrative matters, his role quickly expanded to include services to locals and to union members whose cases were brought to his attention.[14] This practice of using the federation counsel for individual assistance established a model that locals would soon follow as they came to realize the potential value of legal help.

From its beginning the federation legal department sought to promote the organization of legal services at the local level. Its 1938 study of workmen's compensation concluded that little would be accomplished in IAC proceedings without the assurance of competent representation. The legislative program of the federation accordingly included a request that the reasonable attorney fees incurred by the applicant be made chargeable to the carrier or employer.[15] This demand has been reiterated persistently ever since, but has not received more than partial satisfaction. In 1945 an amendment was passed allowing a reasonable attorney's fee in addition to compensation benefits in cases of failure by the employer to insure or obtain a certificate of consent to self-insure;[16] and in 1949, another amendment awarded fees in cases where the applicant "prevails in any petition by the employer for a writ of review . . . and the reviewing court finds that there is no reasonable basis for the petition." [17] The federation's concern for legal aid was expressed again in 1942, when efforts were made to enlist the support of locals in making lawyers available to victims of abusive investigation practices of insurance companies; the aim was to organize a systematic challenge to the admissibility of illegally procured evidence in IAC proceedings.[18]

The development of union-organized legal services received its decisive impetus in the middle and late 1940's. During that period an increasing number of union locals and councils, especially the larger ones in metropolitan areas, began retaining their own lawyers. The federation counsel had become unable to provide all the services demanded and was thus increasingly relieved of responsibility for assistance to locals. At the same time these union attorneys, as well as other lawyers more informally connected with labor circles, began urging local labor leaders to more effectively exploit workmen's compensation benefits, and offered their services for this purpose. Unions were at first reluctant to respond. Labor was generally suspicious of a system that would make the protection of workers' rights dependent upon private litigation, and might benefit lawyers at the expense of injured employees. Its preference went to the kind of action that would have pushed the IAC toward a more committed role in assisting workers. But since little was being accomplished in that respect, the alternative that lawyers proposed had to be considered.

A few unions therefore began referring their injured members to their attorneys. This temporary expedient was rapidly transformed into a fully organized system as its advantages became apparent. Unions evolved standing arrangements with their retained counsel or other lawyers with whom their connections were less permanent or more informal; in addition to normal services to the union, the lawyer would make himself available to prosecute the compensation claims of employees referred to him by the union. Union agents and stewards were given responsibility to see that members in need of legal help would contact the union attorney. Lawyers were invited to participate in "leadership training" sessions for union officers. Those were so many occasions to convince labor leaders of the necessity to watch carefully for systematic infringements of workers' rights by industry; to emphasize the need for and the low costs of legal services; and to leave a supply of business cards for distribution to the membership.[19]

By 1950, this practice had become widespread enough for a specialized claimants' compensation bar to have emerged; it was formally organized in the Applicants Attorneys Association, which became a branch of the National Association of Compensation Claimants Attorneys. The latter had been founded in 1946 and in 1948 began publishing a law journal devoted to the study of workmen's compensation and allied personal injury laws from the point of view of the injured workers' rights.[20] Since 1950, this specialized compensation bar has been rapidly growing; small firms and individual lawyers who had only a part-time compensation practice have developed into large offices with full-time compensation specialists. In metropolitan areas, such as Los Angeles, San Diego, San Francisco, and the East Bay, several firms have some five to ten partners and associates; two firms in the Los Angeles area have over twenty lawyers on their staff.[21]

This system of organized representation has become an established part of the administration of workmen's compensation. In the more aggressive and law-conscious unions, whenever an injury occurs the victim is automatically referred to the union attorney, even before any issue or conflict has arisen; the lawyer then follows up the case and is ready to file a formal application with the IAC at the first sign of trouble. In some unions, a business agent maintains files of all compensation claims of the members, negotiates the more routine matters with insurance adjusters, keeps track of the lawyer's actions through the various steps of the proceedings, and even accompanies the injured employee at IAC hearings on his case. Through the joint efforts of union lawyers and organized labor, a structure of representation has thus been devised, which makes legal services readily available to the compensation claimant; the union provides a reliable intermediary by which the injured worker is immediately channeled to a competent lawyer; and the practice of compensation law on a large scale makes it possible for the specialized lawyer to offer his services at fees that, in spite of the somewhat greater liberality of the IAC, still often deter the general practitioner from taking industrial accident cases.[22]

Characteristics of Organizational Advocacy

But more has been accomplished by this system of representation than simply opening access to the legal profession. For in the process of making legal assistance available to injured employees, the very character of this assistance had undergone critical transformations. By channeling legal services through the union, a new orientation had been imparted to them. The lawyer's responsibility would no longer go solely to the discrete interests of his individual clients; clients would also come to him as members of a class, represented by the union, and sharing common interests by virtue of their common condition as injured workers. When legal services are mediated through a representative group and become oriented to the promotion of group interests, the foundations are laid for a special kind of advocacy, supplementing traditional forms of legal assistance; in *organizational advocacy* the lawyer is transformed from an individual counselor into a legal arm of the representative organization. We shall now examine some of the major features of this type of legal service. In doing this we shall focus our attention on two broad questions: (1) What does organizational advocacy contribute to the lawyer's capacity to meet his client's needs? (2) How does it affect the legal order and the role of law in society? [23]

From Individual to Class Interests.[24] Traditional conceptions of the lawyer's role have given strong emphasis to the highly personal character of his responsibility to the client. In this view, legal problems are seen as individual problems, and the lawyer's role is to avail persons with all protections the law gives to their individual aims. No consideration of group interests should intrude in the lawyer-client relation. As the American Bar Association Canons of Professional Ethics insist:

> The professional services of a lawyer should not be controlled or exploited by any lay agency, personal or corporate, which intervenes between client and lawyer. A lawyer's responsibilities and qualifications are individual. He should avoid all relations which direct the performance of his duties by or in the interest of such intermediary. A lawyer's relation to his client should be personal, and the responsibility should be direct to the client.[25]

This approach can make sense when injustices are seen as isolated experiences and the outcome of personal shortcomings, when the legal world is pictured as a world of disputes among aggrieved individuals, and the main task assigned to law is to settle these disputes. These assumptions are deeply ingrained in our legal tradition, with its emphasis on the adversary system as central to the legal process. They may, however, often not be viable. The injured worker's problem involves more than a narrow conflict between him and his particular insurance adjuster; it calls for more than simply working out some accommodation of contradictory claims. His problem is to come to terms with a system of policies and group practices that consistently work to attenuate his rights; to solve it requires establishing surveillance of company practices, withdrawing the determination of benefits from the discretion of the insurer, securing independent medical care, protecting job security. It requires sustained, organized action directed to the system by which rights are determined. Under such conditions, the law is asked to perform a new role, which is no longer simply to rule on disputed individual contentions, but to correct *patterns* of injustice that affect classes of persons in a systematic way.

In this perspective, organizational advocacy appears as an effort to overcome the traditional limits of the adversary model. With it, the lawyer's responsibility to his client takes on a new character—it becomes a commitment to the interests of the group he serves through the representative organization. The latter does more than simply forward claimants to a lawyer and provide offices with a regular supply of clientele. Through it, individual demands are aggregated, needs are identified, and patterns of injustice are brought to light. Collective grievances can then be articulated and, through the lawyer, fed into the legal and political machinery. The particular aims and needs of individual claimants can thus be reinterpreted in light of the common conditions affecting them as a class. Cases that would otherwise come to the lawyer as isolated instances of hardship now appear as manifestations of systematic deprivations injuring the group as a whole. The lawyer's concern shifts away from short-term remedies to particular misfortunes and turns to the structure of policies and organized practices that determine the fate of all his clients' claims.

A striking feature of the workmen's compensation bar, and a reflection of this commitment to class interests, is the sharp line that separates applicants' attorneys from defense counsel. Both sides have their own distinct associations, and almost no compensation specialist has a mixed clientele. As the head of a prominent defense firm explained:

> It has been some five years since we have represented claimants, not because we feel it is a lesser deal, but I don't think you can represent both sides *on matters of policy*.[26] [Emphasis added.]

To enter the practice of workmen's compensation is to become politically aligned. The compensation lawyer is more than a technical expert in a special field of law; he is also specialized in the kind of groups he can serve, in the values he can uphold and the policies he can defend. As an advocate, his partisanship acquires a *political* dimension.[27] With organizational advocacy, the locus of adversariness in the legal process shifts from the level of individual disputes to that of organized group conflict. Even particular cases become politically meaningful. The union will not infrequently call its attorney about an employee it has referred to him and point out that this claim may be an occasion to challenge some practices of the employer or carrier and to set an example. Conversely, the attorney will notify the union when he finds a similar opportunity or has a chance to set a precedent in a case of "first impression." The strategy to be adopted will then be discussed and the necessary union support obtained. The character of the adversary process is thus changed from a narrow conflict of interests within a framework of established rights, into an arena where clashing political aspirations are confronted. More than a way of settling disputes, law becomes an instrument for the promotion of social values and interests.

To the individual client, the value of this class orientation is of course that it makes the lawyer more sensitive to the system by which claims are processed and thus more able to guide his client's case through it. The IAC itself is sometimes irritated by the naïveté of the nonunion lawyer. A recent staff report to the commission indicates, for instance, that in one office

> . . . all the appearances for the defendants are made by [specialized metropolitan] attorneys and all of the appearances for the applicants are made by local counsel without any specialists in this field of practice. [The referee-in-charge] has been trying to educate the local counsel so that they will more adequately prepare their cases, particularly with reference to medical reports. However no single firm or attorney appears before him often enough for his educational program to have been effective. . . . The result now is that at the conclusion of most hearings the only medical reports are those which have been filed by the defendants and very often they are reports from doctors whose opinions are ordinarily not afforded too much weight when filed in proceedings in [a metropolitan office]. He then has a record that is without conflict and at the same time is often most unsatisfactory.

A specialized applicants' attorney would have his own panel of doctors available for examining the worker and providing rebuttal evidence. A broader and more distinctive contribution of organizational advocacy is its ability to seek change in the legal policies and structural conditions affecting clients' rights. Legal advocacy acquires political relevance and becomes more capable of making law responsive to class needs.

The Broadening of Participation. In our imagery, at least, the role of advocate has been closely associated with the process of adjudication. The tribunal provides the forum where private claims and complaints can be entered and arbitrated in the light of established legal standards; this is where the lawyer has his place as an advocate of individual rights. The judicial process has thus traditionally been the citizen's major institutionalized mode of participation in the legal order.

As advocacy becomes politically oriented, it extends beyond the limited setting of private litigation. The lawyer acquires standing as a representative of organized groups; this opens to him avenues of participation in the legal process that would otherwise remain largely unavailable. Even in adjudication, as emphasis shifts from the particular claim to policy issues and their social implications, the lawyer can appear on behalf of the group itself as a friend of the court. Counsel for unions, especially the state federation, have not infrequently intervened as *amici curiae* on appeal in compensation cases. This adds a new opportunity to insist upon the social needs underlying individual demands.

More important, perhaps, is the extension of legal advocacy to the administrative and legislative processes. A right may be formally recognized and yet remain quite precarious, as when it is attenuated by adverse legal policies or undermined by the conditions in which it is implemented. The injured man's right to medical care can hardly be secure when the responsibility to provide treatment is given to the employer, when the latter is under no administrative surveillance and the legislature shies away from establishing effective protections against abuses. These weaknesses have to be overcome before fuller medical benefits can be obtained. Pressures must be brought on insurance companies to give some range of choice to the employee in selecting a doctor; on administrative authorities to be more liberal in allowing the applicant to procure treatment on his own; on the legislature to limit the discretion of employers and carriers in the selection of their physicians. The applicant's lawyer now has many resources and opportunities to carry his advocacy to these levels. He can do it on his own, since his voice carries the weight of a group demand; as counsel for his client unions; through the union itself, acting on his demand; or through the Applicants Attorneys Association. He is a party to negotiations with insurers, employers, and the medical profession, and to policy decisions within the IAC; he appears at the hearings and meetings of the commission and testifies before legislative committees.

Organizational advocacy can thus come directly to grips with the administrative and political dimensions of legal rights, thereby allowing citizens a fuller and richer participation in the legal process. It emphasizes the significance of political resources for the accomplishment of legal competence. Yet as it turns away from the strictly legal and orients to the scene of politics and administration, advocacy also tends to introduce in these settings some of this concern for orderly procedure and reasoned decision that is distinctive of law. We shall later have occasion to trace this evolution in the IAC. What finally lies behind this broadening of advocacy and participation is an enlarged view of law, which no longer sees the legal as residing mainly in the judicial process, but rather recognizes it in all settings, public or private, where legal rights and values emerge and are implemented.

The Active Creation of Grievances. We have already noted this characteristic feature of union-organized representation: it positively arouses the formation and presentation of claims. This is what the union lawyer does when he seeks to educate union leaders in labor law, when he insists upon the benefits and opportunities they forego by their passivity, when he urges that shop and local officers press employees to assert their rights. He can also directly influence his individual clients, stress the need to fight their claims and avoid quick settlements, secure money for them while their cases are litigated, obtain union support when their jobs are under threat, eventually impress upon them the significance of their case for the law and their fellow employees. By himself or through the union, the lawyer is directly involved in the task of making the injured worker competent and assertive.

This service does not go to the individual employees only. The lawyer performs a similar role toward the union itself. Compensation lawyers have indeed to a large extent been the main guardians of labor's continued interest in the workmen's compensation program. Outside the State Federation of Labor itself, unions' concern for industrial accidents often fades in the shadow of more immediate and pressing issues. The burden is frequently on their lawyers to keep them informed and moving, to formulate their demands and mobilize their support in pressing these before administrative and political authorities. How much political initiative the union exercises and how positively it seeks to exploit legal opportunities will thus often depend upon the commitment and aggressiveness of its legal counsel. The latter may therefore have an important role in preserving the capacity of the representative organization to build up the competence of its membership.

The compensation lawyer has thus assumed an affirmative role in relating injured employees to the law. This new orientation sharply contradicts some professed ideals of the legal profession; to encourage assertiveness often comes dangerously close to unethical "solicitation." The Americal Bar Association Canons of Professional Ethics specifically provide that

> It is unprofessional for a lawyer to volunteer advice to bring a lawsuit, except in rare cases where ties of blood, relationship or trust make it his duty to do so. Stirring up strife and litigation is not only unprofessional, but it is indictable at common law. It is disreputable to hunt up defects in titles or other causes of action and inform thereof in order to be employed to bring suit or collect judgment, or to breed litigation by seeking out those claims for personal injuries or those having any other grounds of action in order to secure them as clients, or to employ agents and runners for like purposes, . . . or to remunerate policemen, court or prison officials, physicians, hospital attaches or others who may succeed, under the guise of giving disinterested friendly advice, in influencing the criminal, the sick and the injured, the ignorant or others, to seek his professional services.[28]

The lawyer has the duty not to "stir up litigation, directly or through agents." This duty rests of course in part upon the profession's desire to avoid corrupting forms of competition within its ranks as well as abusive exploitation of clients. But the rule involves more than this strictly professional concern;

behind it also lies a general legal policy that seeks to inhibit litigiousness and to insure economy in the use of law. In this view,

> . . . the function of the court system is to serve as an impartial tribunal to which disputants can refer their contentions instead of using socially disruptive means of settlement. Under this theory, which emphasizes the peace of the community, it would seem that the judicial machinery is designed to serve only persons who feel sufficiently aggrieved to bring forward their claims on their own volition. If this is true, stirring up litigation is clearly undesirable.[29]

Just as the court is to remain passive, moving only on the initiative of claimants, so is the attorney required to stay withdrawn, waiting for claims to be brought to his desk. Like government, law must be sparingly used; persons will solve their problems by their own means and groups will handle their conflicts by their own instruments of control. Of course, legal standards will often be eroded or circumvented in these private arrangements; but the role of law begins only when peace is threatened. The assumption is that if persons actually need legal protection, they will have the ability and energy to secure it.

Organizational advocacy challenges this conception of law. It does not look at law only as a social technique for securing peace in otherwise unmanageable conflict; rather it sees in it an instrument to be positively used in fulfilling social needs and aspirations. The ideal is to draw the full implications of the values law embodies and to obtain satisfaction of all claims they justify. In this perspective, the citizens' capacity to use the legal order becomes a matter of critical concern. As a part of his role in relating persons and groups to the law, the lawyer acquires a responsibility actively to develop legal competence. By his ties to representative groups, the organizational advocate is uniquely equipped for this task. Organizations provide a valuable resource for reaching individual citizens; through them, as we have shown, compliant victims can be made aggressive claimants. In addition, they make it possible to transform amorphous classes into effective constituencies before legal and political institutions. In exploiting these resources, to some extent the lawyer simply shares in the general functions of the representative group—he spurs initiative and assertiveness. His distinctive contribution is to channel this militancy toward the legal order as opposed to other avenues of social protest and reform. This he does by purposively seeking to identify needs, formulating them in legal grievances, and making legal institutions existentially accessible. Through organizational advocacy, law is thus moved to adopt a more affirmative posture. It comes to search for silent injustices and frustrated rights, it encourages the use of its procedures, it makes its resources available for effecting social change. Above all, it becomes directly involved in the development of a competent citizenry.

Strategic Advocacy.[30] To the lawyer who serves individual and unrelated clients, cases tend to come as a series of miscellaneous controversies, each of them having its own discrete issues. Even if he specializes in a particular field of law, the individual advocate takes and argues his cases as they come, disparate and unrelated. This traditional approach is consistent with an adversary system in which the task of law is seen as settling disputes, and the presentation of legal issues is made dependent upon the emergence of conflicts between defined interests. Rules then appear as the outcome of controversy and the evolution of law tends to be contingent upon the more or less random occurrence of cases.

But when legal representation is organized by a group for a class of similarly situated persons, cases soon come to fall in patterns, revealing recurrent problems and threads of legal issues. Particular claims now appear as potential opportunities for challenging general practices and policies. These opportunities can be sought, created, and ordered so as to prepare the way for desired changes. Advocacy becomes planned and assumes the character of a legal campaign, purposively directed to strategic targets. The specialized applicants' attorney will thus screen the cases that are referred to him and attempt to identify those of special import for the law and its administration; even though the stake may be small to the individual claimants, he will seek to press the issue, avoiding settlement and possibly obtaining union assistance for the injured employee. If a case is weak or untimely, he can evade the problem by a compromise and wait for an appropriate occasion. He may instruct the union to watch for cases of a certain category, so that he can bring one to court when the opportunity arises. With his colleagues and the Applicants Attorneys Association, he can follow up lines of cases and elaborate strategies for extending or curbing them. Thus efforts have been made to extend the meaning of "employment," to broaden the definition of "injury," to liberalize the requirement of causal and temporal connection of injury with employment, to change the interpretation of rules regarding the computation of the "average earnings" on the basis of which benefits are determined. Broadly speaking, strategic advocacy develops whenever a case becomes a test case and the lawyer's work comes to be marked by a direct concern with legal change.

The clearest example of strategic advocacy in workmen's compensation is the systematic effort made by the applicants' bar to extend compensation coverage to a variety of injuries and diseases that were formerly deemed unrelated to employment. To establish compensability often requires expert medical testimony as to the causal relation between the employment situation and the disabling injury. By their control over medical care, employers and insurers held a powerful means of influencing the law in this respect; most industrial practitioners were dependent upon them and, in various ways, captive of their notion of what an industrial injury meant. The employee could seldom afford the costs of securing independent examinations and testimony on his behalf; even if he could, he would often have trouble finding a qualified specialist not already bound to an insurance practice. These conditions had to be changed before medical knowledge could be effectively exploited in extending the scope of compensation. Pressures on the legislature led to passage in 1949 of an amendment granting claimants the right to be reimbursed "for expenses reasonably, actually and necessarily incurred for X-rays, laboratory fees, medical reports and medical testimony to prove a contested claim." [31] With respect to the medical profession, labor had to identify and enlist the services of favorable medical experts.[32] In 1952, for instance, the State Federation of Labor counsel contacted the American Heart Association, seeking its support in getting heart specialists to testify on behalf of cardiacs in compensation cases.[33] Each applicants' law firm uses the same tactics in its area, asking for the assistance of medical organizations, calling on doctors individually to obtain their services, trying them on a couple of cases and then selecting those who can reliably be used. In this way the firm sets up a list of specialists in the major fields relevant to industrial medicine, to whom it can confidently refer its clients. These "medical advocates" are of course most often used for purposes that are specific to the case at hand, such as getting a more favorable description of disability factors. Their major import, however, is that they allow systematic use of medical knowledge for moving the law to cover new *classes* of injuries and disabilities. Formerly, most diseases that did not appear almost endemic to the occupation of the disabled employee—heart diseases, strokes, cancers, mental illnesses—were routinely held not to arise out of employment and hence not compensable; since the late 1940's and under the thrust of persistent advocacy, they have increasingly been brought under compensation coverage. These changes not only broadened the range of compensable injuries; they also tended to make the law more relevant to many occupational classes, such as office employees and executive and professional personnel, for whom it used to have little significance under older, more restricted notions of accidental injury and occupational disease.

The distinguishing mark of strategic advocacy is its immediate concern with legal change as well as the continuity and the organized character of its efforts. It imparts direction to legal change. The latter becomes less dependent upon fortuitous successions of individual claims; cases are sought when needed, and brought up after the way is paved for their consideration. Thus a body of law can be built step by step in a purposively governed fashion. The growth of law can then proceed in a manner more directly and rationally responsive to social aspirations.

Organizational advocacy is of course not such a new development in the legal profession; nor is it one peculiar to the field of labor relations. It is a familiar kind of service in trade associations and defense organizations, such as the NAACP or the ACLU. It can also be recognized in the large law firms that specialize in the service of corporate clients or in the legal departments of insurance companies. In all these cases the lawyer performs essentially the same function of actively promoting the legal competence and the substantive rights of a class of clients.

The law has been progressively giving recognition and legitimacy to the kind of services organizational advocacy provides and to the new meanings and uses of the legal order that it fosters. Of special interest are two recent decisions of the United States Supreme Court affirming it to be a right, protected by the constitutional guarantees of free speech and association, for persons to organize the provision of legal services through representative associations.[34] One of those decisions involved precisely the system of organized representation set up by unions for their industrial accident victims; it overruled a Virginia court decree that had enjoined the Brotherhood of Railroad Trainmen from referring its injured members to specialized lawyers selected by its Department of Legal Counsel. The Supreme Court recognized that

> . . . laymen cannot be expected to know how to protect their rights when dealing with practised and carefully counseled adversaries, and for them to associate together to help one another to preserve and enforce rights granted them under federal laws cannot be condemned as a threat to legal ethics. . . . The right to petition the courts cannot be so handicapped.[35]

The right can therefore not be impaired by common law rules, state laws, and canons of professional ethics prohibiting group legal services or the stirring up of litigation.[36] In the line of other recent cases extending the right to counsel, these two decisions indicate a new and positive assessment of the role law and the lawyer can play in making citizens legally competent. They also place upon legal institutions an affirmative responsibility to open their doors to those in need of their protection. In this perspective, law is no longer the mediator of last resort, whose use has to be discouraged. As the Supreme Court put it in *N.A.A.C.P.* v. *Button,*

> In the context of NAACP objectives, *litigation is not a technique for resolving private differences;* it is a means for achieving the lawful objectives of equality of treatment by all government, federal, state and local, for the members of the Negro community in this country. *It is thus a form of political expression.*[37] [Emphasis supplied.]

Law is a means to be used positively in securing rights, and in promoting social values and class interests.[38]

Conclusion and Caution

We have traced the emergence in the legal profession of a system of organized representation that gave the parties adequate means of pressing their demands through the legal process. As we have argued, when legal assistance is provided by representative groups, a pattern of organizational advocacy develops. This form of representation tends to look beyond the settlement of individual controversies to affect the course of legal development. It is especially needed when individual citizens cannot be relied upon to do this work without the organized support of a group.

This completes our analysis of the transformations that have affected the orientations and capabilities of the parties. We have shown that the administration of workmen's compensation has become increasingly dominated by a special kind of adversary system—the permanent confrontation of organized interest groups.

Before proceeding to examine the consequences of those changes for the IAC, it should be pointed out that, although group-sponsored legal representation is the typical mode of representation in workmen's compensation, the pattern is not nearly so widespread or so firmly organized as our discussion might have suggested. There are as wide variations in the accessibility and quality of legal services in this as there are in other fields of practice. The specialized, union-related firms dominate the applicants' bar. But they have left much room for a variety of other kinds of practitioners. Among those one finds a few personal injury firms, which have one or two part-time or full-time compensation lawyers but have only narrow and tenuous relations with organized labor. And there are large numbers of solo practitioners who from time to time take an industrial accident case but do not have any special interest or special competence in the field. The development of the workmen's compensation bar has been dependent upon the organizational support of unions; by and large, where there is no effective labor organization there is no competent applicants' lawyer. The legal profession has not yet found any alternative to this pattern of "group practice"; indeed, notwithstanding the *Brotherhood* decision, the union-based law firm is still very much frowned upon as illegitimate by the official leadership of the profession.

There has even been a relative weakening of the position of specialized applicants' firms in the 1960's. The emergence and the strength of those firms rested in part on a hard economic necessity; given the low level of fees, the practice had to be on a large scale and depended upon a regular supply of clientele through unions. The rising scale of benefits and the growing liberality of the IAC in awarding fees have in recent years made compensation cases more attractive to the nonspecialized attorney. In addition, the commission has sought, in collaboration with the state bar and local professional associations, to attract a broader range of lawyers to the practice of workmen's compensation. One outcome of those efforts has been the establishment by the reference services of several local bar associations of lists of workmen's compensation "specialists" to whom inquiring claimants can be referred; any attorney who wants to be listed as specialized in compensation will be put on the list on simple request. The IAC information desk sends all unrepresented applicants to those reference services, thereby actually broadening the range of choice open to the claimant well beyond the limited number of truly specialized firms. In effect, the commission encourages the unrepresented employee to base his selection of an attorney on notoriously deceptive information. The practice stems in part from the agency's desire to facilitate access to legal services by nonunionized claimants. But it is also the outgrowth of a growing hostility on the part of the IAC toward the specialized applicants' firms. For reasons that will later become apparent,[39] the commission has become impatient and defensive toward the kind of committed and aggressive advocacy these firms represent.

Notes to Chapter V

1. This point is developed in Philippe Nonet and Jerome Carlin, "The Legal Profession," in *International Encyclopedia of the Social Sciences* (New York: The Macmillan Co., 1968), IX, 66–72.

2. See Chap. IV, pp. 71–72. On the identification of the legal profession with business interests, see A. A. Berle, "The Modern Legal Profession," in *Encyclopedia of the Social Sciences* (New York: The Macmillan Co., 1935), IX, 340–345.

3. To the best of our knowledge there has been no study of the emergence of legal departments and law firms. IAC documents indicate that their growth in casualty insurance companies dates back to the early and middle 1920's. For some information on the present use of corporate counsel in insurance companies, see Charles S. Maddock, "The Corporation Law Department," *Harvard Business Review,* XXX (1952), 119–136.

4. California Statutes of 1917, Chap. 586, Sec. 24(d); California Labor Code, Sec. 4906.

5. See, for instance, *Proceedings of the 25th Annual Meeting of the California State Federation of Labor, 1924,* p. 30.

6. On the role of legal aid in workmen's compensation, see Joseph Bear, "Legal Aid Service to Injured Workmen," *Annals of the American Academy of Political and Social Science,* CCV (September, 1939), 50–56.

7. "Report of the Northern Section of the Committee on Practice and Procedure before the Industrial Accident Commission," *Journal of the State Bar of California*, Vol. VIII, No. 9 (1933), pp. 45–56.

8. "Proceedings, State Bar of California," *Journal of the State Bar of California*, Vol. IX, No. 9 (1934), p. 74. The earlier report had been rejected by a very close vote as sounding too much like an attempt by the bar to extend its monopoly over legal practice at the expense of poverty-ridden employees ("Proceedings, State Bar of California," *Journal of the State Bar of California*, VIII [1933], 240).

9. See *Assembly Bills* (Sacramento: California Legislature, Assembly, 50th Session, 1933), Nos. 194 and 1901.

10. "Report of the Committee on Practice and Procedure before the Industrial Accident Commission," *Journal of the State Bar of California*, IX (1934), 76–78.

11. In 1933, for the first time, the State Bar sent an official delegation to the State Federation of Labor Convention and pledged the profession's cooperation with labor (*Proceedings of the 34th Annual Meeting of the California State Federation of Labor, 1933*, p. 57).

12. On the emergence of a labor law bar and the division of the bar along partisan lines, see Robert M. Segal, "Labor Union Lawyers: Professional Services of Lawyers to Organized Labor," *Industrial and Labor Relations Review*, V (1951–1952), 343–364. The same paper indicates that the union bar has developed more on the West Coast than in any other part of the country (pp. 347, 354, 356).

13. *Proceedings of the 39th Annual Meeting of the California State Federation of Labor, 1938*, p. 33.

14. From 1939 to 1945, the number of individual cases he argued before the Industrial Accident Commission rose to about 250 per year. See *Proceedings of the 40th Annual Meeting of the California State Federation of Labor, 1939*, and *Proceedings . . . 46th Annual Meeting . . . 1945*, and *Reports of Officers of the 40th Annual Meeting of the California State Federation of Labor, 1939*, and *Reports of Officers . . . 46th Annual Meeting . . . 1945*.

15. *Proceedings of the 39th Annual Meeting of the California State Federation of Labor, 1938*, p. 33.

16. California Statutes of 1945, Chap. 520, Sec. 2; California Labor Code, Sec. 4555.

17. California Statutes of 1949, Chap. 223, Sec. 1; California Labor Code, Sec. 5801.

18. *Proceedings of the 43rd Annual Meeting of the California State Federation of Labor, 1942*, p. 46.

19. This account is mostly based on biographical information obtained from several lawyers who were among the first to specialize in workmen's compensation practice on the applicant's side and who currently head some of the largest workmen's compensation law firms in the state. See also Joseph Bear, "Survey of the Legal Profession: Workmen's Compensation and the Lawyer," *Columbia Law Review*, LI (December, 1951), 970.

20. See *National Association of Compensation Claimants Attorneys Law Journal, passim*; see also Samuel B. Horowitz, "NACCA," *ibid.*, VIII (1951), 16–20.

21. An indication of the degree of concentration and organization of the compensation bar is provided by some unpublished statistics gathered by the Industrial Accident Commission in 1959–1960. These statistics indicate that in Los Angeles 58 percent of the fees awarded to the 12 largest applicants' firms were for the first 3 of those 12; in San Francisco about 60 percent went to the first 4 of the 12 largest in that area; at the same time, one firm in San Diego was estimated to have had about 40 percent of the applicants' practice in that area. Typically, the senior partners in these firms do little of the routine workmen's compensation work; they act mainly as counsel for the firm's client unions in labor law

matters and represent them in negotiations with other interest groups and before the legislature and administrative policy-making boards, including the Industrial Accident Commission. Other partners and the bulk of associates take care of the compensation practice. In addition, they perform some side services for individual clients sent to them by the union; these services involve unemployment compensation, personal injury, family relations, and some minor criminal matters.

22. Fees are therefore seldom a problem for the injured worker; he never has to disburse any money, since the attorney is paid out of the award on a roughly contingent basis; and the Industrial Accident Commission keeps the rate at a fairly low level—about 8 percent and seldom exceeding 10 percent of the cash benefits awarded. As for the lawyer, he is assured of recovery by his right to a lien on the award.

23. The following discussion is based mostly on observations made during a stay at one of the largest compensation firms, also famed as one of the most aggressive; these observations were supplemented by interviews with attorneys from all ranks and types of compensation practice.

24. It must be emphasized that the word "class" is not used here in the sense of "social class," but in the sense of "category of persons."

25. *Canons of Professional Ethics* (American Bar Association), Canon 35. On legal ethics, and this rule in particular, see Henry S. Drinker, *Legal Ethics* (New York: Columbia University Press, 1953), especially p. 167. For an extensive discussion of the ethical problems of group practice of law, see "Report of the Committee on Group Legal Services," *Journal of the State Bar of California,* XXXIV (1959), 318.

26. *Transcript of Proceedings,* Senate Committee on Labor, California Legislature, November 9, 10, 1954 (mimeographed, n.p.).

27. A similar point is made in Ann Fagan Ginger, "Legal Processes: Litigation as a Form of Political Action," in D. B. King and C. W. Quick, *Legal Aspects of the Civil Rights Movement* (Detroit: Wayne State University Press, 1965), pp. 195–226; Clement E. Vose, "Litigation as a Form of Pressure Group Activity," *Annals of the American Academy of Political and Social Science,* CCCXIX (September, 1958), 31.

28. *Canons of Professional Ethics,* Canon 28.

29. Vern Countryman, *The Lawyer in Modern Society* (Chicago: The National Council on Legal Clinics, American Bar Center, 1962), Part V, Chap. VIII, p. 5 (mimeographed). See also "Inciting Litigation," *Race Relations Law Reporter,* Vol. III, No. 1257 (1958).

30. On the idea of strategic advocacy, see Jerome E. Carlin and Jan Howard, "Legal Representation and Class Justice," *University of California at Los Angeles Law Review,* XII (1965), 381–437.

31. California Statutes of 1949, Chap. 751, Sec. 1; California Labor Code, Sec. 4600.

32. See Chap. IV, pp. 76–77.

33. *Proceedings of the 50th Annual Meeting of the California State Federation of Labor, 1952,* p. 73.

34. See *N.A.A.C.P.* v. *Button,* 83 S. Ct. 328, 371 U.S. 415; and *Brotherhood of Railroad Trainmen* v. *Virginia,* 84 S. Ct. 113 (1964).

35. *Brotherhood of Railroad Trainmen* v. *Virginia,* 84 S. Ct. 113, at 117. On the legal department of the Brotherhood of Railroad Trainmen, see George E. Bodle, "Group Legal Services: The Case of the B.R.T.," *University of California at Los Angeles Law Review,* XII (1965), 306–326.

36. The *Brotherhood* case buttressed an earlier decision in which the court had affirmed the right of the NAACP to provide legal services to victims of discrimination at its own cost (*N.A.A.C.P.* v. *Button*).

37. *Ibid.*, at 429.

38. Other indications of this shifting emphasis from the dispute at hand to the general values at stake are the growing role of the *amicus curiae* in appellate adjudication, and the recent development of class actions and procedures for declaratory relief. On those points see Carl Brent Swisher, "The Supreme Court and the 'Moment of Truth,'" *American Political Science Review,* LIV (1960), 879–886; "Class Actions: A Study of Group Interest Litigation," *Race Relations Law Reporter,* I (October, 1965), 991–1010; "Developments of the Law: Multiparty Litigation in the Federal Courts," *Harvard Law Review,* LXXI (1958), 874; "Developments in the Law: Declaratory Judgments," *Harvard Law Review,* LXII (1949), 787.

39. See *below,* Chap. VIII, pp. 227–240.

VI Administrative Withdrawal

THE AIM OF THIS chapter is to describe and account for the way in which the Industrial Accident Commission responded to the emergence of organized group conflict. Briefly, this response was a retreat from administrative responsibilities; the commission progressively renounced its powers and repudiated its policy commitments. By the end of this evolution, the agency had lost all the major functions it had assumed as an administrator of the compensation system—control and surveillance over insurers and injured men, education and assistance to the parties, and initiation of new policies and programs.

Clearly, the growth of group conflict cannot by itself account for this outcome. To an administrator, political controversy can be liberating as well as paralyzing. It generates initiatives that he can use to enlarge his programs and consolidate his authority. Specifically, the IAC might have drawn from the growing power of labor renewed support for an expansion of its welfare mission.

The IAC did not do so. The path the agency followed was partly imposed by the particular strategies the parties developed in dealing with the commission. Those strategies were specially apt to erode administrative authority; the parties did not only seek to influence IAC policies, they strove to remove themselves from the scope of agency powers. This was quite apparent on the part of industry; the latter had been given primary control over the implementation of compensation law and had a clear interest in subverting the authority of an agency dedicated to basically adverse aims. Although labor might have been expected to lend political support to the commission, it also chose to make itself independent from administrative powers. Self-help would be its preferred mode of action, rather than relying upon IAC protection and suffering the limitations and controls attendant on such dependence.

But withdrawal was also the result of choices made by the IAC itself, in line with its own doctrine of administrative action. The major aim of the agency, as we have seen, was to "make the law self-administering"; its most developed instruments of action were all geared to that aim. This meant that the commission was committed to encourage self-help and stimulate initiative; by its very action the agency tended to free the parties from its authority. In addition, the IAC had chosen to rest its authority upon consensus and cooperation; conflict and dissent found it resourceless, unable to exercise its power and establish control when needed. This basic incapacity accounts for a number of decisions in the early 1920's, which set in motion the process of administrative retreat.

Retreating from Control

The years 1922 and 1923 were marked by two major setbacks for the IAC. One was the invalidation by the California Supreme Court of the 1919 Industrial Rehabilitation Act, which deprived the agency of its major resource for positive welfare action. Two decisions in 1922 and 1923 held the statute unconstitutional both as an abusive exercise of the police power, violating due process and exceeding the limits of the constitutional mandate for compensation legislation, and as an invalid exercise of the power of taxation.[1] The second blow was a drastic cut in the commission's budget, effective July, 1923. Following twelve years of Progressive rule, a powerful "backlash" had brought the conservative wing of the Republicans back to leadership in the administration and the legislature. Governor Richardson's sweeping "economy" program struck almost all agencies of state government, inflicting on the IAC a reduction of about one-third of its total appropriations. The agency was severely hampered in all its activities, but especially those that lay within its sphere of discretion and initiative and were not strictly required by statute.

These two events mark a radical turn in the history of the IAC; never afterward would the agency recover the initiative and inventiveness it had exhibited in the first decade of its life. This does not mean that the Supreme Court and the conservative administration, by themselves, performed a critical role in shaping the character of the commission; indeed, constitutional interpretations changed in subsequent years, and Governor Richardson's economy drive quickly aborted. What was crucial, rather, was the way the agency responded to these events in the light of its prior commitments. The response of the IAC to the crisis followed from a deep-seated conception of the nature of its mission, a conception that was much strengthened by the way in which industry sought to challenge the agency. As we have seen earlier, in spite of its determination to accomplish the aims of workmen's compensation, the commission had been quite reluctant to assume a role of surveillance. Whatever controls the agency would exercise were to remain limited and incidental to the primary task of the commission, that is, educating, stimulating, and assisting the parties in the pursuit of their common interests. Implementation of the law had to be, or become, voluntary. Priorities in the allocation of agency resources would therefore be given to its programs of education and of assistance in the resolution of trouble cases. The programs of surveillance were the first victims of the 1923 budget cut, and no attempt was made by the agency to reallocate its reduced funds so as to save any part of these programs; nor did the commission seek to restore them when its appropriations were later increased.

Being already predisposed to respond in this way, the commission was further confirmed in this approach by the demands and maneuvers of industry. The early 1920's saw employers and insurers lead a powerful campaign against the IAC, aimed mainly at reducing the scope of the compensation act, weakening the State Compensation Insurance Fund, and limiting agency powers in rehabilitation, safety, and the enforcement of the duty to secure insurance. In reasserting its old faith in voluntarism and self-administration, the commission found a convenient defense against this threat. By redefining its posture as supportive rather than controlling or punitive, the agency was able to preserve the essentials of its powers and administrative resources while accommodating the more pressing demands of industry. At the same time, the doctrine of voluntary compliance made it possible for the IAC to rationalize the concessions it had to make by emphasizing the growing good will and trustworthiness of insurance carriers.

Thus the departments of the IAC that suffered first from the 1923 budget cut were those through which the commission exercised its independent powers of surveillance and investigation. The Department of Investigations was abolished, depriving the whole agency of an important resource. The personnel and activities of the Statistical Department were sharply reduced; the office would henceforth abandon all its research activities and confine itself to examining injury reports, sending information brochures to potential claimants, and computing and publishing quite elementary statistics on accident frequency.[2] Never afterward would the commission attempt to reconstitute a research staff. The Department of Self-Insurance suffered equally; that same year, a bill sponsored by the IAC, which would have strengthened agency powers over the self-insured and in the enforcement of compulsory insurance, was vetoed by the Governor.[3] Although a similar bill, confined to self-insurance, was adopted at the 1925 session of the legislature,[4] nothing was done to ease the budgetary restrictions on the department. The Medical Department was similarly paralyzed; until the 1940's its personnel would consist of only two part-time doctors, appointed at salaries that made difficult the recruitment of competent men. The department abandoned its supervisory functions; all ideas of regulating standards of admission to and practice of industrial medicine were forgotten and the commission confined itself to a role of mere verbal exhortation. Although the IAC formally kept the authority to inspect and approve the adequacy of hospital facilities provided by employers, one finds no trace of this power being used since the early 1920's. Finally, after the schedule of minimum medical fees established by the commission was revised in 1918, no further examination of the medical fees problem was made until 1944.

The fate of the Rehabilitation Department was not more fortunate. The idea of "rehabilitation" expressed the more positive welfare aims of the IAC; besides providing relief, the agency would see that, by appropriate medical care and vocational reeducation, the disabled man be "returned to work." The Industrial Rehabilitation Act of 1919 had given to the IAC broad powers in this domain; it had also provided the agency with a regular source of funds, to be administered under the direct control of the commission. When the Rehabilitation Act was invalidated, the IAC responded by entering an agreement with the newly created Division of Rehabilitation of the State Board of Education;[5] the agreement provided for referral by the IAC of injured workers in need of rehabilitation and general cooperation between the two agencies in matters of common interest. The general policies of the commission would remain unchanged, except that another agency would have responsibility for the administration of facilities for the care and rehabilitation of the disabled. The role of the IAC would be to offer those opportunities and press injured men and carriers to use them. When its budget was cut in 1923, the commission chose to dispense with the services of its welfare and rehabilitation personnel; this decision, together with the elimination of the Department of Investigations, still further reduced the few means the agency had of influencing rehabilitation.[6]

Loss of Autonomy

In renouncing control and surveillance in favor of encouragement and education, the IAC suffered a critical loss that would affect its competence in many other areas of administrative action—it deprived itself of most of its means of inquiry. The two main sources of information that remained available were the evidence gathered in the course of adjudicative proceedings, and various kinds of reports and financial statements employers and insurers were legally required to furnish. In view of the limited capabilities of injured claimants and organized labor, and given the lack of administrative resources for investigation and control, the commission became profoundly dependent upon information supplied by carriers and employers. In effect, the agency was captive of industry in a most crucial phase of its policy and decision-making process.

This dependence had a significant impact on the character of the rehabilitation program. The commission preserved its interest in rehabilitation and continued to uphold its policies in the matter. But its only opportunity for action was through the Statistical and Permanent Disability Rating Departments, which could, on the basis of injury reports, suggest to the worker and the insurer the advisability of a referral to the rehabilitation services of the Board of Education. Subsequent action would depend upon the injured man's initiative and the carrier's desires and would escape agency surveillance. With the end of administrative supervision, "assistance" to the disabled and control over his conduct had passed into the hands of employers and carriers. Rehabilitation became one of the means available to the defense for reducing its liability for permanent disability benefits. Thus rehabilitative care would be given only when it seemed advisable in view of the higher costs of disability indemnities; only then would pressures be put on the worker to accept rehabilitation, including the threat of reducing or terminating benefits; the rehabilitation rationale was used to justify lower benefit payments, when the IAC could be persuaded that the injured man would so be encouraged to return to work.[7] The commission was committed to this system; having lost control, it had retreated to its primary strategy of providing incentives for private action; for employers, this incentive lay in the hope that rehabilitation would reduce their liabilities.[8]

The administration of disability benefits was similarly affected by the loss of means of inquiry. Although the Self-Insurance Department had power to deny or revoke certificates of self-insurance on ground of abuses in the adjustment of claims by the employer, as well as on the ground of financial inability,[9] its only source of information consisted in the financial statements required from self-insurers and similar to those filed by insurers with the Insurance Commissioner's office. The department was hardly able to make a realistic assessment of whether the employer's assets and sureties were adequate to cover his declared liabilities. Never did it obtain or, for that matter, even ask for the resources that would have been necessary for exercising its powers against abusive claims adjustment practices. The latter would be dealt with case-by-case through the adjudication of individual claims.

The Statistical Department confronted similar problems. It had earlier expressed its determination to keep an "ever watchful" surveillance over insurers:

> It ought to be clear that the department is not a passive institution, designed to accept such data as may be submitted by employers and insurance companies.
>
> On the contrary, nearly every report of accident is checked with from two to three other versions of the incident. . . .[10]

Yet, after the commission lost its investigative resources, it was no longer able to do more than accept whatever the carriers were willing to submit. The review of accident reports made it possible to identify only the crudest kinds of inadequacy in benefit payments. Even so, little could be done to follow up these cases; typically they were referred to the secretary's office, otherwise known as the "conciliation desk," which would then call the problem to the attention of the carrier. Subsequent action would generally depend upon the latter's good will.

Problems were perhaps most acute in the area of medical care; the provision of treatment was under the control of employers and insurers, who had quickly come to use the fee schedule established by the IAC as a means of capturing the practice of industrial medicine. The low fees provided in the schedule made industrial practitioners extremely dependent upon the carriers, who supplied their clientele and were able to guarantee their income by regular and massive referrals of patients. "Contract practice" on a large scale tended to foster low standards of medical care and to undermine the integrity of the medical experts, whose judgments were critical for the determination of disability benefits. Although the IAC Medical Department persisted in condemning "contract practice," it had no realistic means of identifying the harms actually done. The reports the agency received from treating physicians were no reliable source of information; and the Medical Department was unable to do more than perform a routine and superficial review of those reports.

The department was equally incompetent in its role as a source of independent expert evidence for the commission. Because of its lack of resources and personnel, it was generally unable to make its own examination of the injured men, and was thereby confined to the role of giving an "opinion" on the reports submitted by carriers.[11] In 1927, formal instructions concerning proper use of the department services confirmed this evolution:

> The Medical Department is primarily advisory to the Commission and should act as an expert passing on the file and not as an examiner furnishing the necessary evidence in the case. It sometimes happens that this is necessary but it should be kept to a minimum.

In effect, the determination of claims by the commission had become dependent upon medical evidence selected by, and gathered under the control of industry.

In the Permanent Disability Rating Department, the "informal ratings" program had originally been conceived as a way of taking over from private carriers the responsibility for rating permanent disabilities in uncontested cases. When the IAC was deprived of its investigative resources, the program quickly lost this aggressive outlook. The department no longer had any effective means of reaching injured workers and examining their condition; no longer could it rely on the Medical Department to check or supplement the medical information furnished by the attending insurance physician. At first, the Rating Department continued issuing ratings in all cases it identified as involving permanent disability, relying on the legally required injury reports and whatever additional information the parties would voluntarily submit. Then, realizing those data were often far too scanty, the department decided it would no longer rate a case unless it received from both parties a formal request for an informal rating; but it positively sought to obtain such a request. Apparently, it had little difficulty in securing one from insurers, who generally welcomed this opportunity of having the IAC rate their cases on the basis of their own files, usually the only and always the most complete source of information the agency possessed. It was harder to get a response from the injured worker; apparently the department came to rely on insurance doctors and adjusters to put pressure on the claimant to fill out and sign his application; it may sometimes even have dispensed with any response from the worker, when the insurers' file was deemed sufficiently complete. At any rate the information contained in the form was seldom detailed and pertinent enough to add much to the insurer's story. Thus, to the carrier, the most likely outcome of the informal rating procedure was that his own handling and assessment of the case were, owing to a seeming ratification by the IAC, given a color of official authority and finality. The commission had sought to avoid this consequence; in response to a practice by some carriers of presenting informal ratings to their claimants as official IAC awards, the agency had specified on its rating forms that such ratings did not carry the legal weight of a formal decision. But this could not prevent the informal rating from expressing an administrative opinion, which, however tentative and legally tenuous, had the signs of official authority and was likely to be seen by unsophisticated claimants as a prejudgment of their case.

The same reluctance to exercise control, and the same belief that the compensation system would rest upon the cooperation of employers and employees, also had consequences for the ability of the State Compensation Insurance Fund to preserve its autonomy and its influence on carriers and employers. The fund had been designed to establish standards for insurance by competing with private carriers. The aim of the IAC was to make it a model in both service to client employers and adjustment practices toward injured workers. Confident as it was that common interests bound employers and employees to the compensation program, the IAC had not perceived the latent contradictions between those two aims. Since competition would normally gear the fund to the interests of employers, whose patronage had to be gained, the only sure protection of workers lay in the authority the commission had over the management and policies of its model carrier. The IAC at first intended to exercise its leadership with the utmost energy:

> . . . we have made the California fund a warm-blooded financial institution. It is a financial institution. It does not give away or throw away any money of the assured. It is careful of that. But it does not stand upon every technicality. It meets the requirements as they come, without very definite regard to strict legality. If a man has been lulled along and the statute of limitations has run without any serious fault on his part, it is not pleaded. There are a good many things we can not compel the other insurance carriers to do directly that we do compel them to do indirectly, because the fund does it, and if they don't do the things the fund does the fund gets the business.[12]

Later, the authority of the commission was progressively eroded. Actually, from its very beginning the SCIF had been organized primarily as a service to industry: its task was to make insurance available to employers at low cost, thereby demonstrating to them the feasibility and legitimacy of workmen's compensation.[13] The fund was therefore conceived in such a way that it would operate under the same conditions as a private carrier, be entirely self-supporting, and by free competition impose its standards on the insurance market. Strong emphasis was put on reducing administrative costs and maximizing profits for the purpose of distributing sufficiently large and competitive dividends to the policyholders. The fund was at first eminently successful in this enterprise. It took a large share of the insurance market, and this gave the IAC some liberty to impose on the fund more liberal standards of claims adjustment.[14]

But in the early 1920's, private carriers became more effective in responding to state competition,[15] and the state fund was put on the defensive. By law the fund suffered from two important competitive disadvantages. First, it was confined to the writing of compensation insurance and therefore, unlike private carriers, unable to provide its clients with coverage for the full range of risks that might need to be insured.[16] Second, the fund was, and still is, forbidden to "refuse to insure any workmen's compensation risk under state law, tendered with the premium therefor."[17] Thereby it was progressively made to function as a rather convenient assigned-risks plan for the whole compensation insurance business; it came to get the worst risks, those that were rejected by private carriers because their too high loss experience tended to depress profits and dividends. Finally, the insurance industry was able to cast suspicion on the fund's integrity; a sustained political campaign pictured the fund as an unreliable arm of government, whose relation to the IAC made it incompetent to serve the interests of employers faithfully.[18] Against such criticism, the fund's most effective defense was to demonstrate how undistinguishable it was from any private insurance firm and to dissociate itself from the commission. The commission yielded increasingly to the fund's demands for greater independence. In 1917 it had already decided to separate the Medical Department of the state fund from its own Medical Department, thereby losing some of its control over the fund's practices in this area.[19] In 1921, the fund's manager insisted that the formal IAC authority should not obscure the fact that

> . . . the operations of the industrial accident commission proper and those of the State compensation insurance fund are separate and distinct.[20]

In 1925, pressures from industry brought the commission to rescind a policy by which it had earlier forbidden the fund to appeal agency decisions to the courts, thereby conceding that the fund would no longer be bound by IAC policies in the determination of benefits.[21]

In 1944, during an Assembly investigation of agency practices, the commission assured the committee that it had "very seldom attempted to influence any activity on the part of the state fund."[22] The committee concluded that the direction of the state fund be removed from the commission; the recommendation was supported by the IAC and the reform was enacted at the 1945 legislature. This completed a process of evolution that had been developing ever since the creation of the fund and the seeds of which were present in its original structure; the fund was placed under a Board of Directors where its policyholders, with four directorships, enjoyed almost absolute control, and the injured workers had only one representative, the Director of Industrial Relations.[23]

The Erosion of Paternalism

When, in the 1930's, labor acquired more effective resources for political action, it could have used its growing power to impart new strength and dynamism to the IAC, and to free the agency from dependence on industry. Instead, organized labor chose another strategy; it did seek to make the agency more responsive to the interests of injured workers, but it insisted on keeping for itself the initiative in defining and promoting those interests. Rather than pressing for more surveillance, more welfare, and a more determined enforcement of the law, labor preferred to rely upon self-help, using the commission only as an arbiter, possibly a supporter, of its demands against industry. In so doing, labor further contributed to the erosion of administrative authority.

This strategy was in part a response to the diminished competence of the IAC, whose programs had all too often been debilitated or even corrupted by dependence upon industry. Labor had little confidence in an agency over which its opponents had such a powerful hold. This is quite apparent in the position the State Federation of Labor took on the issue of "informal ratings." Already in 1934, as agency documents indicate, claimants' lawyers had criticized this procedure for impairing the rights of injured workers, on the ground that the agency allowed itself to issue ratings based almost exclusively on the insurer's file without giving the applicant any genuine opportunity to present his own evidence.[24] When the federation took up the problem in 1938, it did not even consider the potential for control that was at least latent in the informal rating procedure.[25] It requested that the practice be discontinued. In response, the commission tried to correct some of the more objectionable features of the procedure; it insisted on a stricter compliance with the rule that no rating be made without the formal request or consent of the worker, and made it a policy to invite applicants more frequently for a "check-up examination" at the Medical Department. But labor kept insisting that no rating be issued without prior formal determination of all disability factors, with all due procedural guarantees, and that the resources spent on informal ratings be rather devoted to educating and assisting disabled workers in the assertion of their rights. As the then counsel for the federation put it in a recorded discussion with members of the IAC staff in 1942:

> . . . we want to have the Commission discontinue sending these [informal ratings]. . . . We merely want the man advised when he is ready for a rating that . . . the medical reports sent to the Commission indicate that he has a permanent condition and he is entitled to a permanent disability rating, and that the Commission will be glad to advise him of what that rating is, and he has a right to file an application with the Commission to have the Commission ascertain the nature and extent and degree of the permanent disability.

He also suggested that the IAC initiate a program for the education of union members and officers, from whom workers could learn their rights, and concluded by resolving that "as far as we are concerned we will do all we can to educate the people and to discourage the use of this [informal rating procedure]." The commission still felt the procedure was necessary for the protection of the less competent victims, whose cases would otherwise never reach it. To this problem, in the eyes of labor, education was the answer, not surveillance. As the federation counsel indicated at the same 1942 meeting,

> . . . the only argument that has been made so far on the proposition that this [informal rating system] be continued is the statement . . . that in many instances the persons would not otherwise receive any rating. *Of course that has to be overcome by education.* [Emphasis supplied.]

The commission nevertheless decided to preserve the informal rating system. But from a means of control and assistance, the procedure became merely an expedient, that helped the agency to obtain quick and peaceful settlements in cases that might otherwise have added to its growing burden of formal contested claims. In 1945, the IAC was deprived of its Statistical Department[26] and discontinued its efforts to contact reported injured men and secure their consent to a rating. Informal ratings remained as a lower-order arbitration procedure, available to those who were interested.[27] After having long been the overwhelming majority of IAC cases, they increasingly lost their significance; today they make up only a very small part of the agency caseload.[28]

The position of the trade unions on the rehabilitation program was based on attitudes very similar to those that led them to oppose informal ratings. Even though labor gave its support to the ideal of rehabilitation, it had developed considerable hostility to the program as it was conceived within the workmen's compensation system. It found the practice of rehabilitation corrupted by industry interests, and depriving disabled men of due and needed benefits in exchange for sometimes false and always highly uncertain advantages.[29] In addition, inadequate resources and facilities made most rehabilitation programs, public and private, in and out of the compensation system, incompetent to accomplish their proposed aims.[30] Labor chose to focus its concerns on the administration and the adequacy of indemnity benefits. With labor taking this orientation, the political struggle and day-to-day disputes over workmen's compensation came to center on the same problems.

This condition became progressively reflected in the perspectives of the IAC. Emphasis shifted from rehabilitation to relief, from "returning the man to work" to alleviating his losses, from control over the worker's destiny to responsiveness to his demands. In 1939, under the protest of labor, the commission rescinded a policy by which, in certain cases, it reduced the amount of benefits for the purpose of encouraging "rehabilitation" and a return to work, and took jurisdiction over the case until full recovery, irrespective of any compromise between the parties, or of the running of the statute of limitation. The system of referral of cases to the Bureau of Vocational Rehabilitation was formally continued but, from the temporary and partial expedient it had been, referral became a policy, quite expressive of the commission's posture, by which the agency washed its hands from responsibility for rehabilitation. In 1948, the IAC and the bureau worked out a "plan of cooperation," as required by law. It included provisions for the referral of disabled workers to the bureau, and for bureau assistance in investigating and making recommendations on IAC cases involving a petition for commutation of compensation benefits in lump sums.[31] That same year, however, under pressure from organized labor, the commission agreed to relinquish this last power of control it had over injured workers; henceforth it would no longer reject any request for lump sum payment, except for the most serious reasons.[32] As to the referral plan, a letter from the IAC chairman in 1950 is indicative of the extent of the agency's commitment:

> We do not have a follow up system to determine what benefits the injured worker derived from the services of the Bureau of Vocational Rehabilitation. . . . We have no information as to the number of workers who declined to take advantage of the services of the Bureau. . . . We have only two employees engaged in this work. After the case is referred, it has been considered to be the function of the Bureau to proceed further.[33]

All desires on the part of the IAC to exercise control over the injured worker had thus been crushed. In this process, commission policies and perspectives had been cleansed of the quasi-punitive orientation that was implicit in the early paternalism of the agency. This result, however, had been accomplished at a very high cost; the agency had in effect lost all its potential competence for positive action toward the welfare of the disabled.[34]

Labor's strategy can only partly be understood as flowing from distrust toward the agency. Such an interpretation would fail to account for the persistence of the same strategy even at times and in areas in which there were relatively open and genuine opportunities for a more committed and positive action on the part of the IAC. More than diffidence, labor's approach reflected its general perspective on the role of government in the problems of employers and employees. Although the labor movement had increasingly abandoned its earlier suspicion and hostility toward state and law, its posture toward government remained nevertheless colored by some basic perspectives it had fashioned in the previous history of its private struggle with industry. Among those were the emphasis upon voluntarism and self-help as the foundations of the industrial order. Those ideas, to be sure, had lost their negative overtones; the state was no longer perceived as an obstacle to be prevented from interfering with the free pursuit by labor of its private interests. Government would henceforth be positively used and associated to labor's efforts, but these efforts would still be governed by the same values of consensualism and self-government. The state would provide just another bargaining table and grievance machinery, where labor and industry could argue their respective demands, work out common understandings, and evolve the principles of their collaboration. The state would also see to the integrity of this process, and possibly serve as an ally to the worker when the latter's disadvantaged position made this assistance necessary. But in no case would it be permitted to substitute itself for labor in the making and implementation of industrial policy. Government was to be responsive, not prescriptive.

With respect to the IAC, organized labor never saw more in the agency than a "poor man's court" and an arena in which it could press its demands against industry under relatively favorable conditions. As the secretary of the state federation insisted at a legislative committee hearing in 1944:

> We are concerned deeply that the act is administered in such a way that any worker who is injured during his employment can come to the administration of the commission, present his case in the loose lay form without having to be tied up with a lot of legality, particular documents and language, and can state his case and receive a hearing and be granted compensation if justified.[35]

Labor took it for granted that the injured worker would bear the burden of protecting his rights; he would come to the commission rather than let the commission go to him. The compensation law was a workmen's law, for them to develop and protect by their own means; the role of the commission was simply to facilitate this process. This premise underlies all the demands labor made to the agency, which were either for more initiative and participation in the making and implementation of policies, or for more assistance in making workers capable of self-help. The same assumption seems to be present in the persistent hostility toward informal ratings; labor's objections did not go to the defects of the procedure only, for these might have been corrected; they went to the system itself, which failed to give a word to the injured man in the decision of his case and the control of his treatment. Labor did not care for this kind of protective administration, in which rulings were handed down to workers, as to incompetent men, without letting them make their claims and influence outcomes; and if there were indeed incompetent workers, "of course, this had to be overcome by education."

This orientation of organized labor was particularly apparent in the way unions approached medical problems and problems of legal assistance to injured claimants. In both areas, labor had the choice of either pressing the IAC to use its powers and provide assistance in a more committed way, or of developing its own resources for securing adequate medical care, favorable medical experts, and accessible legal services. Although unions did exercise some pressure on the agency to improve its services, the main thrust of their efforts was to enhance their own capacity for self-help.

Instead of demanding that the commission expand its Medical Bureau and use its powers of control over medical fees and hospital facilities, labor focused on developing its own means of correcting deficiencies in medical care. Unions relied on the employee's right, in case of failure on the part of the employer or carrier, to procure his own medical treatment at the cost of the adverse party. They focused on making the exercise of that right more feasible and effective—setting up panels of physicians available to their members, gaining the cooperation of medical associations, obtaining exemption of the self-procured medical treatment from application of the medical fee schedule, pleading that the initial choice of physician be given to the injured employee himself.[36] The problems of "promptness" and "adequacy" of medical care, as well as of "reasonableness" of fees, began coming to the commission only as issues in individual controversies over the adjustment of claims. From a matter of public health and administrative responsibility, medical care became a question of remedy for private losses, that was left for the victim to secure by his own means. The agency would no longer intervene, except as a third party in cases of dispute.

Having lost its supervisory responsibilities, the Medical Department could have focused its resources on making independent expertise available to claimants, whose benefits were usually determined on the basis of opinions from "insurance doctors," and who were seldom able to afford the costs of securing their own medical witnesses. For a while labor did press for an expansion of agency services in this sense; in 1945, after the reform of the IAC, unions succeeded in obtaining that the staff of the department, now called bureau, be considerably enlarged for this purpose. Second, in the late 1930's and early 1940's, pressures were brought on the department to abandon the practice of merely giving informal "advices" on medical files from insurance doctors; it was requested to render opinions only by written reports and after an independent examination of the applicant.[37] The department was therefore increasingly reduced to a source of impartial expertise for the commission and the applicants who requested its assistance. In spite of these changes, labor was reluctant to rely on the services of IAC physicians. There was in part a lack of confidence in the department's staff; civil service salaries did not attract the highly qualified personnel that was needed; there were no specialists on the staff and positions often remained unfilled in spite of earnest recruitment efforts.[38] More important, labor felt that the Medical Department was not sufficiently committed to the interests of employees and the welfare aims of the compensation program. To be effective in confronting its opponents, labor needed to become capable of using medical expertise in the same self-serving way as they did. Since the commission could not be expected to provide such partisan service, unions had to secure it elsewhere and by themselves. At first they managed to get their medical experts at the cost of the claimants. Then, in 1949, they succeeded in obtaining new legislation, by which the applicant's medical expert fees were made chargeable to the employer or carrier.[39] The assistance of IAC doctors would henceforth no longer be needed; their only remaining task would be to act as independent third experts in medical controversies between "insurance doctors" and "applicants' doctors."

The unions' position on the problem of legal aid to injured claimants was inspired by the same basic aims. Although labor repeatedly sought to obtain from the legislature provisions for IAC assistance to claimants,[40] and pressed the agency for more effective education programs, at the same time a great deal of its energy went into developing its own legal resources. Unions took over from the commission the task of providing legal information to their members and developed their own system of organized legal representation. At the same time as it pressed the IAC to provide more effective assistance, organized labor continuously requested from the legislature the adoption of a measure that would have considerably eased the injured man's access to legal services—the payment of legal fees by the employer in addition to the benefits awarded.[41] Here also, labor felt that it could not expect from the agency the kind of commitment and partisanship that was required for the effective promotion of its interests; it had to have a voice and means equal to those industry commanded.

This emphasis upon self-help was undoubtedly strengthened by the growing influence and involvement of lawyers in workmen's compensation administration. Lawyers were the first to insist on the need for partisan advocacy, and to object to the commission's claim that it was providing applicants with all the help they needed.[42] Their growing role undermined the idea that assistance to the claimant was a responsibility of the IAC. Although the value of self-help was profoundly written into the perspectives and institutions of the labor movement, lawyers strengthened it, gave it operational significance, and demonstrated its practical usefulness. Their professional commitment to the values of the adversary system, as well as their special interests as a group, oriented them in that direction.

Withdrawing from Politics

The more insurance freed itself from agency influence, and the more labor developed its resources for self-help and independent advocacy, the more the administration of workmen's compensation was marked by conflict between adverse group interests. This, in turn, created further problems for the agency and led it to retreat further from administrative action.

One of the basic internal contradictions in the IAC was that, although its authority was deeply dependent upon consensus and usually paralyzed before controversy, the agency was bound to arouse conflict insofar as it took an active role. Having lost its means of control, the commission had retreated to its preferred strategy of educating and assisting the parties in the implementation of the law. This meant mainly that it would help injured workers to know and assert their rights; insofar as it was true to this purpose, it had to provoke controversies. The Statistical Department sent information pamphlets to the victims; inquiring injured men were advised by the Information Bureau and, in case of trouble, referred to the secretary, whose office would seek a settlement by informal and amicable means; should this fail, the victim was helped to file a formal application; at the hearing, the referee was responsible for seeing that the applicant's rights were protected. Enforcement of the law was therefore ultimately dependent on the litigation of claims. That was true even where the IAC had formally kept its powers of surveillance. For instance, the agency had the authority to initiate criminal prosecution against employers who failed to comply with the duty to "secure the payment of compensation," that is, to insure. But having lost its other means of investigation, its only opportunity for finding violators was in the course of proceedings in contested claims.

The negative consequences of this dependence on adversariness were at first minimized by several other administrative programs, designed to promote more amicable and cooperative modes of settlement. They were (1) informal adjustment procedures, which apart from informal ratings, were principally the responsibility of the IAC secretary; (2) the role of the Medical Bureau in establishing "incontrovertible" medical evidence; (3) the control exercised by the commission over the presentation of workers' claims as a result of its practical monopoly of assistance to claimants. All those programs were progressively subverted as labor developed its resources for self-help and the agency consequently lost control over the definition and handling of compensation problems. We have already shown how labor developed its own means of legal representation and how it succeeded in weakening the role of informal ratings. A few words should be added on the decline of independent medical expertise and of the functions of the secretary.

Initially, the IAC was determined to avoid the intrusion of adversariness in medical expertise; for this it counted on the integrity of the medical profession and on the reasonableness of employers and workers, as well as on its own supervisory authority and independent expertise. History did not match those expectations and a system of "medical advocacy" progressively developed. It was not visible as long as insurers were practically the only source of medical evidence for the commission, under the weak control of the Medical Department. It became patent when labor began developing its own groups of experts, especially after the 1949 legislation, which allowed claimants to recover the cost of the medical expenses incurred in presenting their claims and thus freed them from dependence upon IAC experts. By this new law, the IAC became fully and officially committed to a system of partisan presentation of medical evidence, to which it had initially been firmly opposed.[43] Instead of the "incontrovertible evidence" it had hoped for, the commission is now constantly confronted with the problem of choosing between or compromising the conflicting partisan reports it is given.

The IAC has also lost the major instrument it had for keeping incipient adversariness under control; with the secretary lay the responsibility for promoting this climate of informal, peaceful, and reasonable discussion which the IAC found essential in compensation administration. His role was to mediate issues and bring voluntary compliance with the law in cases brought to his attention by other offices of the agency or private complaints. After having been quite active in the early years of the agency, the office progressively abandoned its affirmative posture. Deprived of the means of investigation that the IAC had earlier commanded, the secretary lost initiative; calls for action came increasingly through private requests and complaints from without the agency. From an active promoter, the secretary became a rather passive mediator; his responsibilities were largely reduced to the handling of "compromise and release agreements," the validity of which was by law made dependent on commission approval. Even this mediating function was progressively reduced as formal contested cases assumed an increasingly greater significance. The office, which stood for the earlier IAC emphasis on "informal" administration, was criticized for interfering with the process of adjudication by getting involved in the mediation of pending litigated cases. Around 1935, the commission established a distinction between informal and formal compromise and release cases. The latter, arising after formal adjudication proceedings had already been initiated, would henceforth be handled by the referee who had been assigned to conduct the hearings. In 1939, in spite of the fact that the secretary was by law required to keep the minutes of IAC deliberations, a resolution was passed by the commission "whereby in the meetings of the Commission in which cases were to be discussed, the exclusive person presenting the cases for discussion would be the Chief of the Compensation Department,"[44] the office in charge of formal proceedings. The duties of the secretary were so sharply reduced, indeed, that when the incumbent died in 1947 the office was abolished as a civil service position and its responsibilities were distributed among other members of the staff. The supervising referee, formerly chief of the Compensation Department, became the official IAC secretary, in charge of keeping the record of commission proceedings; and the handling of compromise and release cases, that is, the mediating function of the IAC, was entrusted to the referees. By that time, the idea that the administration of benefits could be conducted in a noncontentious and reasonable way had been considerably undermined; claims would normally be litigated.

Thus far, we have shown how the IAC was bound to arouse controversy whenever it sought to obtain compliance with the law, and how its means of controlling the emergence and character of conflict were increasingly weakened. Involved as it was in a continuing confrontation of partisan group interests, the commission found its authority seriously undermined; whenever it sought to affirm its commitments and exercise its powers, its action was inevitably interpreted as a sign of partiality. Its integrity and legitimacy as a public institution were thus always exposed to challenge on the ground of subservience to private interest groups. This problem was particularly significant in bringing the agency to withdraw from its responsibilities of assistance to claimants and from its general role of initiating and making policy.

In the perspective of the early commission, the provision of assistance to workers and the education of insurers were simply two aspects of a single task—that of establishing modes of administration that would promote the rational pursuit by employers and employees of their common interests in the compensation program. The Information Bureau would thus be a service for both carriers and employees; informal ratings would assist both insurers and workers in properly assessing disability factors. The IAC soon learned that the system did not work in this way; the Information Bureau was of little use to insurance companies, and served primarily to assist and stimulate claimants in the assertion of their rights. The report of the agency for 1920–1921 observed a sharp increase of 23.5 percent in the number of claims filed and attributed it to "the effective work done by the Statistical Department and the Bureau of Information in bringing the attention of the injured workmen and their dependents to their rights under the Compensation act."[45] The character of the information services had changed; their commitment was now to the assistance and protection of employees, rather than to the maintenance of a nonpartisan education program.[46]

But as the commitment changed, it also tended to weaken. The commission became somewhat uneasy about the partisan outlook its education services had assumed; it was also concerned about the adversary spirit it was thereby instituting, and the increasing work this litigiousness was throwing upon its staff; in addition, it came under criticism from insurers for encouraging the presentation of "unfounded" claims and raising "excessive hopes" in the minds of injured men. In response to those problems, the letters of advice were progressively toned down. Whereas in the beginning individual letters were sent to each reported injured worker, telling him affirmatively what he was entitled to and should claim in his particular case, in the early 1920's it was decided to replace individual letters by standardized and more carefully worded forms, which simply gave general information about the law without drawing any definite conclusion about the benefits due to each claimant. In a recorded discussion held in 1942, the chief of the Rating Bureau relates how, around 1920, this decision was made:

> . . . up until after the World War, the then superintendent of the Department used to send out letters of advice; they were not on a form, and that wording was, "The man is entitled to such and such for certain disability, age and occupation," but . . . when I came here, to the [Rating] Department, we had further discussion of it, . . . *that it was incorrect, that we had no authority to tell a man that he was entitled to anything or was not,* so we drew up these forms, partly for the purpose of saving time, saving expense. . . . [Emphasis supplied.]

Instructions were also given to the Statistical Department and the Bureau of Information that they should be careful not to incite workers unduly to introduce applications; the following instruction, for instance, was relayed to the staff in 1926:

> On February 26, 1926, Mr. M. [a Commissioner] advised the writer [the Manager of the Compensation Department] that it was undesirable to disseminate information about herniae in order to permit people to use this information to make a case compensable or non-compensable. Letters in hernia cases will of necessity be more or less noncommittal.

After 1930, there was more pressure to attenuate the information services, this time from the Compensation Department, which found itself overworked by its growing adjudicative duties and unable to give enough attention to education and assistance. The very fact of increasing litigation provided an easy rationale for reducing IAC efforts in this area: people had become familiar enough with workmen's compensation and were now simply exploiting a service they no longer deserved. In 1929, the manager of the Compensation Department wrote to a commissioner:

> For the past year there has been such a marked increase in the actual work in the Compensation Department that it is simply staggering. . . . With more and more people becoming familiar with workmen's compensation, we receive more applications from outlying districts where the parties do not know how to get their case together . . . more people are learning ways and means of taking advantage of the Workmen's Compensation Act, such as Doctors and Druggists filing bills. . . . There are too many people trying to get assistance from the Commission who simply give us the smell of a handkerchief and leave the rest in our hands. We are expected to be legal adviser, investigator, make the necessary orders and joinder, notify witnesses, and finally find the property and enforce execution. The Commission has always maintained an attitude of helpfulness,

> but I feel that the time has arrived when we will have to admit that if we give this service to the people who do not do anything to help themselves that it simply means unconscionable delay and congestion in our routine work.

At that time, lawyers had begun entering the field of workmen's compensation practice. After having long resisted this trend, the IAC progressively came to welcome the appearance of applicants' counsel. The old idea that the worker *should* find at the IAC every kind of help he might need, tended to yield to a new policy that the agency would furnish its assistance *if needed,* that is, only to those who were unable or unwilling to obtain help by their own means. The increasing availability of private legal services and labor's own growing capacity and desire for self-help provided ready justifications for reducing administrative information services. In the eyes of the IAC, those services were but a supplement to inadequate private resources; as the latter would develop, the commission would relieve itself of this burden. The old but persistent dream of a self-administered compensation act could then, eventually, be declared accomplished. The agency would finally be able to adopt the role of an impartial third party, and withdraw from a partisan involvement that it increasingly felt illegitimate and incompatible with its true character. In 1944, a new instruction was given to the staff:

> Members of the staff, including referees, shall not recommend individual attorneys or firms of attorneys to litigants but *may recommend that an attorney be engaged* in appropriate cases. [Emphasis supplied.]

Private counsel had first been frowned upon, then tolerated, then welcomed; henceforth they would be encouraged.

The stage was set for what may have been the most dramatic episode in the history of the agency. About 1943, the IAC became the target of violent criticism, emanating mainly from insurance and industry, which challenged the integrity of the agency as corrupted by abuses of political influence. The campaign succeeded in provoking a legislative investigation; in 1944, the Assembly requested a committee to undertake an investigation of IAC procedures with the aim of reappraising "the manner in which, under present conditions, the organization and administrative set-up of the Industrial Accident Commission makes it possible to afford due process of law to persons appearing before it."[47] Throughout the hearings there was continuing criticism of the fact that the commission was "composed of persons who are vigorously professionally active in either union or employer activities":

> . . . in other words you have partisan representation on the bench. For the last six or eight years you have had double representation; in other words, there have

> been at least two persons [out of three commissioners] who by vocation, background and experience would represent labor.[48]

It had become necessary to "bring immediate return of the idea of even-handed justice administered according to due process of law."[49] Therefore:

> Hearing referees should, for obvious reasons, be wholly impartial, of independent judgment and free from nonjudicial interference, domination and control in the hearing and disposition of cases.[50]

The conclusions of the committee were equally critical:

> The Governors of this State have apparently failed to realize the nature of judicial functions required to be performed by the members of the Industrial Accident Commission. This is probably due to the fact that these appointees have a diversity of *other duties involving the welfare of labor. Separation of the Industrial Accident Commission from all functions other than the administration and adjudication of compensation claims,* should result in the appointment of qualified members.[51] [Emphasis supplied.]

Accordingly, the committee recommended stripping the agency of all its administrative responsibilities. Those recommendations were substantially adopted by the 1945 legislature.[52] The statute separated the office of Chairman of the Industrial Accident Commission from that of Director of Industrial Relations, a function he had held *ex officio* since 1927;[53] removed the Safety Department from commission control and made it a separate Division of Industrial Safety within the Department of Industrial Relations; transferred the Statistical Department to the Division of Labor Statistics and Research; put the control of self-insurance under a Supervisor of Self-Insured Employers directly responsible to the director; made the same director responsible for the enforcement of the duty to secure insurance, in conjunction with the IAC attorney; took the direction of the State Compensation Insurance Fund away from the IAC. The Industrial Accident Commission remained within the Department of Industrial Relations as the Division of Industrial Accidents; but in contrast with the authority he enjoyed over other divisions, the director was not given any power over the commission. The chairman and the members were appointed directly by the governor and had all appointive powers within the agency; the commission had exclusive responsibility for the making of compensation policies, under the control of appellate courts.

In spite of the considerable administrative losses it entailed, the reform was welcomed by the commission, and indeed even by labor. The old notion of a single authority responsible for making and coordinating public policy in the whole field of industrial accidents no longer had any appeal. Lost also was the idea that the implementation of the law might require some committed assistance to injured employees. In most respects, the practical import of the reform seemed insignificant, since IAC powers had in effect already been considerably reduced. But even those attenuated responsibilities had become a political burden, of which the commission wanted to be relieved.

For a while after 1945, the IAC kept the task of enforcing the requirement of insurance. But in 1953, as a letter of the chairman indicates, it was decided that "the work could be handled more effectively through the office of the Labor Commissioner"; the director of industrial relations agreed to the suggested change. Similarly, although the reports of injury were now received and processed by the Division of Labor Statistics, they were for a while regularly transmitted to the IAC; as in the past, the latter would screen them, send letters and information brochures to reported victims, and refer problematic cases to the various agencies concerned, such as, for example, the Labor Commissioner, the Safety Division, or the Bureau of Vocational Rehabilitation. But in 1956, according to an instruction from the chairman, the commission decided that "the referral of these reports is not the responsibility of this agency," and that henceforth it would be up to the Division of Labor Statistics to do "whatever is necessary." Shortly thereafter, the old practice of sending information to reported injured victims was discontinued.

The agency still had an "Information Desk" at which inquiring applicants would receive information and advice on their rights and proper procedure. But when, in 1951, a Senate Committee discussed the possibility of expanding this service to provide legal aid to claimants with salaried IAC attorneys, a commissioner objected and

> . . . urged serious examination of the proposal, since a failure to recover compensation by an appointed attorney could lead to great criticism and suspicion of collusion.[54]

The political risks of partisan involvement were too great. Accordingly, rather than letting claimants rely on the assistance of the information service or, at the hearings, of the referees, the commission increasingly urged them to hire their own attorneys. In 1951, the information brochure was amended to include the following advice:

> Injured employees are not required to have attorneys represent them in cases before the Commission. However, in cases where the facts are complicated, or where a close question of law is involved, an injured employee may find it more advantageous to have an attorney.[55]

Since 1963, the advice has become almost a request:

> Where the services of the Industrial Accident Commission are necessary to resolve a dispute, it is ordinarily wise for the applicant to engage the services of an attorney or a person who is well versed in compensation law, although there is no absolute requirement that he do so.[56]

Beyond this advice, there is not much the inquiring claimants can expect from the Information Desk; the policy is that the worker should be referred to an attorney whenever his case seems to call for some sort of action. The information attorney will only give general information on the relevant law and will avoid getting involved in the particulars of the case. His role is to inform, not to counsel. It is to answer, not to raise questions; it should never extend to checking whether the claimant's rights have been respected or exploring the case beyond the problems the claimant himself presents. These few remarks, taken from an interview with an IAC attorney who held the Information Desk, make the posture of the commission quite clear:

> By now the law is pretty well self-operating, because workers are now well educated in their rights and, in an area like here at least, almost all labor is unionized and very strong. Workers are independent enough and look out for their rights. . . .
>
> We cannot force people to press their rights, and we cannot do it in their place; it's none of our business. Like any other rights, parties may waive them by failing to act. . . .
>
> I generally avoid digging deep into the cases. I prefer to get the case worked out by the parties themselves, rather than to get it under our authority. Anyway, it would be a misuse of power to press the interests of the applicant against the carrier.

To render effective assistance to the worker would be both an *unnecessary* waste of energy, and an *illegitimate* abuse of authority.

The same concern for preserving its public integrity accounts for the commission's persistent refusal to exercise responsibility for policy-making. Even medical problems have assumed the character of political issues, in which the IAC must avoid any involvement. The commission sees little difficulty in ruling on the reasonableness of medical fees and the adequacy of medical treatment in legal controversies over particular claims; but it has systematically refused to exercise its remaining regulatory powers in those areas. It has repeatedly rejected demands that it revive its authority to control the adequacy of hospital facilities. After having adopted a new medical fee schedule in 1946, the IAC decided two years later that in spite of past policy it had no authority to adopt such a schedule and would renounce regulating the matter. It was willing to recognize an unofficial schedule, worked out by agreement among the parties, as *prima facie* evidence of the "reasonableness" of fees in cases involving a controversy over that issue. But it objected to proposed legislation that would formally restore its responsibility in that area:

> . . . the practical value of such a schedule-guide at the present time . . . is very little unless the parties most interested . . . give such a schedule their wholehearted support, and agree between themselves to abide by it.
>
> For these reasons, the Industrial Accident Commission, in recent years, has taken the position that the carriers, self-insurers, and doctors should get together and arrive at a schedule of fees which was agreeable to all parties, and which would be observed by all parties.[57]

A bill was nevertheless adopted in 1953,[58] but its actual import was very limited. Rather than taking it as a mandate for assuming regulatory responsibility, the commission has used it simply as a way of giving official authority to compromises that were almost wholly worked out between carriers and employers on the one hand, and the medical profession and labor unions on the other.

Finally, the commission has entirely renounced the major function it formerly had in initiating and sponsoring new policies. After having exercised considerable initiative in its early years,[59] the IAC had increasingly let organized labor share the burden of drafting and lobbying for new legislation. As the leadership was more frequently assumed by labor, the agency found itself confined to the passive role of adding or refusing its support to the demands of organized interest groups. In 1945, the newly constituted commission decided to withdraw from the legislative debate; henceforth it would eschew political advocacy, except on matters of organization, procedure, and personnel that were directly relevant to its internal operations. One rationale for this decision was that there was no longer any need for the commission to intervene in the legislative process. A former commissioner who sat on the commission in 1945 put it this way in an interview:

> For a number of years, we had found ourselves always taking the side of labor against insurance and industry. Now both insurers and employers, and the labor movement had organized strong lobbying systems, with specialized staffs of lawyers and with adequate political connections. We were only duplicating the efforts of the labor movement and we all felt that it would be as good and even wiser to let labor fight for its own interests.

The parties appeared competent enough to take care by themselves of the fate of the compensation system.[60] A more important reason for the new policy was that, with the growing involvement of partisan groups in the legislative debate, the role of the agency had been made to appear increasingly political. The commission was no longer capable of standing as the advocate of a publicly endorsed social aim. It was "always taking the side of labor against industry." In the same interview, the commissioner went on:

> In addition the IAC had for a while been under criticism for its partial advocacy of bills: it was thought in many circles that it was impossible for the Commission to administer in a faithful way bills it had formerly been thoroughly opposed to.

The IAC felt that its legitimacy was in jeopardy; in order to restore its authority, it had to "rise above politics." This is clearly expressed in the following quotation from a letter written in 1953 by another member of the 1945 commission:

> We have felt that we should make no recommendations relative to bills which increased, decreased or otherwise affected benefits. We felt that, since we sat in a judicial capacity, it would be improper and possibly show bias for us to make recommendations concerning "benefit" legislation. We felt there was a very practical reason for not making such recommendations since any that we might make would be either beneficial or detrimental to one or the other of the litigants that appeared before this Commission. We believed that any possible taint of judicial bias should be avoided in so far as possible.

The rhetoric of judicial propriety, expressed here, was gaining wide currency in the IAC at the time. But the issue raised is more general than that of judicial impartiality. More broadly stated, the problem is: How does authority preserve its legitimacy in the context of a continuing and systematic confrontation of adversary interests? To this problem, and in view of its longstanding commitment to self-administration, the IAC had a ready response: disengagement. Henceforth the agency would let the system unfold itself, hoping that a greater aloofness would help to sustain its authority.

The New Doctrine

At the close of this evolution, the IAC was left with the limited competence of a passive and uncommitted third party, mediating between partisan groups which had assumed almost complete initiative and responsibility for the promotion of their interests under the law. This administrative impoverishment was accompanied by significant changes in the doctrine of the agency and the goals of workmen's compensation.

From Initiative to Passivity. Most obvious among those changes was the growth of the idea that the implementation of compensation law no longer required the agency to exercise initiative. The work could be left to the interested parties, who had acquired sufficient competence for assuming this burden. This aspect of the new doctrine remained closely in line with the original philosophy of the commission. The basic aim of the early IAC had been to "make the law self-administering"; it now appeared that this aim had been accomplished. The law was self-administering.

But the move from initiative to passivity should not be seen as flowing from a purely rational and free assessment of needs and circumstances. Many problems remain—such as medical care, rehabilitation, assistance to unorganized workers—that call for administrative action. Although the retreat from initiative was responsive to the growing assertiveness of the parties, something more was involved than is suggested by the self-justifying idea that administrative intervention is no longer needed.

Two features of the early commission doctrine had a decisive influence on the decision to abandon initiative: (1) the determination of the agency to vest the administration of its program in the interested parties themselves; whatever guidance the agency might have to exercise, or whatever assistance it might have to give were to remain provisional and incidental to the major purpose of making the program self-operative; the IAC had embraced a philosophy of government that defined its mission as making itself expendable; (2) the insistence by the agency that compensation was a matter of common interest to both employers and employees, and that its administration would and should rest upon rational understanding and voluntary cooperation between the parties. This idea, which served important functions for the IAC, moved it to flee away from controversy, as the latter developed, and made it reluctant to adopt the aggressive posture that an active use of its authority would have required. The commission had in effect restricted its competence to those areas over which the consensus of the parties had been or could be established.

Initially, this second idea was but a specification of the first, and both were interpreted as summoning affirmative action. They meant the agency would *work* toward a self-administered system by *promoting* consensus and voluntary compliance. Later, however, as conflict grew between labor and industry, these goals came to contradict each other; the IAC was bound to welcome and support the increasing involvement of the parties; yet, in so doing, it was continuously arousing controversy and subverting its own efforts to develop cooperative modes of administration. This, in turn, made the commission more and more reluctant to make active efforts to enhance the competence of the parties. The agency resolved the dilemma by withdrawing from positive action. The two basic ideas were preserved but took an increasingly passive meaning; the IAC would *let* the parties help themselves and *let* them work out their own arrangements among themselves. This was, after all, what both industry and labor had been pressing the agency to do.

But why was the IAC so anxious to preserve cooperative and consensual modes of settlement? The basic source of this concern has to do with the foundations upon which the commission had chosen to base its authority.

Neutrality and the Loss of Commitment. The whole history of the IAC could be described as the history of changes in the nature of its claim to legitimacy. From its very beginning the agency was confronted with a crucial problem—how would it carry out its responsibility for a legislative program, which would seek to promote the welfare of labor, without becoming identified with the special interests of a favored class, and how could it preserve the integrity of its mandate without becoming a target for accusations of bias and thus undermining its authority? In other words, the problem was to define its mission and its role toward interested parties in such a way as to assure its legitimacy as a neutral public institution.

Several features of the early IAC philosophy helped to underscore the neutral character of its role and purposes. The commission strongly insisted on the *public* nature of its program; its mission was to promote the public welfare of the state, its concerns went beyond the special interests of either employers or employees, its action would entail costs as well as benefits for both labor and industry. The emphasis on neutrality appears more clearly when we look at the concrete meaning the notion of "public interest" assumed in the early IAC doctrine. A characteristic tendency of the commission was to *identify public interest with the common interests of the parties.* By itself the commission's insistence on the public character of its purpose would not have ruled out a resolute commitment to the protection of injured employees if this had been declared a matter of public policy. But not only would such a commitment have been hard to sustain in the political circumstances of the 1910's; it would also have run against still firmly entrenched social and legal conceptions of the proper role of the state. The welfare state was hardly emerging and, in its attempts at social reform, had to compromise with traditional views that insisted on keeping government limited and blind to the relative fortunes of its constituents. The appeal to common interests, as well as the emphasis on self-administration, must be seen in this context. By justifying its policies on ground of the promises they held for all affected interests, government was reasserting its continued impartiality, but in a way that enabled it to make new commitments and to move toward a more active role in social affairs. Although formally aimed at public welfare, workmen's compensation sought to appeal directly to the interests of the parties it would affect. The ideal of self-administration itself seemed to require such an interested attachment on the part of both parties to the industrial accident policies. Compensation had to be neutral not only in the sense of being an impersonal pursuit of some higher public interest; it also had to be neutral in its consequences for the private parties affected.

In this perspective, the persistent stress the IAC laid on common interests, rational consensus, and cooperation can be more fully understood; it allowed the agency to assert its integrity and legitimacy in a manner consistent with the active pursuit of its welfare aims. If compensation was the common good of employers and employees, then the commission was legitimately authorized to exercise active guidance and provide assistance in the pursuit of that aim. The concern of the IAC with avoiding adversariness in claims adjustment was but one particular aspect of this generalized denial of conflict; by defining claims as a call for help by both parties in the solution of a common problem, the agency sought to preserve its freedom of action in the accomplishment of its mandate.

Although this notion of common interests was at first useful to the agency in launching and developing its program, it was also costly. First it implied that employers and insurers could be trusted to care for the welfare of injured employees spontaneously, even though they might need to be motivated or educated for this purpose. Therefore the controls the agency would exercise had to remain limited and to take on a special character—they would have to be supportive rather than aggressive, educative rather than compulsory. The same idea also led the agency quickly to accept and rationalize the loss of its means of control. Second, and perhaps more important, the concern for common interests and consensus made it impossible for the agency, in spite of its commitment to the welfare of injured workers, to identify its aims clearly and resolutely with their interests. This tended to give a rather ambivalent character to the protection and assistance the IAC provided; help would be forthcoming, to be sure, but it would have to be consistent with the preservation of an accommodating posture toward defendants.

As long as the IAC remained the main source of assistance and protection for the injured man, it was to a certain extent able to preserve this emphasis on peaceful accommodation, as it had control over the character and the presentation of the workers' demands. But as labor became more competent and took more initiative in its own defense, the agency began to lose this control. Conflict between "defendants" and "claimants" came more and more in the open, challenging the assumption of common interests upon which all action programs of the commission rested. At the same time, as the protection of injured men passed into the hands of unions, the controversy became a confrontation of organized groups and increasingly took on a political character. To its dismay, the IAC saw its posture of neutrality become increasingly precarious; any action it would take or policy choice it would make in this setting of continuing controversy seemed to involve a partisan political commitment. This accounts for much of the ambivalence with which the IAC responded to the growing involvement of labor in compensation administration. On the one hand, the agency felt compelled, in order to protect its authority, to resist the increasing self-reliance and aggressiveness of organized labor; it was reluctant to accept independent legal representation of applicants, it sought to discourage the growth of litigiousness and persisted in keeping its informal ratings system, which did away with involved controversies. On the other hand, the success of its program, dependent as it was upon the participation of interested parties, required it to encourage self-help and assertiveness on the part of claimants; education and assistance therefore remained its preferred modes of action, pointing to labor the way the latter should follow.

Being inescapably bound to this adversary set-up, the IAC was progressively brought to redefine its role and seek a new basis for its authority. The commission would recognize the fundamental divergence of the parties' interests and would henceforth adopt the posture of a third party, basing its legitimacy upon the careful avoidance of any sort of partisan involvement. In practice, this move implied that the agency would renounce any initiative that might compromise its integrity. But more was involved in this new attitude than just a retreat from initiative. The change, to be sure, was rationalized as a move from activity to passivity; given the greater capacities of the parties, the burden of initiating action could be transferred to them, leaving the basic aims of the commission unchanged. In fact, however, those aims themselves had been profoundly altered; the IAC had in effect renounced its commitment to and responsibility for the development of workmen's compensation.

This loss of commitment is implicit in the justifications the IAC gave for abandoning its various action programs. Besides the argument that the necessity for positive intervention had disappeared, there was also the idea that, even if it were needed, such intervention would be illegitimate and incompatible with the true role of the agency. Thus, although the growing competence of labor provided the agency with the necessary opportunity and excuses for withdrawing from action, the thrust behind this retreat was the need for a new and more secure basis of legitimacy, one that could withstand the strains of an adversary system. In so doing *the IAC sacrificed its mission to the preservation of its authority.* The costs were high enough. The full burden of seeing to the implementation and development of the law had been thrown upon labor; no longer could the agency be expected to offer its support in this task, not even to provide it upon demand. Workers would be treated as parties equal to their adversaries; whether they actually were or were not equal would no longer be of concern to the commission.

From Public Welfare to Private Interests. Behind this new posture of impartiality, there was an implicit assertion by the IAC that the welfare of injured workers no longer qualified as a matter of public concern. From the problem of public welfare it formerly constituted, workmen's compensation had become a problem of accommodating divergent private interests.

Had the public character of the compensation program been preserved the IAC might very well have maintained its claim to neutrality and yet affirmed its commitment to the protection of industrial victims. Such a posture seemed untenable in the 1910's, but the conditions were no longer the same in the late 1930's, at a time when public policy was giving government a mandate for making labor a full and competent partner in the industrial order. This new public mandate offered the IAC a new opportunity to reassert its affirmative responsibilities for the protection of injured workers. By that time, however, the notion that government had a stake of its own in the compensation program had practically disappeared.

From the very beginnings of workmen's compensation, the public character of its aims had been quite precarious; the appeal to the common interests of affected parties in support of government action tended continuously to confuse public and private interests in the program. This approach laid the basis for giving the parties a determinant voice in policy-making; self-administration was, in a sense, the practical embodiment of this merging of the public and private spheres. A maximum of responsibility was delegated to the parties in the day-to-day implementation of administrative policies. Both self-administration and the identification of public and private interests were at first concessions designed to make the new government undertaking acceptable. By calling for the participation of interested parties, the IAC sought to commit them more firmly to the purposes of its enterprise, which was to remain eminently public in character. But in seeking this support, the commission had actually made itself profoundly dependent upon the parties. Its measure of administrative accomplishment was the extent of the voluntary compliance it was capable of obtaining; this meant that public aims would have to be redefined operationally so as to coincide with private demands. Even where it had affirmative powers, the agency was hampered by the necessity it felt of preserving its neutrality and justifying its actions by reference to the joint interests of labor and industry.

As the parties became more actively involved in the administration of the law, this whole ideology broke down. The divergence of their interests was increasingly sharpened and their private aims became more and more clearly dissociated from administrative purposes. At the same time the commission found its authority undermined and became steadily less capable of asserting the distinctiveness of its public aims. The agency was put on the defensive; instead of promoting private cooperation toward governmental purposes its energies were absorbed by the more conservative concern of avoiding and resolving private conflicts.

In practice, this process took the form of the Compensation Department, the seat of all IAC quasi-adjudicative functions, assuming a more and more central place in agency operations at the expense of other IAC programs. The significance of this transformation is best shown by the impact it had on rehabilitation and medical care. When the IAC renounced its means of control over rehabilitation, it was compelled to rely more and more on the good will of carriers and employers in furthering its aims. In so doing, it allowed its rehabilitation policies to be subverted by the special interests of the parties; to industry, rehabilitation became a means of curtailing benefit payments, and to labor, a trap to be avoided in order to maximize compensation. The idea of rehabilitation was soon lost in a partisan struggle over losses incurred and indemnities deserved, and the allocation of benefits, the task of the Compensation Department, became the central concern of both the parties and the commission.

Similarly, the loss of resources for supervising medical care allowed insurers to use such IAC policies as the medical fee schedule to capture control of industrial medicine. The employee's only redress was the exercise of his rights to change doctors, to procure his own medical treatment, and to present his own expert witnesses. Problems of medical care and medical expertise were thus absorbed into a conflict between labor and industry over the proper level of benefits, and the Medical Department became an auxiliary service in the arbitration of private controversies. Compensation medicine was no longer a problem of public health, nor was there a public authority responsible for its quality. Medical care had become an award in kind for damages to private interests, medical expertise a means of bolstering private claims. Industrial medicine, in short, had become partisan and self-serving, uncontrolled by criteria of public welfare.

That important losses have resulted from this erosion of public purpose can hardly be doubted. Recurrent complaints from the medical profession and from specialists in vocational rehabilitation have emphasized how the litigious "courthouse" atmosphere of compensation administration frustrates the aims of welfare action. According to a physician speaking at a meeting of the California Medical Association:

> Of all forms of medical practice . . . the treatment of industrial accidents is most inadequate: there is an "inordinately high percentage of complications, delayed

> recoveries and permanent disabilities," and both patients and doctors remain "cautious, defensive and suspicious of each other."
>
> . . . workers who suffer injuries on the job enter "a strange and complicated world unlike any other type of patient." They are surrounded by lawyers, claims agents, union representatives and judges—all of whom, . . . "may have an influential role in diagnosis and treatment."
>
> . . . "Some doctors feel a great deal of hostility toward the industrial accident patient, and behave as though they are all malingerers and exploiters," . . .
>
> "The end result is a medical and psychiatric chaos unlike anything else in medicine," . . .
>
> He [the doctor] proposed that [physicians] seek more strongly to motivate patients to recover, and that their earliest treatments include a genuine concern for the patient as a human being, not merely as industrial accident cases.
>
> Above all, he said, the law that forces so many accident victims into state hearing rooms and courts to press their claims should be changed—to remove the "adversary element" that interferes with good medicine.[61]

One may doubt that the IAC ever was competent to exercise any realistic influence in the promotion of adequate care and rehabilitation. But this used to be one of its major aims. The fact that it has lost this goal is at least partly responsible for the absence of efforts to remedy the inadequacies of care and rehabilitation.

From Pattern-Orientation to Claims-Orientation. As we have already mentioned, the evolution from a philosophy of welfare administration to one of service to private interests was manifested in practice by the ever-growing significance of claims adjudication in IAC operations. This brings us to a final aspect of the change in the administrative perspectives of the commission, that is, the shift of its concerns from *patterns* of practices affecting the implementation of the compensation program, to individual *claims* arising in the application of the law.

The early IAC had no desire to get involved in the adjudication of claims; indeed, it was concerned that the number of applications filed with it would increase and was determined to avoid what, in its eyes, would have been an administrative failure. The agency's concern was to create or foster appropriate practices in the management of claims and the provision of medical care; if its intervention were needed, it would be for education and corrective action toward the development of such practices. Its adjudicative functions were, in its eyes, just a safety valve, designed to handle the small minority of problem cases that the parties would be unable to resolve by themselves. The concerns of the commission were for the *patterns* governing the private administration of benefits; the actions it contemplated were of a *corrective* rather than remedial character.

However, to sustain this orientation would have required a kind of authority the IAC was not able to establish firmly. The belief in self-administration assumed that, on the whole, employers and employees would by themselves evolve the new practices and perspectives that were necessary for a successful implementation of the compensation program. Committed to consensual government, the commission had made itself incompetent to challenge the structure of those private interests it would have had to regulate. Thus, paradoxically, from the very beginning the task for which the powers of the IAC were most clearly and securely defined was also the task in which the agency was least interested—the determination of contested individual claims. Later, with the rise of labor and the growing salience of organized group conflict, the commission came to find it positively useful to shift its concerns from patterns and regulation to claims and case-by-case pronouncements.

In a context of escalating controversy, the *case-by-case approach served as a means of atomizing group demands and stripping the debate of the political character it increasingly tended to assume.* The shift to a claims-orientation must be seen in the perspective of the agency's efforts to safeguard its neutrality; it was an attempt to deactivate a conflict that threatened its authority. By keeping the focus on individual claims and problems, the commission was able, to a certain extent, to make its commitments less visible, or rather less overtly political. The costs of this change were obvious: instead of promoting *reforms* of structure through regulation or the advocacy of new legislation, the agency would limit its competence to the provision of *remedies* in cases of inadequate compliance with compensation policies.

This transformation of the commission's orientation also had consequences for the strategy the parties would follow in pressing their demands. It meant that the IAC would be reluctant to respond to demands for any sort of radical action aimed at changing the conditions of compensation administration; labor's pressures for reforms were thus consistently met by offers of improved remedies to be applied on a case-by-case approach. Instead of developing its means of enforcing the insurance requirement, the IAC proposed and secured an increase of the penalties for noncompliance; instead of supporting labor's demand for giving employees the right to choose their physicians, the commission offered the services of its Medical Department in cases where needed; instead of organizing legal education and assistance in a systematic way, the agency made its help available on individual requests. Therefore the only effective way labor had of pressing its interests was through the introduction of claims and the use of the commission's quasi-judicial facilities. Unions were thus encouraged to focus their efforts on developing their competence and resources in the presentation and advocacy of individual cases; and their political demands to the agency centered on the problem of making its adjudicative services more accessible to employees. Of course, union lawyers performed a crucial role in orienting labor in this direction, and their work was very much in line with labor's own notion of compensation as a right of the employee rather than a state-provided welfare benefit. But what finally, after some reluctance on the part of union leaders, validated this approach was their experience of the commission's incompetence to meet the needs of injured workers with positive action.

In retrospect, the move to a claims orientation did not bring to the IAC the relief it sought. For one thing, it tended to accentuate the growing emphasis on private interests in workmen's compensation, thus further undermining the welfare ideology. The presentation of issues in the form of individual claims was a particularly well-suited means of continuously facing the agency with the consequences of its decisions for the persons immediately affected. Individual problems were placed in the foreground and emphasis naturally shifted from public ends to the private values at stake in decisions. In this way, the move toward a claims-orientation coincided with the displacement of public welfare by private interests.

More important, the focus on individual claims did not long serve its function of disaggregating group demands. Compensation claims, as we have shown, did not remain the unorganized series of individual disputes they originally were. As unions assumed the task of systematically preparing and assisting their membership in the promotion of their interests, as they developed their ties with specialized applicants' lawyers and evolved new patterns of organizational advocacy, individual cases took on the character of a controversy of organized groups. The very process of claims settlement became an arena for those political debates from which the agency had sought refuge. The IAC was compelled to retreat further into the posture of aloof and blind impartiality that it holds today.

Although the move from a pattern-orientation to a claims-orientation was closely linked to the other processes of transformation we have described, it had specific consequences that warrant distinguishing it. With its focus on individual remedies, rather than on correcting patterns of action, the IAC has lost sensitivity and responsiveness to the systematic conditions affecting its work. Although there are wide variations among different local areas in the state in such conditions as the strength of labor organizations and the assertiveness of employees, the structure and quality of the compensation bar, and the degree of autonomy or dependence of the medical profession in its relations with organized groups, these variations are not reflected in the policies of the commission for its different branch offices. The local medical association may be the captive of local firms and insurance agents; it will nevertheless be relied upon to provide panels of independent experts. The commission may be flooded with "compromise and release agreements" for its approval, typically a result of the lack of organization of labor and the incompetence of the applicants' attorneys; each agreement will be assessed on its own merits by the usual standards and methods of the agency. When asked about such variations and what they imply for the work of the commission, members of the staff have a ready answer: "To me there are only individual cases; we never know those statistics (that is, data on unionization, unemployment, the medical profession or the local bar), our job is to process those applications you see on my desk." The point is not only that the IAC does not actively concern itself with such problems, but also that it makes itself unavailable for action upon them even when requested by the parties to act or simply to mediate the issue. This is not simply a matter of preserving administrative impartiality, for, indeed, by assuming this posture the commission objectively tends to let itself become the agent of whatever group—labor or industry—happens to dominate the compensation scene in a given area. To maintain its integrity, the IAC would have to take notice of, and action on, such aspects of its environment as affect its role. Having vested all its energies in the one-by-one determination of claims, the agency has lost its competence to deal with the conditions and the systematic patterns in which those claims are produced.

Notes to Chapter VI

1. *Yosemite Lumber Co.* v. *IAC* (Moore), 9 IAC 11, 187 Cal. 774, 204 Pac. 226 (1922); *People* v. *Yosemite Lumber Co.*, 10 IAC 287, 191 Cal. 267, 216 Pac. (1923).

2. *Report of the Industrial Accident Commission, 1923–1924* (Sacramento: California Legislature, 46th Sess., 1925), Appendix to the *Journals of the Senate and Assembly*, Vol. 4, No. 8, p. 5. Compare the lengthy, detailed, and varied reports of the Statistical Department until 1922 with the short and routine reports of the same department for the years after 1922.

3. *Assembly Bills* (Sacramento: California Legislature, 45th Sess., 1923), No. 260.

4. *Assembly Bills* (Sacramento: California Legislature, 46th Sess., 1925), No. 205; California Statutes of 1925, Chap. 300; California Labor Code, Sec. 3702.

5. The federal Vocational Rehabilitation Act adopted in 1920 organized a program of federal-state cooperation toward rehabilitation of the disabled. In California, a serious conflict between the Industrial Accident Commission and the Department of Education developed as to which agency would administer the federal-state program. Although the IAC had already initiated a rehabilitation program under its Rehabilitation Department, the Department of Education was given control of the new program on the ground that the latter was not intended to benefit injured workers only. A Division of Rehabilitation was

therefore created in the Department of Education, with the understanding that it would coordinate its work with that of the IAC Department of Rehabilitation. This account is based on Warren H. Pillsbury, "History of Workmen's Compensation in California" (Los Angeles: University of California, Institute of Industrial Relations, 1954; unpublished paper).

6. In 1925, after constitutional obstacles had apparently been removed, the Industrial Accident Commission attempted to reintroduce legislation for the creation of a rehabilitation fund under its authority; the bill was defeated (*Report of the Industrial Accident Commission, 1925–1926* [Sacramento: California Legislature, 47th Sess., 1927], Appendix to the *Journals of the Senate and Assembly*, Vol. 5, No. 19, pp. 17–18; *Senate Bills* [Sacramento: California Legislature, 46th Sess., 1925], No. 514; see also *Assembly Bills* [Sacramento: California Legislature, 45th Sess., 1923], No. 895).

7. For examples of such policies and practices, see Chap. IX, pp. 247–251. Similarly, the IAC policy of discouraging lump sum payments was exploited by insurers for their own protection, as a means of avoiding premature disbursements when, for instance, there was a hope of later obtaining a reduced disability rating or the life expectancy of the worker was shorter than the period for which the installment payments would run.

8. As far as encouragement of disabled workers was concerned, the Industrial Accident Commission was paralyzed by its notion that too substantial benefits would destroy in the injured man any motivation to return to work. This idea made the agency reluctant to propose additional advantages for those undergoing rehabilitation. On this notion in the early IAC, see Chap. II, pp. 20–21. This idea was widely shared in compensation circles throughout the country and is still alive today among those preoccupied with rehabilitation. See, for instance, Herman M. Somers and Anne R. Somers, *Workmen's Compensation* (New York: John Wiley & Sons, 1954), pp. 259–261, and *Report of the Workmen's Compensation Study Commission* (Sacramento: State of California, April, 1965), pp. 216–225.

9. California Labor Code, Sec. 3702.

10. *Report of the Industrial Accident Commission, 1914–1915* (Sacramento: California Legislature, 42nd Sess., 1917), Appendix to the *Journals of the Senate and Assembly*, Vol. 5, No. 3, p. 75.

11. Whereas in the year 1921–1922 the department reported having performed 1,533 examinations and rendered only 839 "advisory opinions," ten years later the proportion had been reversed: for the two years 1930–1931 and 1931–1932, there were only 2,506 examinations, as against 5,436 opinions (*Report of the Industrial Accident Commission, 1921–1922* [Sacramento: California Legislature, 45th Sess., 1923], Appendix to the *Journals of the Senate and Assembly*, Vol. 4, No. 10, p. 42; *Second Biennial Report of the Industrial Accident Commission, 1930–1932* [Sacramento: California Legislature, 50th Sess., 1933], Appendix to the *Journals . . .*, Vol. 2, No. 7, p. 31).

12. *Proceedings of the 7th Annual Meeting of the International Association of Industrial Accident Boards and Commissions* (I.A.I.A.B.C.), *September 1920* (Washington, D.C.: U.S. Department of Labor, Bureau of Labor Statistics, 1921), Bull. No. 281, p. 264. Thus, when the Industrial Rehabilitation Act was invalidated, the Industrial Accident Commission used the fund to develop a provisional substitute for its rehabilitation program (*Report of the Examination of the State Compensation Insurance Fund* [San Francisco: California Industrial Accident Commission, October, 1925], p. 9).

13. See Chap. III, pp. 55–56.

14. Between 1914, the year of its creation, and 1921, the fund's share of the total written premiums in California rose from 11.77 percent to 36.93 percent (*Report of the Examination of the State Compensation Insurance Fund*, p. 6).

15. The fund's share of the market fell from almost 37 percent in 1921 to 30.16 percent in 1924, and thereafter fluctuated between 25 percent and 30 percent (*ibid.*). For the years after 1924, see the yearly *Report*(s) *of the Industrial Accident Commission.*

16. This limitation was never fully overcome, even though the fund was authorized in 1929 to write insurance for other employers' liability laws "when written incidental to and in connection with California Workmen's Compensation" (California Statutes of 1929, Chap. 174; California Insurance Code, Sec. 11779, 11780).

17. California Insurance Code, Sec. 11784.

18. *Proceedings of the 7th Annual Meeting of the I.A.I.A.B.C., September 1920*, pp. 236–237. Efforts were also made to pass legislation separating the State Compensation Insurance Fund from the Industrial Accident Commission, or depriving the SCIF of its monopoly of compensation insurance for government agencies. See especially *Assembly Bills* (Sacramento: California Legislature, 43rd Sess., 1919), No. 791, and *Assembly Bills* (. . . , 48th Sess., 1929), No. 489.

19. *Report of the Industrial Accident Commission, 1916–1917* (Sacramento: California Legislature, 43rd Sess., 1919), Appendix to the *Journals of the Senate and Assembly*, Vol. 3, No. 3, p. 20.

20. *Proceedings of the 7th Annual Meeting of the I.A.I.A.B.C., September 1920*, p. 235.

21. *Report of the Examination of the State Compensation Insurance Fund*, p. 17. Sensing the loss, the Industrial Accident Commission made a desperate plea for legislation granting it a monopoly of compensation insurance. Its effort, as well as later efforts by labor in the same direction, failed (*Report of the Industrial Accident Commission, 1925–1926*, pp. 19–22; *Assembly Bills* [Sacramento: California Legislature, 51st Sess., 1935], No. 2418; *Assembly Bills* [. . . , 53rd Sess., 1939], No. 575; *Senate Bills* [. . . , 53rd Sess., 1939], No. 1130).

22. *Investigation of Procedure of the Industrial Accident Commission* (Sacramento: California Legislature, Assembly, Subcommittee of the Interim Committee on Governmental Efficiency and Economy, 1945), hereinafter cited as *Investigation of IAC Procedure, 1945*, pp. 121, 123.

23. California Statutes of 1945, Chap. 1431, Sec. 6; California Labor Code, Sec. 57.5; California Insurance Code, Section 11770. The SCIF has long had, and still has, the reputation among labor representatives of being the most conservative of all insurance companies; this condition is thought to result from the particularly poor risks it carries, strong internal pressures for economy, and an inability to retain competent personnel on its claims management and legal staff. See, for instance, John W. Graves, "The State Compensation Insurance Fund," *Bulletin of the Los Angeles Medical Society* (January 19, 1934), pp. 37, 59, 68; *California and Western Medicine*, (May 5, 1935), p. 396; and more recently, the story, reported in *East Bay Labor Journal* (October 28, 1955), that the manager of the SCIF had publicly declared: "The State Compensation Insurance Fund is not a labor protection agency."

24. In 1936, the insurers countered by asking that the Industrial Accident Commission furnish them with "tentative ratings," based solely on the carriers' records, to the end of assisting them in claims adjustment. The demand was rejected.

25. *Proceedings of the 39th Annual Meeting of the California State Federation of Labor, 1938*, p. 33.

26. See below, pp. 144–145.

27. So low, indeed, that in 1958 the sections of the IAC *Rules of Practice* dealing with informal ratings "were eliminated since the Commission felt that the Rules of Practice and Procedure should only relate to its judicial functions." The procedure was nevertheless continued and new instructions were issued in 1960.

28. See Chap. VII, pp. 172–173.

29. Most discussions of the difficulties of rehabilitation underscore this point. See especially Earl F. Cheit, *Injury and Recovery in the Course of Employment* (New York: John Wiley & Sons, 1961), pp. 284–308.

30. *Ibid.*, pp. 295–299.

31. The text of the agreement can be found in *Partial Report of the Senate Interim Committee on Workmen's Compensation Benefits* (Sacramento: California Legislature, 1951), pp. 238–239.

32. *Proceedings of the 46th Annual Meeting of the California State Federation of Labor, 1948*, p. 78.

33. *Partial Report of the Senate Interim Committee on Workmen's Compensation Benefits*, p. 239.

34. On the inadequacies of industrial rehabilitation in California, see *Report of the Senate-Assembly Joint Interim Committee on Education and Rehabilitation to Handicapped Workers and Adults* (Sacramento: California Legislature, 1959).

35. *Investigation of IAC Procedure, 1945*, p. 59.

36. See Chap. IV, pp. 76–77.

37. Lawyers objected to the provision of informal advisory opinions as violating standards of proper procedure. See Chap. VII, pp. 179–183.

38. The Medical Department recognized those limitations, as in a report in 1958, which concluded that "unless Commission medical jobs are made more attractive, we will be unable to obtain the kind of man we have to have," that is, ". . . doctors capable of rendering opinions upon which referees may rely and which will be recognized by insurance carriers and attorneys outside the Commission." Labor contends that the Industrial Accident Commission can recruit only retired armed forces doctors, whose main expertise is to uncover malingerers and who are unable to reconcile themselves to the welfare aims of workmen's compensation.

39. California Statutes of 1949, Chap. 751, Sec. 1; California Labor Code, Sec. 4600.

40. *Senate Bills* (Sacramento: California Legislature, 53rd Sess., 1939), No. 250; (. . . , 54th Sess., 1941), No. 1034; *Assembly Bills* (Sacramento: California Legislature, 53rd Sess., 1939), No. 1521; (. . . , 54th Sess., 1941), No. 931; (. . . , 55th Sess., 1943), No. 1499.

41. *Assembly Bills* (Sacramento: California Legislature, 51st Sess., 1934), No. 194; (. . . , 52nd Sess., 1937), Nos. 578, 645, 1062, 1536; (. . . , 53rd Sess., 1939), Nos. 1519, 1521; (. . . , 54th Sess., 1941), Nos. 519, 931; (. . . , 55th Sess., 1943), No. 1499; *Senate Bills* (Sacramento: California Legislature, 52nd Sess., 1937), No. 830; (. . . , 54th Sess., 1941), Nos. 1034, 1258; (. . . , 55th Sess., 1943), No. 1044. Labor has actually continued to press for adoption of such legislation at practically all sessions of the legislature; we have mentioned those bills of the late 1930's and early 1940's only to show that they were submitted at the same time as public IAC legal assistance was requested. This latter demand has been almost completely dropped after 1945.

42. "Report of the Committee on Practice and Procedure before the Industrial Accident Commission," *Journal of the State Bar of California*, Vol. IX, No. 9 (September, 1934), p. 74. See Chap. V, pp. 106–107.

43. Of course, the Medical Bureau was still available to solve conflicts of medical testimony, but applicants' lawyers distrusted it and usually objected to its use. The commission also had a fund for covering the cost of appointing "Commission Medical Examiners" from private practice when the report of a specialist was necessary; but the fund was utterly inadequate to fill the needs, and neither labor nor industry was interested in having those

appropriations increased. In 1961, Commission Medical Examiners were appointed in only 88 cases, and in 1962, in 49 cases (*Biennial Report of the California Department of Industrial Relations, 1961–1962* [Sacramento: State of California]). Finally, the agency had the option of appointing "independent medical examiners" at the cost of the parties when they were willing to pay. Since the applicant is usually unable or unwilling to pay, such appointments depend upon the interest or good will of the carrier. In addition, unions and their lawyers have frequently objected to such appointments on the ground that the lists of physicians from which they are selected consist in large part of "insurance doctors," who are allegedly biased against applicants. See *Report of the Workmen's Compensation Study Commission*, pp. 105–111. Thus, the resources of the Industrial Accident Commission for procuring independent medical expertise are seriously limited.

44. *Investigation of IAC Procedure, 1945*, p. 13. See also the complaints expressed by the then secretary, in *ibid.*, p. 14.

45. *Report of the Industrial Accident Commission, 1920–1921* (Sacramento: California Legislature, 45th Sess., 1923), Appendix to the *Journals of the Senate and Assembly*, Vol. 4, No. 10, p. 13.

46. In 1923 and 1925, the Industrial Accident Commission sought to obtain legislation that would have given it a positive mandate to assist injured men in the prosecution of their claims. Both attempts failed (*Assembly Bills* [Sacramento: California Legislature, 45th Sess., 1923], No. 332; *Senate Bills* [Sacramento: California Legislature, 46th Sess., 1925], No. 467).

47. *Investigation of IAC Procedure*, 1945, p. 118.

48. *Ibid.*, p. 45; see also pp. 99, 103–104.

49. *Ibid.*, p. 112.

50. *Ibid.*, p. 124.

51. *Ibid.*, pp. 90–91.

52. California Statutes of 1945, Chap. 1431.

53. California Statutes of 1927, Chap. 440. The purpose of this law was to establish an authority that would coordinate the action of the various branches of the Department of Industrial Relations. The latter had been created in 1921 by putting together various existing agencies in the area of welfare and industrial relations; but the agencies had kept their full autonomy and no office had been made responsible for the coordination of their action (California Statutes of 1921, Chap. 604). The creation of the office of Director in 1927 did not make much difference; his authority was left wholly undefined. Not until 1945 did this office acquire any definite responsibility.

54. *Partial Report of the Senate Interim Committee on Workmen's Compensation Benefits*, p. 285.

55. *California Workmen's Compensation Law* (Sacramento: California Industrial Accident Commission, effective September 22, 1951), p. 10.

56. *California Workmen's Compensation Law* (Sacramento: California Industrial Accident Commission, effective September 20, 1963), n.p.

57. *Partial Report of the Senate Interim Committee on Workmen's Compensation Benefits*, p. 221.

58. Some information on the history of the Medical Fee Schedule can be found in *ibid.*, pp. 217–223. California Statutes of 1953, Chap. 1782, Sec. 1; California Labor Code, Sec. 5307.1.

59. Each session of the legislature from 1913 to 1921, and to a lesser extent in 1923 and 1925, found the Industrial Accident Commission bringing up new proposals for reform. A few important innovations were again suggested in 1929. See especially California Stat-

utes of 1929, Chap. 222, which created a subsequent injuries fund. On the early period, see Chap. II and III, *passim.*

60. Actually, as this commissioner remembered, the new policy had been suggested by a member of the commission who came from, and was closely identified with, the labor movement.

61. *San Francisco Chronicle,* March 23, 1966, p. 7.

VII The Emergence of a Court

THE RETREAT DESCRIBED in the preceding chapter did more than render the Industrial Accident Commission relatively impotent as an administrative agency. A parallel change occurred—the emergence of a new conception of the agency as a court of law. From an administrative authority, which looked to the results of action as the test of policy and decision, the commission was transformed into a judicial body, which sought in rules and principles the guide for and the justification of its determinations. The growth of this orientation toward principled decision-making will be the theme of the present chapter.

Historically, administrative withdrawal and judicialization were inextricably related. The growing judicial character of the commission was often invoked as a rationale for depriving it of some administrative resource. For instance, due process and the principle of separation of executive and judicial powers provided a powerful argument in support of the reform of 1945, which stripped the agency of most of its means of action.[1] At the same time, administrative impoverishment helped lay the foundations for the transformation of the agency into a court; the move toward impartiality, the loss of commitment to welfare action, the growing focus on claims adjustment as the principal task of the agency, established conditions that favored the emergence of a judicial perspective.

But those conditions might as well have led the commission to perform as a sort of mediation service, available for conciliating the conflicting demands of employers and employees on a more or less *ad hoc* basis. The process of administrative retreat cannot by itself account for the growing commitment of the IAC to a system of governance in which partisan demands are treated as claims of right and criteria of decision are sought not in agency purposes and expertise, or in the need to reach some balance and preserve harmony between the contending interests, but in a set of standards that are recognized as binding without respect for particular merits or needs. Nor can we account for the withdrawal of the agency solely as a consequence of its transformation into a court; for, indeed, as we shall later argue,[2] the loss of authority and commitment suffered by the commission has itself tended to prevent the agency from becoming fully committed to principled adjudication. The two processes—judicialization and administrative withdrawal—must therefore be kept analytically distinct; it is the purpose of this chapter to disentangle them and to identify the specific conditions and consequences that are associated with the process of judicialization.

The retreat of the IAC, as we have shown, can be accounted for by the growing adversariness that characterized the relations of the parties before the agency, and by the consequences this evolution had for the foundations of agency authority. By itself this evolution did not entail pressures to make the IAC more principled in the exercise of its authority. Adversariness as such, that is, the commitment to a system in which conflict and partisan initiative assume a prevailing role in moving authority to act, may, indeed, be compatible with quite a variety of modes of governance. It flourishes in the legislative process, before mediation boards, and in corporate management, as well as in court proceedings; and conversely, adjudication may develop in settings that are not characteristically adversary. Which mode of governance prevails depends less upon the presence of conflict than upon the character of the controversy as it is perceived by the parties and by the deciding authority. What matters is the *kind* of appeal that is made in support of the contending claims; appeal can be made to the weight of power, or to the requirements of reciprocity and consensus, or to the test of knowledge and expediency. Or, indeed, appeal may be made to the moral support of authoritative principles and rules without respect for considerations of power, consent, or expediency. It is this moral appeal that makes a controversy "legal" and puts pressure on the decider to take a principled stance in the exercise of his authority; for his legitimacy then depends upon his ability to meet this appeal and justify his decision. He is held *accountable to rules and principles.*

We shall now attempt to show how the controversy between injured employees and employers was progressively transformed into a legal debate over rights and duties, and how this change resulted in putting upon the IAC an increasingly heavier burden of accountability.

The Legalization of Controversy

As we have shown earlier,[3] the history of workmen's compensation was marked by important changes in the patterns of participation by labor and industry in the administration of workmen's compensation. Not only was there a significant increase in the extent of their involvement, but the very nature of their participation was profoundly transformed. Employers and employees developed greater resources and invested more energies in administrative and political action; but they also evolved a new perspective on the nature and purposes of their action. Instead of simply attempting to secure adequate consideration of their interests by the IAC, the legislature, and other groups, they increasingly took the view that those interests involved legally protected rights that lay beyond compromises and administrative manipulations and were to be asserted as grounded in principle. This change was particularly salient for labor in view of the insecurity, the lack of resources, and the general alienation from law that characterized both unions and individual workers at the beginning of the period studied. With the growth of its political competence, with the emergence of a more positive view of law and government, with the changing character of authority in industry and the increasing security and moral autonomy gained through organization, and finally with the support of the legal profession, labor progressively acquired the moral and social resources that enabled it to make its demands in the principled and assertive manner of legal advocacy.

As the conflict between employers and injured employees grew, a shift occurred in the nature and object of the controversy. Initially, under the welfare philosophy that prevailed in the early commission, although the "benefits" of the employee were legally defined and conditioned by a "liability" on the part of the employer, this liability tended to be treated as providing *resources* for administrative action, and the benefits tended to be conceived as categories of *needs* to be fulfilled by the agency with those resources—medical needs, need for relief during unemployment, need for rehabilitation after a permanent disability. The dominant problem with which the agency was confronted, or at least the problem it saw as significant and worthy of its attention, was one of *adjusting available resources to existing needs.* This was to be done "without incumbrance of any character"; law, the legal limits of liability, the legal extent of compensation rights, would not be allowed to become an obstacle to this major task. Procedure was to be kept "informal" and free of "technicalities," so as to maximize opportunities to gather information and provide broad discretion in working out appropriate solutions to the problems raised. Claims were not suits, but "applications"; hearings were not trials, but "inquiries"; the process of determination was not adjudication, but "adjustment." This definition was in large part accepted by the parties themselves. This is quite understandable for employees, since they were heavily dependent on administrative assistance, and the commission took it upon itself to introduce and press their claims in accordance with its own conceptions of the issues and of the proper manner of resolving them. As to employers and insurers, although the agency approach could potentially have been a costly threat to their rights, it actually tended to give them much the same discretion in their own handling of claims as the IAC sought for itself. That insurance and industry went along with the commission's desire to deemphasize the legal aspects of compensation problems is indicated by the fact that until the late 1920's their representation before the agency was generally assumed not by lawyers but by lay members of their claims management staff.[4]

The transition to the use of attorneys, the change in the nature of controversies, and their effect on the work of the commission are aptly summarized in this quotation from a report of the manager of the Compensation Department to the commission chairman in 1929:

> There has been a marked increase in the number of attorneys appearing before the Commission, and I believe everyone will concede that an attorney, speaking generally, will make the case harder to try and cause more proceeding and more testimony, and will often end by ordering a transcript and petitioning for rehearing. The hearings are necessarily delayed on account of *lengthy arguments and objections by counsel,* with the result that a referee could try three more cases in the same time with the same effort under the old practice of having the man appear in person and the insurance carrier represented by an adjuster. There has been a practice lately among many insurance carriers to turn their insurance cases over to a firm of attorneys and two or three such firms have apparently specialized in this work. Without in any way discussing the ultimate desirability, the whole effect is at least 50 per cent more work per case.
>
> . . . *If we take a chance, we encourage a petition for rehearing or a letter of complaint.* . . . In formal orders terminating [compensation] after notice where a man is represented by an attorney, the average attorney *does not feel that he is doing justice by his client unless he fights the petition and insists on a hearing. His first move is to send in an objection.* . . . I do not believe it is an exaggeration to say that to have an attorney represent an applicant brings in, in the average case, as much work as the original case of itself would have caused. [Emphasis added.]

The commission was losing its free hand; objections, petitions, complaints, hearings, and rehearings were pressing it more and more insistently to account for its actions by justifying standards. Not only did this mean "more work"; above all it meant another *kind* of work—the focus of energies had to be at least partly displaced from assessing needs and finding means of providing for them; to *discussing, scrutinizing, and justifying the standards used in the process of assessment and decision.* Everything was being questioned, no longer was it possible to "take a chance" without running the risk of "encouraging a petition for rehearing or a letter of complaint," one had to be "cautious" in the presence of lawyers whose "first move" was always "to send in an objection." Further quoting from the same report, we read that:

> Due to many complications . . . *we are all more cautious* in preparing final orders and the Commission are watching the orders with the result that *we oftentimes have to recommend an order now that would not have been recommended a few years ago.* In addition to this *each order covers matters that either did not come up or were not handled as carefully heretofore.* . . .
>
> The Commission has been requesting more and more information per case, including the qualifications of doctors testifying; a statement as to who called the witnesses; the amount of fee paid an attorney and agreement if any; due to the fact that the Commission will often ask a Referee for further information or criticise his memorandum because certain information was not in the memo, there has been a subconscious tendency to increase the length of memos in reporting hearings. . . . Under the old practice the Commission would redecide the case on the rehearing as it then stood. . . . Now . . . in a large per cent of the cases where rehearings are granted the case is again set for hearing. . . .
>
> A few years ago we did very little work for the Legal Department. At the present time we copy practically all the court opinions and briefs prepared by the attorney. . . .
>
> There is a tendency throughout the United States in workmen's compensation to include more and more cases under the compensable list that would have been considered diseases heretofore. These are known as medical cases and are very difficult to try and involve lots of analyses and hearings. Due to the fact that the Commission has broadened out in this field it encourages similar cases, and as more people become familiar with a possible hope in such cases *we have more and more of these borderline, questionable cases.*
>
> In addition to the above, *people make an active study of our line of decisions with a view of creating borderline cases,* hoping to have the case just outside the line. [Emphasis added.]

We see here *the intrusion of legal argument into administrative policy-making.* The issue of the debate was no longer the "wisdom" of policies and decisions as such, that is, their adaptation to aims and circumstances. It was their *authority.* Rules were becoming the central focus of controversy. The change had two closely related but separable dimensions. First, the parties were no longer simply requesting that the agency consider their particular interests and needs in applying its policies to their cases. They were addressing their claims to the policies themselves, challenging or invoking them, testing their scope and limitations. In the words of our quoted administrator, they were "creating borderline cases." That is, the policies of the IAC were no longer taken for granted; they were beginning to be systematically subjected to *criticism.* Test cases were being brought up with increasing frequency. In addition, policies were no longer treated only as guides for the agency, which the commission could more or less freely set and follow in accordance with its purposes and expertise. They were now taken as *entitling* employers and employees to a determinate conduct on the part of the agency, whatever the latter's wishes might be; they were held as binding the IAC toward the parties themselves. Any claim to authority by the commission would thus be met by a corresponding claim of right by the parties; employers would insist that the commission define and respect the limits of their liability instead of letting this liability be used as a manipulable resource under unexamined standards; employees would test the conditions and extent of their benefits rather than let those hinge upon unspecified administrative notions about their needs and best interest.

This change can be described as an effort to *transform policies into rules.* A policy becomes a rule when it is charged with such authoritativeness as to warrant holding the decision-maker *accountable* to it; it is then withdrawn from the realm of adaptive problem-solving, or of unexamined routine, and made a governing standard by which conduct and decisions are systematically and consciously assessed. Both criticism and the emphasis on entitlement tend to underscore the authoritativeness of policies and to confer on them the status of rules; the former makes their authority an issue for debate, thus offering it the conditional support of reasoned argument and persuasion; the latter affirms their authority by holding them to be sources of obligations and warranted expectations.

The result has been a legalization of controversy. The agency would henceforth be pressed for recognition of the interests and needs of employers and employees as legally defined rights and duties. This movement corresponded to the emergence within labor of a new approach to workmen's compensation, in which benefits were no longer seen as welfare advantages administered by and under the discretionary control of employers but as indemnities owed on grounds of principles that had to be actively asserted and promoted.[5] This legal posture adopted by injured employees in their relations with employers and carriers was carried over to the IAC, before which unyielding defendants had to be brought. Labor was thus largely responsible for the initiation of this process of legalization of the controversy. The first wave of "legalized" cases, the first massive, although yet unorganized, attempt to test and extend the principles of compensation struck the commission in late 1929 and 1930, precisely at the time when the depression and rising unemployment were beginning to be felt. Although there is no way to verify this interpretation, it seems likely that this wave came from a class of unemployed injured workers who had little to lose and all to gain from taking the risk of a more aggressive legal action against their employer.[6] This is also how, judging from a 1932 statement of their point of view, insurance and industry accounted for the phemonenon, which seems to have been quite general throughout the country.[7] The same statement illustrates quite clearly the legal character the compensation controversy was then assuming. The conflict as perceived was not primarily political; it involved a moral issue of "fidelity to law."

> . . . now there is an obvious determination on the part of some to make the compensation laws a medium through which to accomplish by indirection what they have failed to accomplish directly by independent legislation: *viz.*, practically a redistribution of wealth through highly socialistic measures providing for a wide range of social insurance. . . .
>
> Compensation insurance funds must be protected from the powers that prey; compensation insurance must be restricted to its own proper functions; the process of perpetually extending it to provide relief, more and more, for misfortunes other than the consequences of injuries for which industry is truly responsible must be halted, indeed reversed; and relief for such other misfortunes must be provided in other ways—where appropriate, by other insurances.
>
> . . . I think we have all been at fault, that we all started off to treat the workmen's compensation law as too much of a general panacea, to be applied "generously" and its bounties distributed readily, without regard to any legal technicalities. Experience now shows that we have run wild. . . .
>
> *Let's get back to first principles.*[8]

The movement toward legal representation in compensation cases was both a result and a cause of the legalization of controversy. The view of compensation as a matter of right made law and lawyers more relevant in the eyes of the parties, while lawyers in turn worked to strengthen the new conception and articulated it before the IAC. A count made by the IAC in 1932 indicated that 57 percent of the applicants were represented either by union business agents or by lawyers, but mostly by the former, as an inquiry of the state bar in 1934 suggests.[9] In 1948, still on the basis of agency data, 58 percent of the applicants and 78 percent of the defendants had legal representation; for 1950 the figures were 64 percent and 89 percent. Since that time, statistics have been kept only for applicants; the proportion of the latter who were represented by an attorney reached 84 percent in 1960 and 87 percent in 1963.[10]

Another indication of the growing legalization of the compensation controversy is found in the changing patterns of use by the parties of the arbitration services of the IAC. From the very beginning and throughout its later history, the commission has maintained a distinction between two kinds of claims adjustment services it provided—the "formal" and the "informal." The former were and still are initiated by a formal "application" filed by the injured claimant with the IAC; from the beginning they were characterized by a more detailed and careful examination of the legal and factual issues, in accordance with more formalized procedures. The "informal" claims settlement services were those of the commission secretary, and the informal rating procedure, which we have described in the preceding chapter.[11] Their emphasis was on assistance, mediation, and *ad hoc* problem-solving; rules and evidence remained basically unquestioned, and procedures remained largely inarticulated routines. As employers and employees increasingly saw their conflict as a legal controversy, a steadily larger proportion of compensation claims came to be formally litigated; that is, many claims that in the early years would have been directly settled by the employer or carrier or would have been solved with the informal intervention of the commission now resulted in the filing of applications for "formal" adjudication by the agency. Whereas, according to IAC statistics, until 1925 the number of formally contested cases amounted to only 6 to 9 percent of the estimated number of lost-time compensable injuries, this number began rising from about 9 percent in 1925 to more than 12 percent in 1929; 1929 marks a sharp break and is followed by a booming increase up to 22.5 percent in 1932.[12] This proportion has since then more or less steadily risen up to about 30 percent in the middle 1950's and more recently has jumped from 34 percent in 1958 and 1959 to 38 percent in 1960 and 48 percent in 1963.[13]

Agency statistics on permanent disability cases reflect the same movement toward increased reliance on the "formal" services of the commission. The Permanent Disability Rating Department (now Bureau) can become involved in permanent disability cases in three ways: in reviewing "compromise and release" agreements the IAC is requested to approve, in recommending "informal" advisory ratings to the parties who apply for one, or in making "formal" recommended ratings in formally contested cases. Figures on the caseload of the department indicate a sharp decrease in the reliance by the parties on "informal" ratings. Of all the cases rated by the department, excluding the "compromise and release" cases, only 11.5 percent were formal cases in 1924; this proportion rises to almost 20 percent in 1929, reaches 33.5 percent in 1932, jumps to more than 40 percent in the immediate postwar period, 57 percent in 1953, and currently amounts to about 75 percent of the bureau's caseload.[14] The clients of the informal rating services are typically employees who do not have a lawyer, do not belong to a union, and basically do not challenge the truth or lawfulness of the treatment they have received from their employer or carrier; in all these respects they contrast sharply with their fellow workers who file an application and get their cases formally heard and rated after having hired an attorney and secured their own medical evidence.

The growing use of the commission's "formal" settlement procedures is, of course, not quite a reliable indicator of the degree to which the compensation controversy has been legalized. Many claims that are filed as "formal" applications and are "formally" rated are not perceived by the parties as involving any issue of right. The filing of a claim may be just a bargaining maneuver, an attempt to gain a better contractual settlement; or the parties may simply be gambling on the uncertainty of their cases. Thus many "formal" cases end in a compromise before an official decision issues. The growth of formal litigation has been accompanied by a sharp increase in the use of "compromise and release" (C&R) agreements as means of settling controversies.[15] Yet the significance of this evolution is not altogether clear. To some extent, the greater use of contractual settlements is a reflection of the greater legal assertiveness of injured claimants; it affirms the principle that the administration of claims shall not be left to the discretion of the employer or carrier, that the worker has a right to dissent as well as agree with the treatment offered, that compensation benefits constitute a kind of property of the injured man, which he may claim, use, and bargain with according to his own assessment of his interests; furthermore, a compromise involves at least a limited appeal to the authority of the IAC, since its validity depends upon the agency's approval. That this interpretation is at least partially true is suggested by the fact that the movement toward growing use of contractual settlements started exactly at the time when the incidence of formal litigation of claims also increased, that is, around 1930, and followed a closely related pattern of development. Nevertheless, settlements constitute also quite frequently a sign of weakness and dependence on the part of the employee, of inability to assert his rights effectively. This is indicated by the fact that the percentage of C&R's has, in recent years, risen more sharply and reached higher levels in some areas of the state where labor is poorly organized and the specialized union-connected bar has remained relatively undeveloped.[16] The C&R is particularly advantageous to the employer or carrier, because it gives legal and nearly final authority to the private arrangement he has made with the employee; even though the arrangement may be more unilateral than genuinely contractual, it is shielded against future challenges.[17]

Data on the incidence of formal litigation and contractual settlements are therefore admittedly ambiguous. Nevertheless, seen in the context of the growing assertiveness of unions and of the growing use of legal advocates in claims adjustment, they do confirm the existence, ever since about 1930, of a rather sweeping trend toward legalization of the compensation controversy. Indeed, they even tend to underestimate the extent and significance of the change, for they ignore the profound transformations that have, in the course of the same period, affected the character of agency procedures. By the standards of the early IAC the claims and procedures that are today called "informal" would then have been deemed highly formal and "legalistic." In the last thirty years, the "conciliation" services of the secretary have been abandoned, the handling of C&R's has been made subject to formal rules of procedure, informal ratings have been regulated so as to institute minimal safeguards for the rights involved, and a wealth of detailed procedural standards has been developed to govern the process of formal adjudication. The significance of the changes we have observed cannot be properly assessed without an understanding of changes in the legal *quality* of the process of settlement and adjudication.

The growing emphasis on rules and rights as the focus of controversy has, indeed, been accompanied by considerable efforts to establish standards, which would secure within the commission a firmer accountability to those rules and a more deeply bound respect for those rights. It is to those efforts and changes that we now turn our attention.

The Growth of Procedural Standards

A major obstacle to the effectuation of the new "legalized" approach to compensation problems was the extreme indefiniteness of the procedural standards that governed the IAC in its early period. Even though rules were more and more insistently invoked, and this insistence by itself entailed considerable moral pressure, nevertheless it was relatively easy for the commission to evade the arguments it was confronted with and to render them meaningless. There were many barriers against legal challenges. The opportunities for argument and criticism were subject to many restrictions; channels of appeal appeared ineffective; regulations and policy statements, substantive and procedural, were open to discretionary qualifications and sometimes even remained undisclosed. What was needed was a set of standards designed to govern the operations of the agency and to compel it to meet the legal challenges that were put to it. If accountability to rules was to be secured, there had to be *rules of accountability*, rules that would govern the making, identification, and implementation of rules. It is in large part the making of such rules, or metarules, that marked the transformation of the IAC into a court of law.

As initially conceived, commission procedures were intended to provide "an inexpensive, non-technical and expeditious system for the disposal of litigated cases."[18] Inexpensive: fees and court costs, except for witness fees and attorney fees—the latter to be controlled by the IAC—were eliminated. Expeditious: very short delays were specified at all stages of the proceedings, in order that benefits be quickly dispensed to the needy applicants. And above all nontechnical: since the purpose of the proceedings was adjustment rather than formal adjudication, rules had to be minimized in order to preserve the initiative and the discretion of the decider.

The commission was aware of the risks of abuse and arbitrariness that might result from such uncontrolled discretion. A defense of the agency's procedures was offered in a 1915 paper written by one of its referees and legal counsel.[19] It pointed out two forms of restraints that would operate on the agency as guarantees of essential fairness. First appealed to was the political balance that had been built into the structure of the agency; decisions, it argued, were made by a board, rather than a single administrator, so that the errors and biases of any commissioner would always be checked by the other board members. The second restraint lay in the administrative competence of the agency; the IAC would have the constant advice and services of a staff of specialized experts, doctors, raters, welfare workers, engineers, referees, and lawyers. This argument did not solve the problem of what ends this competence would serve, and how compatible those ends would be with fairness to either party. Nor did it anticipate that the commission's expertise might later be questioned and considerably eroded under the assault of the parties and their organized interest groups. Administrative competence, both in the purposes it served and in the limitations it suffered, was, indeed, *the* target of the parties' rebellion.

It is worth observing that what the commission was thus offering as guarantees of its fairness was its own *self-restraint.* Political moderation and administrative expertise were invoked as warrants of trustworthiness and not as values to be effectuated and protected by the agency's constituency through some game of political influence and rational criticism. Furthermore, both ideas carefully avoided setting any predetermined limit on agency discretion. The commission's preferences went clearly to nonlegal restraints. Thus, even in the restraints it invoked as warrants of its fairness, the IAC expressed its fundamental distaste for outside criticism and legal processes.

Problems quickly began pressing the agency to concern itself with rules. At first these problems remained largely internal. The staff needed instructions as to how it was expected to proceed, and the commission was concerned with putting some order and regularity into its operations. In a 1927 report, the manager of the Compensation Department felt obliged "again to emphasize the necessity of procedure in some way resembling legal procedure." Informality had gone too far, even from the sheer standpoint of administrative reliability. Some discipline was needed also to protect the agency's integrity. In the absence of rules, the staff was often too prone to adopt whatever order was pressed upon the agency by the more articulate and better organized parties, that is, insurance carriers. In 1925–1926, the commission issued a series of instructions on the proper distance to be maintained between referees and insurance adjusters. All those rules, however, remained internal; they were not made public; they were not meant to be used by the parties for the preservation of their rights, but simply to provide guidance in the conduct of administrative business.

Beginning in the late 1920's and early 1930's, the IAC was rather abruptly confronted with a wave of challenges to its procedures, coming this time from the parties who sought to secure effective means of gaining recognition for the rights they claimed. Before that time, there had been a number of cases brought to the courts for procedural errors; but they had remained few and isolated. The decisions that had resulted were largely taken as granting redress for particular errors in the particular cases involved, without much consequence for the general procedural system of the commission. The new wave had a different meaning; cases were more numerous, they came back repeatedly to the same issues, they formed patterns, they were accompanied by constant complaints and criticisms addressed to the commission and by appeals for new legislation; the courts were forming lines of decisions; the challenge was to the system itself.

The campaign had a legal slogan—that "the Industrial Accident Commission is a court, and is thus bound by the constitutional standards of due process governing judicial procedure." The principle had actually been announced by several judicial dicta in the early cases in which the constitutionality of workmen's compensation had been tested. In *Pacific Coast Casualty Company* v. *Pillsbury* (1915), the court had stated that any action of the IAC in the exercise of its power "to settle disputes concerning the liability" of employers under the act "would be an exercise of judicial power. For that purpose it [the commission] is, in legal effect, a court."[20] But those cases seemed to have lost their authority after the IAC won the adoption of the 1918 constitutional amendment, which explicitly characterized it as an "administrative body" and freed it from "common law and statutory rules of evidence and procedure."[21] After 1918 and until the early 1930's, very few cases were taken up to the courts on procedural or evidentiary issues. The courts did not have an occasion to reassert the principle of the judicial nature of the IAC until 1935.[22] By that time, the old cases of 1915–1916 had suddenly been discovered to have new significance: to the parties they provided a leverage for bringing IAC procedures under the common rules of fairness; to the courts, they offered an authority to accomplish this result. A series of cases in 1939–1940 confirmed the doctrine that "the industrial accident commission is a 'judicial' body and its decisions and awards are subject to the general legal principles which circumscribe and regulate the judgments of all judicial tribunals and sufficiency of evidence to sustain the commission's findings must be determined in light of the rules applicable to procedure in the courts."[23] In the reform of 1945, the principle was implicitly incorporated in the legislation; Section 111 of the California Labor Code was rewritten to read: "The Industrial Accident Commission . . . shall exercise all judicial powers" vested in it by the law.[24] What this principle accomplished can best be shown by tracing the history of the major procedural controversies that shook the agency.

Before doing so, it will be useful to indicate the broad outlines of the proceedings in formally contested cases. Legal action is initiated by the filing with the commission of a written application, which is then served on the adverse parties together with a notice of hearing; the defendant may file an answer. Hearings are then held and the commission issues its "findings and award," which are served on the parties. Thereafter, and for a period of five years from the date of the injury, the case may be "reopened," either on "petition" of a party or on agency initiative, if there is any change in the claimant's disability. The law provides for a first channel of appeal within the agency itself; the commission may grant a "reconsideration," formerly called "rehearing," on the petition of a party or on its own motion. Finally, and only after a petition for reconsideration has proved ineffective, the parties may petition the appellate courts for a writ of review; the scope of judicial review is, however, strictly limited to issues of law. The law gave the IAC the authority to "adopt reasonable rules of practice and procedure,"[25] and to hire a staff of referees who would assist the commission in hearing cases.[26]

Opportunity to Be Heard. The first procedural issue the commission was confronted with was that of the right to an opportunity to be heard, including the right to notice of hearings, to be served evidence presented outside a hearing, and to submit and rebut material evidence. Although this right was formally granted in the workmen's compensation act,[27] several reasons often pressed the IAC to infringe it. In a memorandum written in 1931, a commissioner expressed the thought that a party has a right to cross-examination, "but that we should try to avoid such a procedure whenever possible and resist it in every possible way until the court tells us not to do it." One reason, the most trivial but also the most urgent, was expediency; given its increasingly overwhelming caseload, the commission found it difficult to reconcile its concern for quick justice with procedural "niceties." Cross-examination was seen as a useless and time-consuming luxury. The following instruction addressed by a commissioner to the referee staff in 1932 makes the point quite clearly:

> In a recent case . . . when the Expert Medical Examiner's report was received and served, the defendant immediately asked for a further hearing in order to call the E.M.E. as a witness and cross-examine him. The referee was told not to grant the further hearing as the Commission has learned from many years of experience that the cross-examination of competent doctors by attorneys *gets nowhere and is a waste of good time.* Section 19-c authorizes the filing of medical reports and subdivision 7 has a proviso that opportunity be given to produce testimony in explanation or rebuttal before decision is rendered. *Due to the abuse of this latter provision by attorneys* practicing before the Commission, *the Commission will disregard this provision in appropriate cases,* and a referee should be prone to deny such requests. [Emphasis supplied.]

This was not just a response to a temporary crisis. The policy had long standing at the IAC. A document of 1915 states:

> While cross-examination is not prohibited, that kind of cross-examination which seeks to "rehash" the whole of the testimony previously given without knowing in advance of any variation to be brought out, is not allowed.[28]

The agency had little regard for the value of partisan submission or contradiction of evidence. The taking of evidence was the commission's responsibility:

> The purpose of the hearing is not to listen to such proof as may be presented by either side, but it is to get at the facts, largely upon the initiative of the commission itself. . . . The proceeding is looked upon as in the nature of an investigation instead of a trial.[29]

The parties were allowed to participate only because they were generally recognized as *useful to the agency* in the performance of its task. But this participation was a privilege, always liable to be withdrawn when it appeared useless or harmful to administrative efficiency:

> No arguments are made at the hearing, although the privilege of stating contentions of law or fact is permitted. Written memoranda of points and authorities, or comments upon the evidence are freely received provided the case will not be unduly delayed in waiting for them.[30]

Together with expediency, a concern for the welfare and interests of injured workers often lay behind the commission's impatience with protracted hearings. This appears in the following instruction of 1929:

> The abuse of requesting further proceedings by carriers, and unnecessary examinations, irritate and worry an injured man and oftentimes causes neurosis. Parties are expected to file their documentary evidence, including medical reports, at the first hearing. . . . They should be prepared to put in their defense at the hearing and have the case submitted then and there or, at most, to be submitted 5 days thereafter. When it is not possible to submit a case then and there, and it is desired to file further medical reports or an employer's report, the substance of the disposition should be: case open 5 days for filing medical reports and to then stand submitted without further proceeding.

The point is not that bias was thereby introduced in the decision process, even though sometimes it was; but rather that the pursuit of agency goals, even when carried out quite impartially, tended to interfere with the duty to respect procedural rights. Indeed, encroachments on the right to notice and hearing often worked as much to the objective disadvantage of the claimant as of the employer or carrier. For instance, the IAC had for a long time taken the view that the reports and opinions from its Medical Department should be kept confidential and not be made part of the official case records or served on the parties. In the late 1920's, the commission came under strong criticism because of this practice. In 1929, the IAC decided to reverse its policy "in order to be as fair as possible to all parties concerned in the proceedings"; at the same time it specified an interesting exception:

> Please note, however, that all reports from the Medical Department which are marked "confidential" are not to be served. In some cases the Medical Department may find it necessary to criticize other doctors or possibly the applicant. In some neuroses or hysterical cases it would be very bad therapeutics to have the applicant informed of the contents of the report of the Medical Department.

This distinction was reformulated in 1930; medical reports of the Medical Department following a personal examination of the claimant would be filed and served, in order to "avoid the charge that we are deciding cases on the opinions of experts which are not made part of the record. . . ." However:

> . . . there are some reports from our Medical Department advisory in nature, which in our opinion should not be filed and served. These are reports of the Medical Department approving reports of medical examiners; reports of the Medical Department stating that the medical director or either of his assistants believes that the case should be decided according to the medical report of Dr. ———; also memoranda in which the Medical Department expresses doubt as to how the case should be decided and possibly suggesting a compromise, which need not be served unless the referee thinks that it will help to bring about a settlement of the case.

The reluctance of the IAC to submit the opinions of its Medical Department to the scrutiny of the parties points to another reason behind its general impatience with this procedural guarantee; this was the need to protect its own authority. It was all right that evidence be subjected to the scrutiny of the parties; but the *judgments* of the staff, which engaged the authority of the commission, had to be guarded from criticism. It is the case, indeed, that the agency's resistance to rules of fairness was particularly strong where the opinions of its own staff of experts were involved. Until 1940, it was the general practice that the reports of the Permanent Disability Rating Department, in which the claimant's disability was evaluated and a rating was recommended to the referee or the commission, were not filed in the case record nor served on the parties. These reports also were "advisory in nature," just as were the confidential reports of the Medical Department. They were more than just a piece of evidence, with the same standing as any other lay or expert testimony. They constituted steps in the process of assessment of the claim. This point is made explicit in the following memorandum addressed in 1932 by the superintendent of the Permanent Disability Rating Department to a member of the commission:

> I see no more reason for the copy of the rating sheet to be filed on the parties than there is for the referee's memorandum to be filed on the parties, or for the results of a discussion of the case with the Commission, or with the Medical Department, being served on the parties. The referee is making the decision and is entitled to secure his information from those sources within the Commission's organization which will enable him to make an intelligent and just decision. These sources are the advice he receives from the Medical Department, either oral or written; or from discussion with the resident Commissioner, which is usually oral.

In a similar document of 1930, the same officer argued:

> Under our present practice, it would be equivalent to giving advance information on a decision to show anyone the rating before the order . . . issues.

Not only did rating reports enjoy a special weight, coming from the IAC's impartial experts, as opposed to the partisan evidence submitted by applicants and defendants; they also involved the exercise of a portion of the power, vested in the commission itself, to evaluate and determine compensation claims. The reports of the raters and IAC doctors, like the reports of referees, were *occasions for the commission to exercise its expertise in industrial accident problems and its discretion in the making and application of compensation policy.* The IAC felt that subjecting all opinions expressed in the course of its handling of cases to constant scrutiny and criticism would have paralyzed its authority and made impossible the use of its expertise.

A series of cases in the 1930's and early 1940's culminating in a few landmark decisions about 1940, took care of most of these problems. The right to notice of hearing, to an opportunity to present and rebut evidence, and, most importantly, the right to service and cross-examination of the reports of the Rating Department, were successively reaffirmed as constitutionally protected guarantees of due process.[31] The cases, especially the *Young* decision on rating reports, were backed by opinions that were sharply critical of IAC procedures and left no doubt as to the courts' determination to put some order in the agency. The IAC complied, but not without prolonged resistance in the detailed implementation of the new rules, especially as they affected the Rating and Medical Departments. Before the *Young* case, the practice generally followed by the commission and the referees in requesting a disability rating was simply to send the whole case file to the Rating Department with an attached note, "Please rate." In the absence of any special instruction, the rater was supposed to make his own assessment of the effects of the injury, on the basis of filed medical reports; only then could he figure out what disability rating the Rating Schedule provided for the identified infirmities. As we have pointed out, his work was a part of the total adjudication of the case. The import of the *Young* case was to *redefine the status of the rating report as that of a mere piece of evidence*, subject to the same rules as other expert evidence, as opposed to a kind of recommended award, to be incorporated in the final award and subject to the rules governing IAC decisions. The implementation of this decision required that "the functions of the rater be distinguished from those of the fact-finder." The parties were prompt to protest that the Rating Department, in making its own assessments of disability factors, was exceeding its proper role as witness and taking over the judicial functions of the commission and referees. Instructions were thus made to the effect that it was the responsibility of the referee to determine what the disability factors were and that the rater had to make his computations solely on the basis of factors so determined. The Rating Department expressed much dissatisfaction with the new system; it found the referees' instructions frequently inadequate for the purposes of rating. In a memorandum of 1940, it insisted on the need for raters to be able to make their own evaluation:

> I would suggest that the referees be required to write out for the information of the Rating Department accurately the disability factors which are to be rated. The Rating Department will then *edit or revise* the description of disability for the purpose of rating and computing the rating thereon. However even though

> the referee accurately describes the disability to be rated, we should also have the medical reports in order to properly evaluate the disability, as frequently the weight to be given to subjective factors depends upon the discussion of such factors by the medical examiners and the referee's summary of his impressions obtained at the hearing. [Emphasis supplied.]

The suggestion was adopted; the file was always sent with the instruction of the referee, and frequently these instructions were simply to rate on the basis of some specified portion of the file selected by the referee. The practice was soon criticized as subverting the purported separation of the functions of rater and referee. The issue became particularly critical when the demand was made that the referee's instructions to the rater be made part of the record and served on the parties; without them, it was argued, cross-examination of the rater was made meaningless. The Rating Bureau in a memorandum of 1946, firmly opposed the request:

> I don't think it wise to file and serve the Referee's description of disability because *the Rating Bureau frequently substantially modifies the description of disability by eliminating superfluous factors* which do not constitute permanent disability, substitutes correct terminology for incorrect terminology, reedits in general the often confusing, disorderly and unscientific phraseology and wording of the description. If the Rating Bureau even so much as changes a comma or transposes an impossible fraction representing loss of function into a proper fraction, this gives the parties the chance to come in and want to find out why we corrected the error. It has been done. . . .
>
> I note another suggestion that the rating formula which is used be put on all copies [of the rating report] and filed and served upon all parties. The formula is put on the Referee's copy and on the Rating Bureau's copy for their own information. Most Referees don't understand the formula. . . . If the Referees don't understand the formula, how can the applicant or his attorney understand it? The only ones who would benefit by serving the formula would be the insurance carriers. It would give them an opening to come in and ask for additional cross-examination. It would not stop cross-examination but would create further litigation. If the applicant or his attorney don't understand the formula, they might also want to cross-examine the Rating Expert to find out what all the symbols mean. This would create rather than prevent further litigation and cross-examination. Rather than file and serve the formula I would prefer to leave it off all copies except the Rating Bureau copy. [Emphasis Supplied.]

The old practice was allowed to continue until, in 1951, at the occasion of a large revision of the Rating Schedule, increased pressures from practising lawyers brought the commission to adopt a new set of rules.[32] Over the strenuous objections of the Rating Bureau, that the rules "would only increase delay and litigation and cross-examination," the commission required that requests for permanent disability ratings should include "specific instructions concerning factors, both objective and subjective, on which the rating is to be based";[33] that the rating report should contain "the factors of permanent disability, unless they are specifically set forth in the instructions, the percentage of the recommended permanent disability rating, the weekly rate of permanent disability payments . . . , and the formula used." [34] Both the request and the report were required to be filed and served on the parties.

The issue was nonetheless not closed yet. For the rules continued to allow that the file or a portion of the file be sent to the rater together with the request for rating. Opportunities were therefore still left for the rater to exercise his own judgment on disability factors, especially the "subjective" factors, such as pain and discomfort, which can seldom be determined and described by reliable tests. "Judgment ratings" became a target of criticism, on the ground that raters were again usurping the functions of the referees. Finally, in 1958, the Rules of Practice were amended to require referees to describe subjective factors in terms specifically determined for that purpose, and which were almost automatically associated with a definite rating percentage.[35] Instructions were also made from time to time, prohibiting rating on any basis other than the referee's formal request: *ex parte* discussions between rater and referee were thus forbidden.[36]

Identification of Responsible Authority. Efforts to subject agency experts to the scrutiny and criticism of the parties were closely connected with another problem, often referred to as the problem of "institutional decisions."[37] In their attempts to secure the right to be heard, the parties were confronted with a *diffusion of responsibilities* for decision-making among a variety of administrative staff members to whom they had no sure and immediate access. Opportunities for proof and argument were most of the time fairly open; yet they often seemed meaningless in view of the fact that there was no guarantee that arguments would actually reach the deciders and have a bearing on what they would decide. A referee heard the case and signed the award; but the decision was seldom only his. As we have shown, it was the outcome of an institutional decision process in which raters and agency doctors frequently performed important responsibilities. What sense was there in presenting a witness at the hearing, if an absent rater was later to recommend, and for all practical purposes make, the evaluation of the disability without having his attention brought on the testimony? One of the purposes of subjecting raters and IAC physicians to the rules of cross-examination had been to remove them from the process of adjudication; their role had been stripped of its "judicial" aspects and redefined as that of mere witnesses.

The problem of institutional decisions was brought into sharp focus in a prolonged controversy over the respective responsibilities of the commission and its referees. Responsibility for the determination of controverted cases had been statutorily vested in the commission itself acting as a board; but the commission had been authorized to refer particular cases to subordinate hearing examiners, called "referees," who would hear the evidence and recommend appropriate findings and awards.[38] Beyond this, the law had left the process of decision-making almost totally up to the commission's discretion:

> Upon the filing of the report of the referee, the Commission may confirm, adopt, modify or set aside the same or any part thereof and may, either with or without further proceedings, and either with or without notice, enter its order, findings, decision or award based in whole or in part upon the report of the referee, or upon the record in the case.[39]

The commission used its power very freely. Initially the board or its individual members heard, or at least read, the record of most of the cases. But as the caseload became heavier, the commission was compelled to delegate more and more of its adjudicative tasks to its referee staff, keeping only some distant control over their work, until practically all cases were heard and decided by the referees. At first, all referee decisions were reviewed by the manager of the Compensation Department before being signed by the members of the commission. Then a distinction was made between "referee decisions," which were signed and issued by the referees themselves and only occasionally reviewed by the manager, and "commission decisions," which were more systematically reviewed and were issued under the commissioners' signatures. This latter category included only the more serious cases, cases on rehearing, and cases reopened under the agency's power of continuing jurisdiction. The system made it possible for the IAC to keep control over policy-making; instructions were thus frequently sent to the referee staff, advising that decisions made in violation of some new or continuing policy would not receive confirmation.

It was the responsibility of the manager of the Compensation Department to enforce those instructions by regularly reviewing the decisions made or recommended by the referees. Generally such review did not involve any thorough reexamination of the case; the reviewers and, when necessary, the commission were able to limit their reading to two convenient documents the referee was required to write. One was the "report of hearing" in which they summarized the evidence received at each hearing held on the case; the second was the final report or "memorandum" in which the referee stated the reasons of fact and law for his recommended findings and awards. Even in "rehearing" cases, no actual rehearing was required unless it was found necessary to take further evidence. Finally, although the "reports of hearing" were a part of the case record and were thus available to the parties,[40] the IAC was quite careful to keep the "memoranda" of decisions confidential;[41] this left the commission free to exercise its control without the interference of outside criticism.

Criticism of this procedure began with the 1933–1934 investigation of the IAC by the state bar.[42] It gained momentum when, in 1936, the U.S. Supreme Court rendered its decision in the *Morgan* case.[43] The court invalidated an order of the Secretary of Agriculture, issued on the basis of staff recommendations but without direct personal acquaintance with the issues involved. In so doing, the court laid a broad principle, that "the one who decides must hear." To vest the authority to decide in a person other than the one who has heard the case is to make a sham of that hearing, which is constitutionally guaranteed as a requirement of "due process."

> The "hearing" is designed to afford the safeguard that the one who decides shall be bound in conscience to consider the evidence, to be guided by that alone, and to reach his conclusions uninfluenced by extraneous considerations.[44]

The principle was forcefully exploited by the parties before the IAC.[45] In a rapid succession of cases, the issue of the respective powers of commission and referees was brought to the California courts. Two decisions in 1940, four in 1941, two in 1942, three in 1944, and two in 1946, and five more spread over the following ten years,[46] affirmed and reaffirmed the rule that the commission is empowered to issue a decision, even though it has no acquaintance with the record of the case, if its decision follows the recommendations of the hearing referee; but that it denies due process of law when it departs from those recommendations without having personally read the record. A similar rule applied to cases that were transferred from one referee to another in the course of the proceedings—the award would be valid only if the deciding referee had read the record of the part of the proceedings that he had not attended. Concerned with maintaining an effective review over the implementation of its policies by the referee, the commission did its best to resist the new rule. In this it was considerably helped by the secrecy that protected referee recommendations. The commission had by a rule of procedure "exempted" its referees from compliance with the statutory provisions that required that referee reports be made in writing and formally filed in the record of the case.[47] Shortly after the court decisions were announced, the policy was reemphasized in an instruction sent to the staff:

> You are familiar with the recent decisions in the case of *Taylor* vs *Thomas* and the *Young* case. Attorneys on one side or the other are looking for possible ways and means to attack decisions with which they are dissatisfied and the Commission is finding itself somewhat embarrassed in cases where there is at least an intimation that somebody has been talking too much or to wrong people.
>
> This memorandum is sent out with the expectation that every member of the staff who has anything to do with the litigation of cases will realize the sanctity of any information that is not open to the public and will be exceedingly cautious not to either make any statements or drop any hints that will be embarrassing to the Commission or the Legal Department should the case go to court. While there are many things that give us trouble, the number one difficulty is an intimation that the decision which issued was not in truth the referee's decision or consistent with his recommendation.

The system of review by the chief of the Compensation Department was maintained.

After the practice had been condemned again by the state bar in 1941,[48] the issue came up before the Assembly committee that investigated the IAC in 1943–1945.[49] Protest against the secrecy of referee memoranda was so violent and so firmly supported by the committee that in 1944 the commission was brought to reverse its old practice; henceforth, referee reports would be made part of the record, in compliance with the California Labor Code.

The report of the Assembly subcommittee concluded with a strong condemnation of the review system used by the IAC. It invoked the similar conclusions reached in 1941 by the U.S. Attorney General's Committee on Administrative Procedure, and quoted from a statement of its chairman to the effect that "the entrance of anonymous reviewers to winnow out the essentials of the case makes for loss of confidence and suspicion as to the real seat of decision."[50] It found that:

> 5. That the commission has concealed from the public and from the appellate courts the true facts as to the irregularities in the procedure of the commission. . . .
>
> 23. The statute should be amended so that original decisions may be made by the referee who hears the evidence and observes the witnesses. That the referees be required to make specific findings on all probative facts on issues involved and separately stated from conclusions of law. . . . That such original decisions made by a referee become final unless appropriate action is taken for a rehearing. . . .

25. Assuming the adoption of the foregoing recommendation under which referees would be given authority to make original decisions, all petitions for rehearing should be referred, first, to the referee who made the decision. He should be given the power to grant, but not to deny, such a petition . . . if the referee remains satisfied with his original decision, the petition for rehearing should be considered and acted upon by the members of the commission. Such action shall be upon the entire record, with opportunity to the parties or their counsel to present oral or written argument. This function must be performed by the members of the commission sitting as a body and not delegated in any degree. . . .[51]

Those recommendations were not adopted[52] until after further protest from the state bar in 1950,[53] and a new legislative inquiry by the Senate Interim Committee on Workmen's Compensation in 1951.[54] Legislation was then introduced and adopted, by which the referees were granted authority to adjudicate cases in the first instance.[55] The powers of the commission remained unchanged except in cases in which the original decision was made by a referee; in such cases, the commission would perform as an appellate body, acting on petitions for "reconsideration," a new name for what was formerly called "rehearing."[56] The supervisory powers of the board were preserved in a provision that authorized it to reconsider a case upon its own motion.[57] The old review system was therefore maintained and the dissatisfaction of the parties kept alive. In 1955, a further amendment was passed that required that decisions on reconsideration be made "by the commission or a panel thereof *and not by a referee*."[58] The amendment was the product of a *Joint Statement of General Principles* proposed by the State Chamber of Commerce and the State Federation of Labor, which read in part:

That the commission or its panels should serve as an appellate body to pass upon petitions for reconsideration. In that connection it is recommended: . . .

B. That the commission or panel should not refer a petition for reconsideration to any referee for further study or for an expression of opinion or recommendation as to action upon it, and the commission or panel should not be allowed to adopt the opinion of the referee in lieu of its own reasons for decision.

The statement recognized the need for the commission to avail itself of the help of some legal assistants in making its decisions, but warned that "such staff should not exercise judicial powers similar to those exercised by referees," but should act in a manner similar to appellate court law clerks. The office of Reviewing Referee was therefore abolished. With its end came the effective end of the commission's power to reconsider cases upon its own motion.[59]

At the end of this prolonged battle, IAC experts had been transformed either from "advisers" into "witnesses," as in the case of raters and agency doctors, or from "advisers" into final "judges" of first instance, as in the case of referees. Not only had the commission lost the freedom to exercise its expertise in making and implementing its policies; it had also lost a part of its authority over policy. The only authority it kept in this regard was the limited power to decide on appeal issues that had grown outside of its control, which were brought before it by partisan advocates and in a process of adversary arguments that threw upon it a heavy burden of justification. What the parties had accomplished was the identification of targets within the agency to which they could aim their arguments with the assurance of getting a response. No longer could they complain, as the chairman of the Attorney General's Committee on Administrative Procedure had, that:

> The agency is one great obscure organization with which the citizen has to deal. It is absolutely amorphous. He pokes it in one place and it comes out another. No one seems to have specific authority. There is someone called the commission, the authority; a metaphysical, omniscient brooding thing which sort of floats around the air and is not a human being. That is what is baffling. . . . There is an idea that Mr. A. heard the case and then it goes into this great building and mills around and comes out with a commissioner's name on it but what happens in between is a mystery. That is what bothers people. . . . I myself have felt baffled in presenting cases because I know that the man who was listening to me was not the man who was going to decide the case and what I wanted to do was to get my hooks into the fellow who was going to decide the case.[60]

Now they had found the fellows who had to be hooked; each step of the decision process had been isolated in the open, and each authority had been identified and brought to answer. To the opportunity to be heard had been added the certainty of being listened to.

Justification and the Right of Appeal. The parties still needed to be answered. The quest for justification is intimately tied to the right of appeal; the greater the burden of justification that is put on the decider, the richer the opportunities for criticizing his decisions and appealing them for deficiencies in their support. Several features of the early IAC procedure tended to limit both the agency's duty to justify its rulings and the parties' right to appeal those rulings. Among those features were the statutory provisions exempting the agency from common law limitations on the admissibility of evidence, and freeing it from review of its factual determinations by the appellate courts.[61] They have been a focus of continuing controversy.[62]

A first amendment was successfully introduced in 1933. It required that "all oral testimony, *objections,* and *rulings* shall be taken down in shorthand by a competent phonographic reporter."[63] The new rule, by prescribing that a complete record be made of all proceedings, entailed a threat to the commission that this record would be used against the agency in petitions for review. A body of case law progressively developed and imposed some definite restrictions on IAC discretion in the assessment of evidence. The principle upon which this law was built was stated in a 1934 case, in which the California Supreme Court invalidated an award on the ground that "it is not sufficient that the referee or commission be satisfied as laymen of the correctness of their view, but the law requires that they shall reach their conclusion on the basis of legally competent evidence."[64] Therefore mere "speculation or surmise" will not do; nor will an expert opinion based upon false factual premises; nor will the courts uphold an award based upon lay testimony when expert evidence denies its truth. Nevertheless, whenever there was any genuine conflict in the evidence, the commission remained free to determine the issue as it felt, unbound by any standard of "preponderance of the evidence" as governs civil courts. The IAC was then accused of abusing this freedom and making decisions that were not supported by more than a "scintilla of evidence." [65] A 1951 statute extended the review powers of the appellate courts to the determination of whether "the order, decision or award was not supported by substantial evidence."[66] But, as it turned out in the wave of cases that followed this amendment, the courts took the new rule as merely a restatement of the policy they had been following before.[67]

The true effectiveness of these changes in the law of evidence and court review does not appear until one considers them in the context of a number of other legal changes affecting procedures within the agency. Of special significance is the growth of a more meaningful right of intra-agency appeal. To develop this right was an important aim and result of the long fight against "institutional decisions," which we have described in the preceding section. The "monitor" system, as it existed in the early agency, tended not only to diffuse responsible authority and hide the decision process from scrutiny; it also made the process of appeal highly uncertain and often indeed indistinguishable from the process of decision on original cases. Appeals were administratively confused with the system of review to which original cases were subjected. Cases on "rehearing" were one kind of "commission decisions" among others; and the rehearing of a "commission decision" was just another "commission decision." The same people "reheard" the cases as had "heard" them before, and the reexamination afforded was not likely to be more extensive. The confusion was particularly apparent in the blurring of the lines between two statutorily quite distinct procedures: the "rehearing" of a case under appeal, and the "reopening" of a case for good cause under the continuing jurisdiction of the commission. Dissatisfied with the rehearing obtained, the parties would seek to "reopen" the case, since delays for petitioning to reopen were usually much longer than for asking a rehearing. Although it was ambivalent about the practice, the commission usually went along, with the results described in the following memorandum of 1931:

> The Commission realizes the difficulty if people are to be allowed to file petitions to reopen . . . for good cause *ad libitum.* The petition now being considered in the . . . case is the third petition, and the basis of the petition is that the Commission made a mistake in the first instance. If this is to be considered sufficient cause to reopen cases, there would be no end of litigation and the Commission would simply have an unsettled condition in all the cases during our 245 weeks of jurisdiction. . . . It is difficult to state concisely just what petitions should be treated with caution . . . and what petitions should be filed and set or handled as desk work as a matter of course. . . . We have always been granting [certain] petitions freely, and Mr. A. [a commissioner] approves the continuation of such a procedure as it would be most unjust to an employee to deny him further relief. . . . The above will be true regardless of what name is given to the document, [petition for rehearing or petition to reopen].

The indefiniteness and uncertainty of appeal procedures worked both to undermine the quality of the reconsideration afforded—not all petitions would be "treated with caution" and some indeed would "be filed and set or handled as desk work as a matter of course"—and to erode the authority and finality of original orders, since there would be "no end to litigation and the Commission would have an unsettled condition in all the cases."

The growing separation of the functions of referees and commission, the increasing pressures to have the commission perform a genuine role on reconsideration, and increasing restrictions on what is good cause for reopening cases[68] contributed to make the process of appeal more determinate, more restricted perhaps, but more effective and meaningful. This evolution was accompanied by the growth of rules governing the character and content of agency decisions at all levels.

The only requirement of the early law in this respect was that the commission "make and file (1) its findings upon all facts involved in the controversy and (2) its award which shall state its determination as to the rights of the parties."[69] Since the IAC had by rules forbidden the filing of the reports of referees,[70] no detailed statement of the reasons behind agency decisions ever came to the parties. Legally, it was sufficient that the "findings of fact" to be made with the awards be confined to "ultimate facts," as opposed to "probative facts"; the commission was not required to discuss the evidence upon which it relied, but only to state the presence of the legally defined conditions upon which its decision as to rights and liabilities rested—for example, "X is an employee of Y," "the injury arose out of and in the course of employment," "the disability is permanent and stationary."[71] Such findings already involved legal conclusions that the agency had no duty to justify. Efforts were, however, attempted in the late 1940's and 1950's to make the requirement of findings more stringent and more specific. In a case of 1947, the State Supreme Court, while refusing to invalidate the award of the IAC, nevertheless warned of its preference for more specific findings, for the reason that they would

> . . . in many cases not only be fairer to the parties who may wish to seek a review of the final determination reached, but will also be helpful to the reviewing court in its efforts to determine whether the determination may be sustained.[72]

Several awards were subsequently annulled for lack of finding on a material issue, and a standard was formulated that findings of ultimate facts were sufficient only when they could be made certain by reference to the case record.[73]

Efforts to secure more thorough justification of agency decisions focused on developing new administrative and statutory rules. The 1944 instruction that restored the publicity of referee reports left their content quite indeterminate:

> 12. Findings of fact may be in *summary form*.
> 13. Conclusions of law shall be *succinctly* stated.
> 14. *In his discretion,* the referee may discuss the weight of the evidence and give his reasons for specific conclusions. [Emphasis added.]

But when the 1951 legislation granted the referees authority to issue original decisions, the IAC was brought to adopt a new rule, that "the report on decision . . . shall set forth clearly and concisely the reasons for the decision made, including a discussion by the referee of the evidence, together with essential findings of fact and conclusions of law." [74] A 1953 amendment gave statutory authority to the rule.[75]

A similar evolution took place in the rules governing commission decisions on reconsideration. In 1951, new agency rules organized a procedure by which petitions for reconsideration were first referred to the trial referee for recommendations on their merits, and then to a new referee, if additional evidence was needed, for a recommended decision; they specified that both reports would include supporting reasons and would be served on the parties.[76] But no special requirement applied to the commission itself, which held the ultimate power to decide. What the commission had not conceded was secured from the legislature. A 1953 statute required that commission decisions "state the reasons for the decision or . . . specifically adopt reasons already stated by a Commissioner or referee."[77] But suspicions were not quieted yet and, on the joint request of labor and industry, the 1955 legislature strengthened the standard by requiring that decisions on reconsideration be made by the commission "and not by a referee," and that they "state the evidence relied upon and specify in detail the reasons for the decision."[78]

Administrative Purpose and Judicial Accountability. The commission resisted demands for accountability because it was reluctant to offer justifications that would tie its hands or expose its decisions to challenge. The IAC wanted to be free to tailor its decisions to its practical purposes. That is why, before 1944, the agency insisted on the secrecy of referees and other staff reports. The point was stated in a book of rules made for the use of the referees: to make their reports public "would make it impossible for the referees *to express themselves freely and without restraint.*"[79] The commission wanted to be free to reduce a permanent disability award when it found this would "encourage" the worker to return to work; it was concerned when word of this practice apparently began spreading in late 1931. It did not want to be too detailed in explaining certain awards to the parties because, as stated in a memorandum of 1919, "it does not seem that it would be advisable to create dissatisfaction with the award." It did not want to commit itself to any specific doctrine of what is a "good cause" for reopening a settled case; in a report of 1929 we read:

> The basis for reopening . . . should be any cause that to the Commission is sufficient reason for reopening the case. This gives the insurance carrier the opportunity to try out the effects of a settlement agreement *without in any way preventing the Commission from giving any relief that they might otherwise give.* [Emphasis supplied]

Nor did it want to specify what "good cause" is for reapportionment of death benefits among the dependents of the victim. An instruction of 1938 advises that "in such cases, the referees should make a finding that good cause appears for reapportionment. It is not necessary to state what the good cause is; in fact, it is undesirable to do so." The commission did not see itself as applying rules regardless of "where the chips may fall"; rather it felt it had to be free to manipulate its "rules" with a view to the specific results it wanted to accomplish.

Although commission practices were on the whole as likely to offend and hurt applicants as defendants, criticisms of the intrusion of administrative purposes in the adjudicative process found their main leverage in the idea of political bias. Legal standards of judicial impartiality and separation of powers were exploited, mainly by insurance and industry, to press the view that the commitments of the IAC to the welfare of injured employees made it unfit to perform a task of adjudication fairly. This point was the central focus of the 1944–1945 Assembly investigation, the outcome of which was to strip the commission of a "diversity of duties involving the welfare of labor,"[80] and to separate it from most administrative functions it had formerly carried.[81] Further efforts in the same direction were made in the course of a recent investigation of the agency by a "blue ribbon" committee,[82] whose conclusions were substantially adopted by the 1965 legislature. The independence of the commission would be strengthened by increasing the tenure of its members and selecting them from among experienced attorneys "with due consideration of their judicial temperament and ability"; in addition, all remaining responsibilities in the areas of medical care, rating, information services, and rehabilitation would be transferred to a separate agency, thus confining the authority of the commission, now rebaptized as "Workmen's Compensation Appeals Board," to purely judicial matters.[83]

The problem of administrative bias has been and remains peculiarly salient in controversies over standards of evidence. The indefiniteness of evidentiary rules creates continuing suspicion, especially among defendants, that rights are being subverted by partiality in the assessment of facts.[84] And it is the case indeed that the major basis for exempting the IAC from common rules of evidence and limiting judicial review of factual determinations has been a deliberate policy of making the burden of proof less onerous on injured claimants, in view of their limited resources. As a member of the commission argued in objecting to proposed changes of the law in 1951, "It seems quite obvious even to the uninitiated that a change in the law, were it to be made, would permit the side having the most money to obtain the greater number of reports and witnesses and hence on a numerical preponderance basis win the case." The consequence of the policy, however, has been an increasingly strong feeling by defendants that the judicial process was being corrupted. To defense lawyers, and even to those among them who are not politically committed to the interests they represent, advocacy before the commission often tends to appear meaningless: "Whatever I say, they'll go for the worker." The IAC has come to be known in the defense bar as "the gift shop." It is argued that the requirement of "liberal interpretation" has been used to establish a new principle, that "doubt benefits the applicant," with the result that all rules pertaining to the burden of proof are practically nullified.[85] The following quotation is from a letter written by a prominent insurance counsel to the Senate committee that investigated the IAC in 1951:

> Some referees seem to regard [their discretion in taking and assessing evidence] as license not only to permit, but to invite almost any type of leading question, hearsay or self-serving evidence. . . . Despite the fact that a majority of the referees do not abuse the statutory discretion, there are a few who do so by their own type of examination, by the type of questioning they permit by counsel, or by both forms of action. Seldom does this produce a truthful record or an equitable result.
>
> . . . [Some referees] seem to regard themselves as counsel, or associate counsel, for the claimant and throw themselves whole-heartedly into the process of trying to 'smoke out' facts, however tenuous, which may make the case compensable, but never anything which might have the contrary effect. Such referees, of course, seldom find a case non-compensable, having placed themselves so thoroughly in the role of advocate that they never recover their judicial balance sufficiently to view the evidence impartially.

Efforts were thus made to deprive the commission of whatever control and initiative it still had in the gathering of evidence. This was a last remnant of the old conception of hearings as "inquiries," in which the referees assumed the full burden of what was viewed as a "neutral" investigation of "neutral" facts. With the growing initiative exercised by the parties and their counsel, this system had been progressively undermined. The theory had nevertheless partly survived because it permitted the referee to protect the still-numerous unrepresented applicants against expert defense lawyers. The referee would "investigate" the worker's side of the case, but, as indicated in this instruction of 1932,

> In the average case where the defendant is represented by an attorney or an adjuster the referee is not expected to watch his case for him as he is well able to take care of his company's interests.

But this posture was hard to sustain in hearings that increasingly took on an adversary character; the production of evidence appeared as a partisan act, and "facts" were always suspect as self-serving. The problems raised by referee initiative are well illustrated in a 1958 account of the difficulties of a branch office of the IAC, established only a few years earlier in an area in which no specialized applicants' bar had yet developed:

> The result now is that at the conclusion of most hearings the only medical reports are those which have been filed by the defendants and very often they

> are reports from doctors whose opinions ordinarily are not afforded too much weight. . . . As long as this situation persists, it is necessary that [the referee] exercise a somewhat wider discretion in describing and evaluating subjective complaints in order to do what he considers to be just in a particular case. In reviewing his cases, I think probably we [the commission] should have this in mind. . . .
>
> [The referee in charge of the office] notes that the local [applicants'] attorneys, having through the years become accustomed to referees . . . who did most of the questioning, expect him to do the same. It may take some time before he can get them to realize that the burden is on them to prove their client's case and that they should not expect the Commission to indulge in too much paternalism, where there is an attorney present to protect the employee's rights.
>
> [The referee in charge] is rather disturbed because of the fact that he received fifteen petitions for Reconsideration last month. . . . Two Los Angeles [defendants'] firms of attorneys, which have been rather critical of [the referee,] have filed a disproportionate number of these petitions. . . .

The practice was casting doubt on the judicial integrity of the commission. With the increasing availability of counsel to injured claimants, the agency has in recent years found it more and more easy to relieve itself of its responsibility for the rights of claimants. It has become a settled rule that, rather than advising and helping an unrepresented claimant, referees should request him to hire an attorney;[86] also that a referee should not raise issues on his own initiative; that "leading" questions from either counsel or referee should not be admitted, and that a referee will in principle restrain from taking over from counsel the examination of witnesses.[87] The IAC has finally given its allegiance to the very conception of the judicial office that it had been created to challenge and had consistently fought for the best part of its history: the passive legal umpire of the common law courts.

Rule-Making. The early IAC posture toward rules and accountability is again illustrated by the way it treated its own *Rules of Practice and Procedure.* The commission had been empowered to enact "reasonable" rules that would specify and implement the broad procedural policies the compensation law had instituted. It was quite characteristic of the early commission that it hardly exercised that authority. Until as late as 1947, the published official *Rules of Practice and Procedure* remained little more than an information brochure, in which the statutory provisions on procedure were put together in a restated and more or less expanded form, together with a collection of blank forms. They were meant to inform the *parties* of the general standards they would be expected to observe. They said little or nothing as to the rules and process the *agency* itself would follow in handling cases; such regulations existed, of course, but they were primarily contained in collections of instructions for internal office use and were available to the staff only. In this way, the IAC was able to avoid committing itself to the policies it followed; even the published rules were declared "subject to amendment at any time without notice"; [88] and the agency felt free to "amend" them in its internal office regulations.[89] In holding so fast to its freedom, the commission paid a heavy price, since it almost denied itself the use of regulatory powers that might have been quite useful. Indeed, the first genuine regulatory act of the agency through the *Rules of Practice* did not come until 1942, when the commission decided to require that all parties, upon filing of any application with the IAC, send all medical evidence in their possession to the commission and serve copies to all adverse parties.[90] For the first time a determinate duty, which went significantly beyond simply restating statutory standards, was thereby imposed with the backing of powerful sanctions. The same low regard for rules is apparent in the little attention the IAC paid to its Permanent Disability Rating Schedule; in spite of sweeping changes in the technology and occupational structure between 1918 and 1945, the schedule was not revised a single time in that period, even though it had crucial effects on the level of benefits.

To the IAC, the failure to exploit the potentials of regulation did not seem too high a price. The agency had put all its hopes and invested all its energies in informal, consensual means of administration. Formal proceedings, with which the *Rules of Practice* were primarily concerned, were but an unfortunate necessity, from which nothing of value could be expected.

It may seem paradoxical that the potentials of regulation were not seriously realized by the IAC until the time when it was being deprived of its administrative powers and emptied of its sense of purpose. But quite apart from the fact that, with the agency reduced to the role of a passive tribunal of limited authority, the use of regulatory powers became possibly less threatening to the interested parties, this was also the time when rules first became a prominent issue and the object of a systematic scrutiny. Until then there had been policies, but few rules. The system gave broad discretion to the IAC in the implementation of its policies, but it also afforded the parties, especially insurers and employers, broad leeway in working out accommodations with those policies. Policy-making remained as unexamined and unarticulated as it was formally uncontrolled.

Concern for the rule-making process developed in the course of the fight for procedural rights. It became apparent that the official *Rules of Practice* were inadequate in accounting for processes of decision within the agency and that a wealth of procedurally relevant administrative instructions had to be made known and exposed to scrutiny. The state bar inquiry of 1941 concluded with the request that "by appropriate legislation the Industrial Accident Commission be bound by its own rules."[91] The issue of publicity came up again before the legislative committee that investigated the IAC in 1944–1945; the committee found that:

> This commission has labored under a system of secret rules, policies, regulations and instructions affecting its ultimate decisional power . . . . In some cases they represent the will of an administrative officer and are not of considered commission action. Some of these directives were contrary to law. Some showed a clash between "executive" policy and "judicial" considerations. The practice of permitting such directives may constitute an abridgment of the constitutional guarantees. . . . There are . . . Rules of commission practice which set aside the positive requirements of law. Other Rules were published but are disregarded.[92]

The pressures aroused by the investigation brought the commission finally to comply with a 1941 statute that had required and organized the publication of all state administrative regulations.[93] The *Rules of Practice* were revised and published in 1947 as part of the Administrative Code.[94] At the same time, the agency wrote and adopted a *Manual of Procedure* for the use of its staff; although the document was not published, the commission was careful to make it easily accessible to interested parties.

Publicity meant that the rules would be more easily criticized. In 1949, the commission's authority to enact a Medical Fee Schedule was placed in doubt after having always been taken for granted. The IAC cautiously retreated, until its power was formally restored in 1953.[95] In 1950, the adoption of a new Permanent Disability Rating Schedule confronted the commission for the first time with the issue of retroactivity. In the past, as the chief of the Rating Bureau acknowledged,

> . . . on various occasions between 1914 and 1939 the commission made amendments in the Permanent Disability Rating Schedule, but without qualification regarding any effective date of such amendment, and . . . once made the schedule in its amended form thereafter was applied to all cases presented for rating irrespective of the date of injury.[96]

Were changes in the schedule purely evidentiary and procedural, and thus to be applied immediately to all pending cases, as labor argued? Or did they amount to substantial modifications of the benefit schedule, and should they then govern only injuries occurring after the effective date of the change, as industry claimed?[97] The commission resolved the issue in favor of industry. Labor brought it up again before the legislature in 1951, but a new statute confirmed the commission's policy.[98]

With the growing salience of formal rule-making, labor and industry became concerned with institutionalizing modes of participation in administrative rule-making. In 1947, the IAC had succeeded in being exempted from the new California Administrative Procedure Act, which had established minimum standards of notice, hearing, and judicial review for rule-making in state administrative agencies; the rationale invoked for this exemption was that the commission was a "court," subject to special standards not to be confused with those governing administrative bodies, and that the Workmen's Compensation Law already covered the matters of rule-making power and judicial review.[99] This argument no longer satisfied the parties, and when in 1953 the legislature restored the authority of the IAC to regulate minimum medical fees, it also required that "public hearings" be held before the adoption of any fee schedule.[100] In 1955, labor and industry jointly requested that no change in the *Rules of Practice* be made without prior notice and hearing of interested persons and groups. Furthermore, they insisted:

> In addition to the rules of Practice and Procedure there should be an operating manual governing internal operations.
>
> A. Copies of the manual should be available to practitioners . . . and current changes should be available promptly. Notice of the existence and availability of the manual should be given to all interested parties.
>
> B. Any matters contained in the manual which affect parties in the presentation of cases before the commission, and which are not contained in the Labor Code, should appear in the formal Rules of Practice and Procedure.

The 1955 legislature passed a statute that adopted almost literally the recommended requirement of notice and hearing.[101] Further legislation in 1957 imposed the additional requirements that "all meetings of the commission, except for the purpose of judicial deliberations of cases, shall be open and public," and that all records of the agency be open to public inspection.[102] A revised set of rules was adopted by the IAC in 1958.

The Formalization of Informal Processes

The movement toward greater accountability has affected "informal" as well as "formal" proceedings before the IAC. The often quoted *Joint Statement of Principles* presented by labor and industry in 1955 had its word on this point too: it requested "that the commission review its procedure in nonlitigated matters in the light of principles recommended for handling of litigated cases."

We have already traced part of the process of decline of informal procedures: the suppression of the informal adjustment services of the secretary, the transfer of the handling of compromise and release agreements to the referees, the decline of informal ratings and the extension to this procedure of minimal standards for the protection of the worker. Much of this process, as we have argued, can be accounted for as an erosion of administrative competence following the increased involvement of partisan groups. But the demand for accountability has added its own weight to the trend. This is particularly apparent in the changes that have affected the handling of compromise and release agreements (C&R's).

While permitting the parties to enter compromises, the workmen's compensation law required that those agreements be approved by the IAC.[103] The rationale for this provision was that compromise should be tolerated only where the commission was satisfied that there was some genuine uncertainty as to the rights of the parties; otherwise contractual arrangements should not be allowed to subvert public policy. For a while, the commission held firmly to this notion, as the following statement of policy of 1914 indicates:

> The Industrial Accident Commission will not approve any settlement agreement entered into between an injured person and his employer or insurance carrier, without having first made a careful investigation into all the facts of such case and determining the issue in accordance with the facts and law as would be done if a formal hearing were held, except that when it is impossible to determine from the evidence obtainable that the injury or death arose out of the employment . . . , a reasonable compromise may be affirmed.[104]

Agreements were thus approved only if they fully conformed to the law or if, in cases of doubt, they were "reasonable," that is, clearly in the interest of the injured man, whose protection was the primary responsibility of the agency. In general, settlements were frowned upon and discouraged, since they tended to withdraw issues from the authority of the commission. In practice, the cases were reviewed by both the Rating and Medical Departments before the secretary, and later a referee, would recommend a decision to the commission.[105]

In the 1930's, the commission began relaxing the restrictions it had placed on compromises. The old principle remained, as indicated in this 1939 statement of policy concerning settlements in cases of hernia:

> In general the Commission recognizes its administrative responsibility to prevent the abuse of hernia settlements finally terminating in a substantial racket. Speaking generally, one of the prime purposes of the Compensation Act is to restore the injured person to industry physically fit to compete in the open labor market. A settlement . . . where the employee does not in fact secure medical treatment gives him a few dollars which are soon spent and leaves him a public liability

and a hazard. . . . The Commission therefore starts out with the general rule that hernia claims should not be settled; that it is contrary to public policy.

But the same statement provided a long list of exceptions and, indeed, two months later, after "careful study to the problem giving rise to general dissatisfaction and complaint," particularly from labor, the commission decided to rescind the policy. Both industry and labor had become increasingly irritated by administrative intrusions that they found either abusively biased or unduly paternalistic. The applicants especially insisted that compensation benefits were their property and resented IAC surveillance as interfering with the management of their private affairs.

The principle of agency control did not have to be challenged; labor found in it a necessary guarantee against abusive adjustment practices by employers and insurers. But it had to be made a safeguard, and nothing more; from an occasion for positive control over parties' affairs it had to be transformed into a minimal restriction on otherwise free private contracts. This would be accomplished by removing control over C&R's from the commission and placing it in the hands of those members of the staff who, by their work, were least committed to active administration and most attuned to the standards of restraint and impartiality of the legal process, that is, the referees. In 1946, the office of the secretary was abolished; all C&R's would henceforth be handled by the referees,[106] but the latter were still subject to the control of the commission through the system of internal administrative review. While giving referees the authority to issue original decisions in contested cases, the 1951 legislation had left in the commission itself the power to approve compromises. The parties did not obtain satisfaction in this respect until 1955, when the legislature yielded to the joint insistence of labor and industry, and gave referees full authority to approve C&R's.[107] A final obstacle was the IAC requirement that all settlements be referred to the Medical and Rating Bureaus before being ruled upon by the referee; the parties insisted that both offices be removed from the process of review, at least in cases where the compromised issues were "purely legal." The commission did not yield until 1959, when new instructions dropped the requirement and allowed the referee to decide in his discretion whether he needed advice from the staff. The parties could henceforth rest assured that the intrusion of administrative concerns in the process of decision would be minimized.

There remained the problem of imposing restraints on the referees themselves; insurers were particularly insistent on this point, as in this letter written to the commission by an insurance executive in 1954:

Some referees . . . almost always request additional payment in settlements submitted to them for approval. Too often, no real basis for the requested increase is apparent, and we would appreciate having reasonably complete explanations for them, in justification of the added payments requested of us.

This insistence on impartiality has not been reflected in any formal agency rule but it has nevertheless deeply penetrated the perspectives of the commission and its staff. The standard by which referees as well as raters and IAC doctors operate in their review of C&R's is that any compromise will be approved if it comes reasonably close to or above a "middle point" between the original demands of claimant and defendant. The routine procedure in permanent disability cases is to evaluate the two ratings that would be obtained on the basis of the worker's and the carrier's medical reports; if the rating to which the proposed compromise corresponds comes near the middle between the two extremes, the settlement is approved. Almost never is an inquiry made to check on the relative plausibility of each side's allegations; only in the minority of cases in which the worker has not been represented by counsel will some caution be exercised in reviewing the record. Although there are variations in practice, most referees positively avoid influencing the process of settlement, on the ground that it is improper for "judicial" officers to risk prejudging issues they may later be called to adjudicate. The agency has become equally careful not to upset the compromises that are submitted; it is very seldom that approval is denied or made conditional. Indeed, in recent years the IAC has positively encouraged settlement as a way of relieving the growing burdens of decision. We shall return to this point in the following chapter.

From Administration to Adjudication

This chapter has traced the emergence of demands for justification in the exercise of administrative authority and the formation of rules of accountability in response to those demands. But accountability, the main focus of our discussion so far, cannot by itself accomplish the transformation of an administrative authority into a court of law. Accountability is constitutional government, that is, government restrained and guided by rules; but the rules may leave a wide range of freedom for political choice and administrative expediency. What distinguishes adjudication as a mode of governance is a special principle of accountability: where there is no rule to decide a particular claim, the decider must make one. It is this commitment to governance *by* rules—and not only restrained by or even guided by rules—that characterizes adjudication as a special way of exercising authority.

The foundation of this commitment is a primary concern for the interests of the person affected by governmental authority. If the person is at stake, then special care should be taken in the exercise of discretion and power; the means to that end is justification that is acknowledged as authoritative. It is this special burden of justification that compels the adjudicator to search grounds for his decisions in standards that can be accepted as generally binding. Rules, in turn, are particularly competent to protect the person against abuses of discretion: for, being binding on the decider, they lend their authority to the demands of the subject, thereby transforming his interests into vested rights.

It is precisely this concern for the claims of affected persons that was at issue behind the striving for accountability in IAC proceedings. We have underscored the role of partisan legal criticism in subjecting administrative authority to standards of accountability. The thrust behind this movement was very much the same effort to make the agency responsive to private demands that we have seen operating in the retreat of the IAC from its administrative responsibilities. Legal argument was only a special strategy to accomplish that aim; interests would best be secured by treating official policies as entitling parties to recognition of their claims. As a strategy, legal advocacy had a special appeal; to employers, it appeared as a defense against the threat to their interests associated with the turning political tide of the 1930's; to employees, it was a means of freeing themselves from this dependence upon managerial discretion, in which the welfare approach of the commission together with the system of self-administration tended all too often to keep them. Given this purpose of affirming private claims, accountability would have to be more than a restraint on agency discretion—a check on bias and arbitrariness, a safeguard against invasion of other established rights—and more even than a positive assurance of rationality in the administrative process; it would have to become the guarantee of a fully principled decision process. All demands would be claims of right; all decisions would have to be justifiable by authoritative rules and principles. The IAC would have to become a court.

This interpretation helps explain the connection between administrative withdrawal and the transformation of the IAC into a court. The key to both developments is the growth of adversariness. In Chapter VI, we were interested in adversariness as a political process; we saw how partisan groups strove to capture the power of initiative in the making and implementation of public policy, and what consequences their efforts had upon the character of administrative goals and authority. The changes that were thus wrought in the mission and doctrines of the IAC made an important, albeit partial, contribution to the emergence of adjudication. They committed the commission to a conception of its role as primarily one of responding to the demands of its constituency; the interests of affected employers and employees were thus placed in the foreground of agency concerns. To recognize, protect, or conciliate those interests would be the primary, if not the sole, responsibility of the IAC. Accountability to rules was a way of institutionalizing that responsibility. It had the effect of vesting interests as rule-protected rights. In order for this additional development to occur, *adversariness had to evolve from political confrontation into legal controversy.* Claims of right and legal criticism would then be the strategy by which the parties pursued their interests. But the basic impetus still lay in partianship. The confinement of the IAC to the role of third party had supplied a major institutional condition of its development into a court.

Notes to Chapter VII

1. See Chap. VI, pp. 144–145.
2. See *below,* Chap. VIII, pp. 234–240.
3. See Chap. IV and V.
4. Although precise figures on the character of representation are not available for this period, documents from within the agency are quite revealing. Up until 1926, at least, the agency referred to carriers' and employers' representatives as "insurance adjusters," and not until 1929 did the commission begin to be alarmed about the growing involvement of legal counsel in compensation cases.
5. See Chap. IV, pp. 78–96.
6. The later experience of the Industrial Accident Commission shows that rise in unemployment is typically followed by an increase in the number of claims filed, and therefore tends to confirm this interpretation.
7. F. Robertson Jones, "Ominous Abuses Threatening the Insurability of Workmen's Compensation," address delivered at the Annual Convention of the International Association of Insurance Counsel, September 8, 1932, p. 5.
8. *Ibid.*, pp. 6–7, 23–24, 17.
9. "Report of the Committee on Practice and Procedure before the Industrial Accident Commission," *Journal of the State Bar of California,* Vol. IX, No. 9 (September, 1934), pp. 72–82.
10. Evidence from a survey of death and permanent disability cases of the late 1950's indicates that legal representation is quite frequent even in uncontested claims; for that time the data show that the claimant had legal counsel in 65 to 80 percent of the uncontested cases surveyed, and in 90 to 100 percent of the contested cases, depending upon the monetary value of the claim. See Earl F. Cheit, *Injury and Recovery in the Course of Employment* (New York: John Wiley & Sons, 1961, p. 266.
11. See Chap. VI, pp. 130–131, 134–135, 141.
12. These figures come from unpublished statistics gathered by the Industrial Accident Commission in 1935 and covering the preceding 20 years of its history. The estimated number of compensable injuries was apparently established by a review of the injury reports that employers, insurers, and treating physicians were required to make to the commission. The duty to report is still effective, but the reports must now be made to the Division of Labor Statistics and Research, and no longer to the IAC. The duty covers all injuries "arising out of and in the course of employment" and that result in absence

from work for one day or more, or require medical treatment beyond ordinary first aid. See California Labor Code, Sec. 6407. A number of these injuries are not "compensable" in the sense that they do not entitle the victim to any payment of disability indemnity; such is the case when an injury results in temporary disability only, and for less than the seven days "waiting period," that is, the first seven days of disability for which the employee does not receive compensation. The employer is obliged to furnish only medical treatment. See California Labor Code, Sec. 4650.

13. The basis of those figures is the estimate suggested in *Report of the Workmen's Compensation Study Commission* (Sacramento: State of California, April, 1965), p. 162. This estimate differs slightly from the one precedingly used, in that it includes in the "compensable" category all injuries that have necessitated hospitalization. It reflects the effects of a 1959 amendment to the law that required payment of temporary disability benefits from the first day of disability in case of hospitalization. See California Labor Code, Sec. 4650.

No records of the estimated number of compensable injuries are available for the years 1934 to 1967. The Industrial Accident Commission continued to record and publish, as it did before 1934, only the yearly number of reported injuries.

The comparison of those figures actually understates the extent of the increase in formal litigation. With the development of the law, especially in the last 30 years, the category "compensable injuries" has considerably enlarged and now covers a wide variety of injuries that it would not have covered in the early years of workmen's compensation. In addition, one can confidently assume that a larger proportion of industrial injuries actually occurring are reported to the administration, since compliance by employers and carriers with the duty to report injuries has improved with the growing care exercised by unions and employees in the defense of their rights.

14. We have drawn our figures for the period up to 1949 from unpublished IAC statistics; the figures for the later years are those of the *Report of the Workmen's Compensation Study Commission*, p. 76. By itself, the declining use of informal ratings might mean that the commission came to review, formally or informally, a lesser proportion of permanent disability cases; actually, however, the number of cases rated has amounted at first to a fairly constant 8 or 9 percent of the estimated number of compensable lost-time injuries, and in recent years this percentage has even increased up to 15 percent in 1962. Rather than losing cases, the Rating Bureau has thus been gaining cases—but of a different, more "legalized," character.

15. Whereas the number of C&R's, as they are called, remained below 1 percent of the estimated number of lost-time compensable injuries almost throughout the 1920's, it suddenly rose to more than 2 percent in 1930 and thereafter steadily increased to more than 10 percent in the middle 1950's, 19 percent in 1960, and 24 percent in 1962. This trend has been particularly striking in the last 10 to 15 years. In 1950, C&R's represented 24.5 percent of the total number of IAC decisions; in 1963, the figure had reached 45 percent.

16. As, for instance, in the San Diego and Bakersfield areas, in which C&R's in 1963 amounted to 57 percent and 72 percent, respectively, of the number of decisions issued by the local IAC offices.

17. Although a C&R case is, like other cases, subject to being reopened during the continuing jurisdiction of the Industrial Accident Commission, such reopening requires an "exceptionally strong showing" of good cause, such as fraud, duress, or incompetency at the time of execution; the reason is that C&R's are held to have the binding authority of a contract. See Warren L. Hanna, *The Law of Employee Injuries and Workmen's Compensation*, Vol. I, *Practice and Procedure* (Albany, Calif.: Hanna Legal Publications, 1953), pp. 157–159. A variety of other interests have contributed to the recent rise in the number

of compromises. The IAC finds them helpful in reducing the burden of a growing case load; doctors and claimants' attorneys may also seek a settlement in an otherwise uncontested case in order to secure payment of their fees through a lien.

18. Warren H. Pillsbury, "An Experiment in Simplified Procedure: Proceedings before the Industrial Accident Commission," *California Law Review,* Vol. III, No. 3 (March, 1915), pp. 181–194, at p. 181.

19. *Ibid.*

20. 2 IAC 529, 171 Cal. 52, 151 Pac. 658 (1915). The statement was reiterated in Western *Metal Supply Company* v. *Pillsbury,* 3 IAC 109, 172 Cal. 407, 156 Pac. 491 (1916); and again in *Carstens* v. *Pillsbury,* 3 IAC 215, 172 Cal. 572, 158 Pac. 218 (1916). Numerous cases had also sought to challenge the validity of the provision exempting the Industrial Accident Commission from "technical" rules of evidence, but the constitutionality of the provision was upheld. See *Western Ind. Co.* v. *IAC* (Robson), 4 IAC 39, 174 Cal. 315, 163 Pac. 60 (1917); in support of admissibility, see *Shell Co.* v. *IAC* (Fleming), 5 IAC 50, 36 C.A. 463, 172 Pac. 611 (1918); *P. G. & E. Co.* v. *IAC* (Kendall), 6 IAC 112, 180 Cal. 497, 181 Pac. 788 (1919); admissibility denied in *Engelbretson* v. *IAC* (Wells), 2 IAC 1021, 170 Cal. 793, 151 Pac. 421 (1915); *Employers Liability Assur. Corp.* v. *IAC* (Marsters), 2 IAC 1024, 170 Cal. 800, 151 Pac. 423 (1915); *Connolly* v. *IAC*, 3 IAC 439, 173 Cal. 405, 160 Pac. 239 (1916); *Western Ind. Co.* v. *IAC* (Pavlovic), 4 IAC 328, 35 C.A. 104, 169 Pac. 261 (1917).

21. California Constitution, Art. XX, Sec. 21. The same text was incorporated in the workmen's compensation statute in 1917 (California Statutes of 1917, Chap. 586, Sec. 60; California Labor Code, Sec. 5708–5709). A new case in 1920 again characterized the Industrial Accident Commission as a court, but the actual holding of the decision was too remote from the issue to be of much consequence (*Gouanillou v. IAC* [Michaud], 7 IAC 204, 184 Cal. 418, 193 Pac. 937 [1920]).

22. *Bankers Ind. Ins. Co.* v. *IAC* (Merzoian), 20 IAC 357, 4 C. 2d. 89, 47 P. 2d. 719 (1935), in which the court used the principle as ground for holding that the Industrial Accident Commission had equity powers. See Whitney R. Harris, "Is the California Industrial Accident Commission a Court?" *California Law Review,* XXIV (March, 1936), 328–335.

23. *Lyydikainen* v. *IAC,* 4 CCC 264, 36 C.A. 2d. 298, 97 P. 2d. 993 (1939). See also, for example, *Walker Mining Co.* v. *IAC* (Galeazzi), 4 CCC 211, 35 C.A. 2d. 257, 95 P. 2d. 188 (1939); *Young* v. *IAC,* 5 CCC 67, 38 C.A. 2d. 250, 100 P. 2d. 1062 (1940); *Holmes Eureka Lumber Co.* v. *IAC* (Hansen), 5 CCC 230, 41 C.A. 2d. 150, 106 P. 2d. 23 (1940); *Taylor* v. *IAC* (Thomas), 5 CCC 61, 38 C.A. 2d. 75, 100 P. 2d. 511 (1940).

24. California Statutes of 1945, Chap. 1431, Sec. 18; California Labor Code, Sec. 111.

25. California Statutes of 1917, Chap. 586, Sec. 57; California Labor Code, Sec. 5307.

26. California Statutes of 1917, Chap. 586, Sec. 59; California Labor Code, Sec. 5309–5315.

27. California Statutes of 1917, Chap. 586, Sec. 19, 20; California Labor Code, Sec. 5700, 5701, 5703, 5704, 5803. Note, however, the important qualifications implicit in those texts, especially California Labor Code, Sec. 5701 and 5703.

28. Pillsbury, *op. cit.*, p. 185.

29. *Ibid.*, p. 184.

30. *Ibid.*, p. 185.

31. *Lyydikainen* v. *IAC*; *Walker Mining Co.* v. *IAC* (Galeazzi); *Evans* v. *IAC,* 10 CCC 271, 71 C. 2d. 244, 162 P. 2d. 488 (1945); *Holmes Eureka Lumber Co.* v. *IAC* (Hansen); *Young* v. *IAC.*

32. In 1946, the Industrial Accident Commission instructed the referees to furnish the

Rating Bureau "with a full description of the permanent disability factors" and required that "only this description, and not the file, be referred to" the bureau. But this new policy was not even mentioned in the revised *Rules of Practice* that were issued a couple of months later, in January, 1947. Actually, the old practice of sending the file to the rater was continued.

33. California Administrative Code, Title 8, Chap. 4.5, *Rules of Practice and Procedure of the Industrial Accident Commission,* Sec. 10927.

34. *Rules of Practice and Procedure,* Sec. 10928.

35. *Ibid.,* Sec. 10927, as amended August 5, 1958; *California Administrative Register,* Vol. LVIII, No. 14.

36. The Medical Bureau has been subjected to much the same criticism, and with similar results. The parties insisted that whenever it reviewed a case, its report was to be written and served. The bureau protested, in a 1951 memorandum, that "if this were done, then any conversation that any referee might have with the Rating Bureau or the Medical Bureau in regard to a case should also be reduced to writing and served on the parties." Although no formal rule was adopted, the continuing threat of criticism has brought actual agency practices in line with the principle that all case reviews must be reported and served. On this issue, see also *Partial Report of the Senate Interim Committee on Workmen's Compensation Benefits* (Sacramento: California Legislature, 1951).

37. For a general discussion of this problem in administrative law, see Kenneth Culp Davis, *Administrative Law Text* (St. Paul: West Publishing Co., Hornbook Series, 1959), pp. 187–212.

38. See California Statutes of 1913, Chap. 176, Sec. 4; California Labor Code, Sec. 115; California Statutes of 1917, Chap. 586, Sec. 69; California Labor Code, Sec. 5309.

39. California Statutes of 1917, Chap. 586, Sec. 64; California Labor Code, Sec. 5315. The Industrial Accident Commission was specifically authorized to "refer matters arising out of the same proceeding to different referees." See California Statutes of 1917, Chap. 586, Sec. 59; California Labor Code, Sec. 5310.

40. *Rules of Practice and Procedure* (Sacramento: California Industrial Accident Commission, 1933), Rule IV, Sec. 2.

41. *Ibid.,* Rule XI, Sec. 6.

42. The investigating committee concluded with definite condemnation of the secrecy in which referee memoranda were held, but in its answer the agency expressed its firm opposition to any change in this practice ("Report of the Committee on Practice and Procedure Before the Industrial Accident Commission," pp. 75, 77).

43. *Morgan* v. *United States,* 298 U.S. 468 (1936).

44. *Ibid.,* p. 480.

45. Although the Supreme Court later retreated from its 1936 opinion when the Morgan case came back before it (*Morgan* v. *United States,* 304 U.S. 1 [1938]; 313 U.S. 409 [1941]), the principle that "he who decides must hear" remained in the foreground. In 1939, two law review articles addressed severe criticisms to the Industrial Accident Commission on that basis, one of them arguing that all agency decisions were and had been legally void. See Donald Gallagher, "Power of the Industrial Accident Commission to Settle Disputes Arising under Workmen's Compensation Legislation," *California Law Review,* Vol. XXVII, No. 3 (March, 1939), pp. 241–277; D. O. McGovney, "Proposed Modification of Framework and Functions of the Industrial Accident Commission," *ibid.,* pp. 278–284.

46. *Taylor* v. *IAC* (Thomas), 5 CCC 61, 38 C.A. 2d. 75, 100 P. 2d. 511 (1940); *Bethlehem Steel Co.* v. *IAC* (Foy), 5 CCC 284, 42 C.A. 2d. 192, 108 P. 2d. 698 (1940); *O'Hare* v. *IAC,* 6 CCC 134, 44 C.A. 2d. 629, 112 P. 2d. 915 (1941); *Dater* v. *IAC,* 6 CCC 190, 45

C.A. 2d. 664, 116 P. 2d. 112 (1941); *Helmick* v. *IAC*, 6 CCC 238, 46 C.A. 2d. 651, 116 P. 2d. 653 (1941); *Santa Maria Gas Co.* v. *IAC* (Huffman), 6 CCC 258, 46 C.A. 2d. 775, 117 P. 2d. 951 (1941); *Colonial Mutual Compensation Insurance Co.* v. *IAC* (Miller), 6 CCC 266, 47 C.A. 2d. 487, 118 P. 2d. 361 (1941); *Pacific Empl. Insurance Co.* v. *IAC* (Ehrhardt), 7 CCC 71, 19 C. 2d. 622, 112 P. 2d. 570 (1942); *Stoll* v. *IAC*, 7 CCC 157, 20 C. 2d. 440, 126 P. 2d. 865 (1942); *California Shipbuilding Corp.* v. *IAC* (Gaddis), 9 CCC 132, 64 C.A. 2d. 622, 149 P. 2d. 432 (1944), *cert. denied*, 324 U.S. 843 (1944); *Darling* v. *IAC* (Fernholtz), 9 CCC 329, 67 C.A. 2d. 300, 154 P. 2d. 421 (1944); *California Shipbuilding Corp.* v. *IAC* (Baker), 11 CCC 14, 27 C. 2d. 536, 165 P. 2d. 669 (1946); *Lumberman's Mutual Casualty Co.* v. *IAC* (Cacozza), 11 CCC 124, 289, 29 C. 2d. 492, 175 P. 2d. 823 (1946); *National Automobile & Casualty Insurance Co.* v. *IAC* (Guest), 14 CCC 100, 34 C. 2d. 20, 206 P. 2d. 841 (1949); *Power* v. *IAC*, 19 CCC 49, 123 C.A. 2d. 591, 267 P. 2d. 85 (1954); *Allied Compensation Insurance Co.* v. *IAC* (Lintz), 26 CCC 241, 57 C. 2d. 115, 17 Cal. Rptr. 817 (1961); *Industrial Indemnity Co.* v. *IAC* AHicksQ, 26 CCC 246, 57 C. 2d. 123, 17 Cal. Rptr. 821 (1961); *Durae* v. *IAC* (Mansker), 27 CCC 240, 206 C.A. 2d., 23 Cal. Rptr. 902 (1962).

47. *Rules of Practice and Procedure* (1933), Rule XI, Sec. 6.

48. "Report of the Committee on Administrative Agencies and Tribunals," *Journal of the State Bar of California*, Vol. XVI, No. 8 (1941), pp. 36, 37.

49. *Investigation of Procedure of the Industrial Accident Commission* (Sacramento: California Legislature, Assembly, Subcommittee of the Interim Committee on Governmental Efficiency and Economy, 1945). Hereafter cited as *Investigation of IAC Procedure, 1945, passim.*

50. *Ibid.*, p. 87. The reference there is to *Report of the Attorney General's Committee on Administrative Procedure* (Washington, D.C.: U.S. Department of Justice; Senate document No. 8, 77th Congress, 1st sess., 1941), especially pp. 243–244.

51. *Ibid.*, pp. 88, 91–92.

52. California Statutes of 1945, Chap. 1431, Sec. 18–21, intended to solve the problem by increasing the number of commissioners, to the end of enabling them to review cases personally before deciding. In addition, protest against the review system was so bitter that in 1946 the Chief of the Compensation Department resigned, and his office, as a civil service position, was allowed to lapse. His duties were transferred to supervising referees who were chosen by the commission from the referee staff, without any change in civil service status.

53. "Report of the Committee on Administrative Agencies and Tribunals: Industrial Accident Commission," *Journal of the State Bar of California*, XXV (1950), 315.

54. *Partial Report of the Senate Interim Committee on Workmen's Compensation Benefits*, p. 161.

55. California Statutes of 1951, Chap. 778, Sec. 1, 4, 6; California Labor Code, Sec. 115, 5309, 5314.

56. California Statutes of 1951, Chap. 778, Sec. 8, 13, 20, 21; California Labor Code, Sec. 5315, 5900, 5906, 5907. In practice, petitions for reconsideration were referred to the referee who had issued the award against which the petition was filed; this referee had power to recommend granting reconsideration and to propose a decision on reconsideration for the commission's signature. If he did not recommend reconsideration, the petition was then transferred to some other referee, who would make his own recommendations. If some new evidence had to be heard on reconsideration, those further hearings were held by a referee who had not sat on the hearings in the first instance. Substantially the same procedure is effective today under Sec. 10878 ff. of the *Rules of Practice and Procedure.*

57. California Statutes of 1951, Chap. 778, Sec. 8, 13, 27; California Labor Code, Sec. 5315, 5900, 5911.

58. California Statutes of 1955, Chap. 1822, Sec. 1; California Labor Code, Sec. 5908.5.

59. The power is still exercised once in a while, but only on the request of a party who has found some error in a decision and is too late to petition for reconsideration. Since the commission's delay for acting on its own motion is 60 days, instead of the 20 days given to the parties for petitioning, a party whose delay has expired has 40 more days to ask the agency to reconsider "on its own motion" (California Labor Code, Sec. 5900 [b] and 5903). Even that is rarely done. Indeed, Rule 10877 of the IAC *Rules of Practice and Procedure* forbids the commission to use its power on request of the parties.

60. Davis, *op. cit.*, p. 202.

61. California Statutes of 1917, Chap. 586, Sec. 60, 67; California Labor Code, Sec. 5708, 5709, 5952, 5953.

62. On an early but unsuccessful challenge to those provisions, see *above,* p. 176, and fn. 20. The commission was also able to avert a similar challenge at the legislature in 1931 (*Assembly Bills* [Sacramento: California Legislature, 49th Sess., 19311], No. 955; *Journal of the Assembly* [Sacramento: California Legislature, 49th Sess., 1931], p. 586).

63. California Statutes of 1933, Chap. 864, Sec. 1; California Labor Code, Sec. 5708 (emphasis supplied). Up to that time, the law explicitly required the recording of only the testimony the agency took without notice and outside a hearing (California Statutes of 1917, Chapter 586, Section 19 [c] [7]). The reports of hearings, summaries prepared by the referee after each hearing, were the only required record of what happened during agency proceedings.

64. *Hartford Accident and Indemnity Co.* v. *IAC*, 20 IAC 267, 140 C.A. 482, 35 P. 2d. 366 (1934).

65. "Report of the Committee on Administrative Agencies and Tribunals," *Journal of the State Bar of California,* XXV (1950), 316–318; *Partial Report of the Senate Interim Committee on Workmen's Compensation Benefits,* pp. 242–247.

66. California Statutes of 1951, Chap 606, Sec. 8, 9; California Labor Code, Sec. 5952.

67. See *Columbia-Geneva Steel Div.* v. *IAC* (Coffee), 18 CCC 44, 115 C.A. 2d. 862, 253 P. 2d. 45 (1953). The "substantial evidence" test had, indeed, long been used by federal and state courts as a means of freeing administrative agencies from standards of "preponderance of evidence" applicable in civil courts; it had actually already been used in a few California cases involving the Industrial Accident Commission. On this doctrine see Davis, *op. cit.*, pp. 521–525; Hanna, *op. cit.*, pp. 212–216; and the cases cited in Warren L. Hanna (ed.), *The Workmen's Compensation Laws of California* (Albany, Calif.: Hanna Legal Publications, 1963), pp. 325–327, 368–371.

68. *Glendaniel* v. *IAC*, 6 CCC 85, 17 C. 2d. 634, 111 P. 2d. 314 (1941).

69. California Statutes of 1917, Chap. 586, Sec. 20 (a); California Labor Code, Sec. 5313. The apellate courts were empowered to determine on review whether "such findings of fact support the order, decision or award under review" (California Statutes of 1917, Chap. 586, Sec. 67 [b]; California Labor Code, Sec. 5952 [e]).

70. See *above,* p. 185 and fn. 41.

71. *Lumberman's Mutual Cas. Co.* v. *IAC* (Cacozza); *California Shipbuilding Corp.* v. *IAC* (Rogers), 12 CCC 310, 31 C. 2d. 270, 188 P. 2d. 27 (1947); *Transport Ind. Co.* v. *IAC* (Cooper), 23 CCC 30, 157 C.A. 2d. 542, 321 P. 2d. 21 (1958); *Argonaut Ins. Exch.* v. *IAC* (Bellinger), 23 CCC 34, 49 C. 2d. 706, 321 P. 2d. 460 (1958).

72. *California Shipbuilding Corp.* v. *IAC* (Rogers).

73. *California Shipbuilding Corp.* v. *IAC* (Sharp), 13 CCC 109, 85 C.A. 2d. 435,

193 P. 2d. 61 (1948); *Pierson* v. *IAC*, 15 CCC 188, 98 C.A. 2d. 598, 220 P. 2d. 794 (1950); *Whitaker* v. *IAC*, 15 CCC 191, 98 C.A. 2d. 838, 220 P. 2d. 780 (1950); *California Comp. Ins. Co.* v. *IAC* (Moore), 19 CCC 249, 287, 128 C.A. 2d. 797, 277 P. 2d. 442 (1954); *Horn* v. *IAC*, 19 CCC 258, 129 C.A. 2d. 837, 276 P. 2d. 673 (1954); *Simien* v. *IAC*, 21 CCC 10, 138 C.A. 2d. 397, 291 P. 2d 951 (1956); *Urquiza* v. *IAC*, 21 CCC 286, 144 C.A. 2d. 322, 300 P. 2d. 871 (1956).

74. California Administrative Code, Title 8, Chap. 4.5, *Rules of Practice and Procedure,* Sec. 9747 (c).

75. California Statutes of 1953, Chap. 1256, Sec. 1; California Labor Code, Sec. 5313.

76. California Administrative Code, Title 8, Chap. 4.5, *Rules of Practice and Procedure,* Sec. 10878.

77. California Statutes of 1953, Chap. 1256, Sec. 4; California Labor Code, Sec. 5908.5.

78. California Statutes of 1955, Chap. 1822, Sec. 1; California Labor Code, Sec. 5908.5.

79. *Investigation of IAC Procedure, 1945,* p. 78.

80. *Ibid.*, p. 90.

81. See Chap. VI, pp. 144–145.

82. This commission was established by California Statutes of 1963, Chap. 2040; California Labor Code, Sec. 6200–6240.

83. *Report of the Workmen's Compensation Study Commission*, pp. 61–63, 65–68; California Statutes of 1965, Chap. 1767.

84. Although the parties have a right to object to the assignment of their case to a referee they suspect of bias (California Labor Code, Sec. 5311), and the courts have repeatedly reminded the Industrial Accident Commission of its duty to give a "fair and impartial hearing" (see especially *Boswell Co.* v. *IAC* [Owings], 9 CCC 334, 67 C.A. 2d. 347, 154 P. 2d. 13 [1944]; *Bethlehem Steel Corp.* v. *IAC* [McClure], 10 CCC 162, 70 C.A. 2d. 369, 161 P. 2d. 18 [1945]; *Argonaut Ins. Exch.* v. *IAC* [Thrasher], 18 CCC 228, 120 C.A. 2d. 145, 260 P. 2d. 817 [1953]), the indefiniteness of standards casts doubts over all decisions.

85. *Partial Report of the Senate Interim Committee on Workmen's Compensation Benefits*, p. 246; *Second Partial Report of the Senate Committee on Labor* (Sacramento: California Legislature, 1955), p. 21.

86. This is true even in the branch offices of the agency, where referees are responsible for the legal information service, which is handled by IAC attorneys at the main offices in San Francisco and Los Angeles (*Office Manual*, California Industrial Accident Commission, p. 6).

Even IAC attorneys in charge of the Information Desk are to some extent subject to the same principle. They must avoid "getting involved" (see Chap. VI, pp. 146–147). One of them was reprimanded by the chairman of the commission because he had adopted the practice of notifying employers he found violating certain legal duties—for example, the duty to insure, to post notice of the name of one's insurer—of the legal sanctions to which they were exposed.

87. This is not to say that actual practice always conforms to those rules, although it most often does. But such are the standards by which practice is uniformly judged by defense lawyers, for obvious reasons, and indeed by most applicants' lawyers, who resent "paternalistic" intrusions by the referees in their cases and see them as interfering with the presentation of their arguments.

88. *Rules of Practice and Procedure, 1942*, p. 2.

89. For instance, an internal instruction of 1940 stated that "appointments of independent medical examiners should be the exception and not the rule," in spite of an

explicit rule of practice to the contrary (*Rules of Practice and Procedure 1933*, Rule XVIII, p. 23; the rule remained in the 1942 revision, quoted *above* in fn. 88).

90. *Rules of Practice and Procedure, 1942,* Rule XIX. Before that time, the parties were not required to submit their medical evidence before the hearings at which they wanted to produce it. This system worked very much to the disadvantage of the claimant, who never knew the grounds upon which the insurer had assessed his case before the hearing, and therefore did not know what rebuttal evidence he might have to produce.

91. "Report of the Committee on Administrative Agencies and Tribunals," *Journal of the State Bar of California*, Vol. XVI, No. 8 (1941), p. 327.

92. *Investigation of IAC Procedure, 1945*, pp. 121–122. One of the regulations referred to there was a book of rules made for the referees, probably in the late 1930's from which the report quotes at pp. 78–79.

93. *Ibid.*, p. 19. The statute referred to was the first step in the creation of a law of administrative procedure in California (California Statutes of 1941, Chap. 628, Sec. 1, adding California Political Code, Sec 720–725.5; those sections were later recodified in California Government Code, Sec. 11350–11415).

94. California Administrative Code, Title 8, Chap. 4.5, *Rules of Practice and Procedure of the Industrial Accident Commission,* Sec. 9700 ff. This followed a reenactment of the 1941 statute as part of the California Government Code (California Statutes of 1945, Chap. 111, Sec. 11350–11415).

95. California Statutes of 1953, Chap. 1782, Sec. 1, adding California Labor Code, Sec. 5307.1. See also Chap. V.

96. *Partial Report of the Senate Interim Committee on Workmen's Compensation Benefits,* pp. 169–183; California Statutes of 1951, Chap. 1683, Sec. 1; California Labor Code,

97. A series of cases in 1947 had brought this issue to the foreground. The Industrial Accident Commission had decided to apply a change in the legal schedule of benefits to all cases pending before it, irrespective of the date of injury; in *Aetna Casualty and Surety Co.* v. *IAC* 11 CCC 258, 12 CCC 123, 30 Cal. 2d. 388, 182 P. 2d. 159 (1947) and other cases listed in 12 CCC 144, 145, 184–188, the Supreme Court had held this retroactive application of a statute illegal.

98. *Partial Report of the Senate Interim Committee on Workmen's Compensation Benefits,* pp. 169–183; California Statutes of 1951, Chap. 1683, Section 1; California Labor Code, Sec. 4660 (c).

99. California Statutes of 1947, Chap. 1425; California Government Code, Sec. 11445.

100. California Statutes of 1953, Chap. 1782, Sec. 1; California Labor Code, Sec. 5307.1.

101. California Statutes of 1955, Chap. 1822, Sec. 2; California Labor Code, Sec. 5307.

102. California Statutes of 1957, Chap. 2211, Sec. 1, 2; California Labor Code, Sec. 136, 137.

103. California Labor Code, Sec. 5000, 5001.

104. *Rules of Practice and Procedure, 1914,* p. 20.

105. The proposed settlement could be either approved or denied—if denied, the case would then be treated as a formal application—or approved on condition that some of its provisions be changed. In this third case, the parties remained free to reufse the change suggested and proceed to trial.

106. A first move in that direction had already been made in the late 1930's when the handling of C&R's arising from formally controverted cases had been transferred from the secretary to the referees in charge of the cases before the settlements. See Chap. VI, p. 141.

107. California Statutes of 1955, Chap. 1822, Sec. 4; California Labor Code, Sec. 5001.

VIII Uses of Judicialism

THE STORY TOLD in the preceding chapter is incomplete in two major respects. First, although the parties have performed a crucial role in subjecting the Industrial Accident Commission to judicial standards of accountability, the process has not been solely one of reluctant agency concessions to outside pressures. In the last two decades, the parties have found increasing support for their demands within the agency itself, and the commission has come to affirm the view of itself as a court that was being pressed upon it. To the IAC, the new doctrine appeared increasingly useful as a symbol and warrant of impartiality, a means of protecting its legitimacy in the midst of political controversy.

Second, at the same time as it was more and more eagerly cultivating the symbols of its judicial status, the commission was developing new patterns of resistance to standards of accountability. This development was in large part triggered by an overwhelming growth of the caseload of the agency; the requirements of efficiency and mass production have made the commission increasingly impatient with often exacting demands of judicial fairness. Claims have to be "processed" and decisions "produced"; the "output" of the referees must be kept up to standards of "efficient" management; issues and controversies come to be looked at as points of friction in the production line. The rhetoric of the IAC has become a strange mixture of judicial symbolism and managerial parlance. The ethics of court and factory are verbally reconciled by the maxim, "Justice delayed is justice denied."

More important is a continuing effort, underlying this concern for efficiency, to evade legal controversy and avoid the burdens of decision that accompany it. To the commission the adoption of a judicial posture was a way of withdrawing from politics and reducing the risks of overtly political controversy. But the growing involvement of organized groups in the process of adjudication itself has increasingly underscored the political significance of legal issues and judicial decisions; policy problems and group interests were continuously brought to the foreground of seemingly insignificant individual cases. Thus the very tensions that made the symbolism of judicial office attractive to the IAC also pressed it to evade the responsibility for policy-making that is always latent in adjudication.

This accounts for the peculiar selectivity with which the IAC has interpreted the idea that it is a court, that is, an eager affirmation of the symbols of the office, coupled with increasing impatience toward the burdens of judicial decision and justification.

The Court

Apart from the vigilance of the parties, the main internal support for the development of a judicial ethos in the IAC has come from the referees of the Compensation Department. In many controversies with the agency, the parties found in them a group of eager and strategically located allies. The referees were those among the staff of the commission who, by their professional background as lawyers and by their continuing confrontation with the demands of the litigants, were most sensitive to the growing need for a more orderly legal process. They were also those, down the line of compensation administration, and in the midst of controversy, who were most exposed to challenges to their authority. They found in the judicial model a useful way of meeting this problem and enhancing their status.

Ever since the early days of the commission, the referees had been prone to point out the similarities between their role and the function of judges in civil courts; the analogy gave meaning and importance to their responsibilities in the agency. On the whole, however, this idea had little momentum in the early IAC; agency doctrine laid strong emphasis on those distinctive characteristics of the commission that set it apart from ordinary courts. The legal staff, including the referees, fully shared the conviction that judicial traditions were but an anachronism, unable to meet the legal problems of modern society; that the IAC was tracing the path of the future and offering a *model* for other courts, which would all in due time adopt its "simplified procedures."[1] In an unpublished paper written by a referee in 1917 and modestly subtitled "A Short Treatise on the Functions and Qualifications of a Referee," the writer emphasized how the office of referee "requires something decidedly *more* than a strictly judicial service":

> The judge is in no sense an inquisitor or an investigator. His duties are judicial in the strict sense and the burden of the investigation rests upon the advocates before him.
>
> But the Referee is first and foremost an *Investigator*. The duty is incumbent upon him to search for, and find, all the facts necessary to support a decision. His position is in some sense analogous to that of *amicus curiae*: his care is to be able to present to the Commission a complete history of all the facts involved in the

> controversy, and not let the case pass out of his hands for decision until such history is complete.
>
> He cannot and must not depend upon counsel for this investigation. Advocates may, in the interest of their clients, suppress facts which should appear. . . .

The author saw the pride of the referee in this distinct and avant-garde character of his role and concluded that "to aid in the administration of an industrial and social scheme such as Workmen's Compensation is a service calculated to stimulate ideals," and that referees should be "spurred by the simple thought that they are helping to do good."

The low regard of the IAC for "formal" adjudication, the still relatively small extent to which formal procedures were used, and the subordinate role in which referees were maintained as mere advisers to the commission further contributed to hold down whatever "judicial" ambitions the referees might have had. These conditions, as we know, began changing about 1930; the increasing incidence of formal controversies suddenly transformed the Compensation Department from a peripheral service of last resort into the central and most critical office of the IAC. In this process the referees became the most powerful and, indeed, the character-defining group in the IAC.

Signs of the view among referees that they were "judges" to be treated like the judges of civil courts can be traced back to 1929–1930. At a meeting of the referee staff with members of the commission in December, 1929,

> The problem of creating a proper identification and respect for the Commission and the referees while holding hearings, was freely discussed. Some referees suggested that we follow the court procedure and have the bench elevated slightly. The Commission realizes the desirability of proper respect and decorum, and with this in mind and with a view of uniformity it was suggested that the referee sit at the end of the table with the witness occupying the end seat on the side of the table to his right and the reporter to his left and just opposite the witness.

In the reformist enthusiasm of the early IAC, the commission had banned from its proceedings all reminders of court symbolism—everybody sat around a conference table as for an informal discussion. Now the perspectives were reversed—instead of offering a model for the courts, the IAC was turning to the courts as a model for itself. The referees realized that, instead of being "more than judges," they were in effect much less than the judges they should have been. Practicing lawyers and the organized bar were continuously pressing the idea as a means of forcing changes in procedural practice.[2] In 1937, after repeated demands from the bar, the commission adopted the following instruction:

"MOUNT THE BENCH"

> We have received suggestions from the Bar generally, [which we believe are psychologically sound] and we request that, effective this date, all Referees and Reporters, when using out of town hearing facilities, take their respective positions upon any rostrum or bench available, and so far as possible conform to the usual decorum of a court of record.

The compensation bar has never withdrawn its support to the referees' later demands for fuller recognition as judicial officers.

The referees quickly assumed leadership in promoting this new conception of their role. The latter would indeed serve them quite effectively as a means of enhancing their status and independence within the IAC. Resentment against the supervision of their work and decisions by the commission was rampant among them. As a referee who joined the IAC in the early 1930's remembered in an interview: "We were not free to decide cases in accordance with our conscience; our work was to find out what the men who happened to sit on the Commission wanted us to decide." As lawyers, they resented this control of lay "politicians" over their professional work. As early as 1930, the commission had met some grievances on that issue. The following instruction was then adopted:

> It has been reported to us that some of the referees feel that they are not entirely at liberty to disagree with the instructions or suggestions of the Compensation Department regarding decisions in specific cases. The Commission has in no way departed from its policy of leaving the final responsibility for the decision of cases by referees to them, and no member of the Commission desires to compel any referee to issue a decision as a referee decision which he does not fully approve of. . . . if after careful consideration a referee feels that he cannot in conscience make the decision suggested by any superior in the Compensation Department, he is entirely at liberty to prepare the decision as a Commission decision and forward it without his signature.

In the 1940's, after the parties had begun taking issue with the commission's review of referee decisions, the rebellion became open. In 1943, the referees formally requested that the power to issue original decisions be transferred to them,[3] and throughout the 1944 Assembly investigation they acted as the chief witnesses for IAC critics.[4] The chairman of the commission had some bitter remarks on the referee staff:

> They hold court—they have a little court of their own, and gradually they are inclined to become more inflated. . . . They bitterly resent any correction or discipline, and not only resent it, they show it, take exception to it. . . . The referees are for life, and I am only for four years, you gentlemen for two years; they regard all of us as passing affairs in their life—we walk along the stage.[5]

In its findings, the investigating committee concluded:

> That the members of the commission claim a lack of authority over referees. . . . Related to this is a fundamental difference of opinion as to whether the referees are *judicial officers* with the necessary independence of conscience and judgment inseparable from that status or are *mere employees* acting under "directives" carrying out more or less mechanical functions assigned to them by the members of the commission.[6]

As we know, the committee recommended that the referees be given authority to issue original decisions and that they be fully recognized as judicial officers.[7] The recommended transfer of adjudicative powers was not implemented until 1951;[8] this reform largely freed the referees from commission authority.

The same legislation also granted another major claim of the referees. An amendment to the labor code directed that the salaries of the referees would henceforth be set by the State Personnel Board "for a class of positions which perform judicial functions."[9] Until then, salaries had been determined by comparison with those of other legal employees in the state civil service.[10] The 1951 statute compelled the State Personnel Board to separate the referee class from other legal classes and to provide for it a special salary range substantially above the prior level. The next issue became to determine what other judicial office the referee position should be compared with for purposes of salary determination. In the eyes of the referees, the most comparable job was that of Superior Court Judge. Therefore, they sought to raise the standards of professional qualification for referee positions to the level of those required of members of the judiciary,[11] and to make their official job description sound closer to their high ideal. The following is the draft of a job description suggested by some referees in 1955:

> Judicial officer assigned to hear and decide controverted adversary proceedings arising out of disputes between employees, insurance carriers and employers under the Workmen's Compensation and General Laws; having the duties and responsibilities required of a judge of a court of record; making original findings of fact, conclusions of law, and orders and decisions based thereon; approving compromises and releases; and, in addition, having the power to punish for contempt.

In addition they demanded that their position be exempted from a State Personnel Board Policy, which requires that an "appropriate" salary differential be maintained between agency heads and their staff, arguing that

> Commission members, as such, have no direct or indirect supervisory authority over the Commission's referees. . . . The judicial function of the referee is not in

> itself subject to the usual line supervision. The . . . referee's decision is an entirely independent one, subject to no review prior to its issuance. . . . The foregoing represents a singularly high and distinguished degree of responsibility for civil service personnel.[12]

The referees have not won their case yet; a new job description, adopted in 1955, characterizes the referee as conducting "judicial proceedings," but it also insists that he "does other work as required."

In recent years, the referees have sought to free themselves from the supervision of the chairman, who by law is charged with the control of the manner and efficiency of their performance. The Referees' Conference—an association organized by the referees to represent them—has created a committee that has jurisdiction to examine and dispose of all cases involving the discipline of referees in accordance with their own self-made canons of ethics. On the theory that judicial officers can be judged only by their peers, the conference has demanded that the chairman delegate his disciplinary powers to this committee. Although the commission has not relinquished its authority, it has nevertheless been led to listen to the committee on several occasions. The referees have actually become almost a distinct organization within the organization of the IAC; their conference has its own policy committees on all IAC problems; it promotes its views before the legislature, the administration, and the bar, independently from and not infrequently in opposition to the commission; it has its own liaison programs with the compensation bar; and indeed it maintains its own paid lobbyist in Sacramento.

Nowhere is the acute status-consciousness of the referees better revealed than in their long, strenuous, and quite successful efforts to mold the style of the IAC after the image of the courts. Every reminder of "administration," from the most important policy to the most harmless word or sign, had to be removed from the agency. Judicial impartiality and above all the appearance of impartiality became a core value; referees were to refrain from questioning witnesses, from communicating with the parties, from publicly calling attorneys by their first names; phone calls and correspondence with litigants had to be handled by their secretaries, who were to protect them from partisan approaches. They insisted that they, and not the Medical Bureau, should have power to select and appoint medical experts, in spite of an IAC rule to the contrary.[13] They requested and obtained in 1952 that the power to punish for contempt be transferred from the commission to them in cases of contempt committed in their presence.[14] As one of them wrote to the chairman:

> Take away that power and with it you take the ability of our referees to maintain order and dignity in the hearing room; thus charging them with the responsibil-

ity of being judicial officers while rendering them impotent to effectively meet that responsibility.

This was asserted in spite of the fact, acknowledged by the writer, that the problem had hardly ever arisen. The physical structure of offices and hearing rooms became a critical issue. In a report written in 1956, the referees argued:

> There is marked difference between holding hearings in court room than in some of our regular hearing rooms. If the room be adequate, litigants feel they have had their day in court. Everyone is constantly reminded where they are by the physical surroundings. It is not good to have the referee conduct a hearing with everybody sitting around.
>
> The hearing room should include the following:
>
> 1. Absence of any office atmosphere; no reporter's typewriter desk, typewriter, ringing telephones, file cabinets, or desk piled high with files.
> 2. Elevated bench for referees, not a table. When elevated he can write without the "up-side-down-reader" seeing what he is writing.
> 3. Witness chair placed away from attorneys and referee.
> 4. Adequate counsel table preferably one separated from spectators.
> 5. Furnishings need not be elaborate but nevertheless be dignified.
> 6. Proper acoustics.
> 7. Should have flags of the same size as are found in any court room instead of the little flags such as we have in Los Angeles.
>
> Many applicants' attorneys have told that after leaving the hearing room in cases where the applicant feels that he has probably lost his case, he then insists that the attorney take the matter to court. He does not have the feeling that he has been in court at all.

In addition, it was requested that each referee be assigned his own hearing room adjacent to his private office; the latter would be protected from public access by a reception room in which his secretary would sit. In support of this demand, a referee argued on behalf of his colleagues that

> privacy of the referee is no different from that of any judge; chambers of the judge are always located adjacent to the court room.

The referees got their private offices and reception rooms, and in several places even their own personal hearing rooms. Some of them proceeded to refurnish their "court rooms" at their own cost, replacing the metallic tables and chairs supplied by the IAC with more "dignified" wooden benches and witness stands.

Finally, almost everyone and everything at the IAC had to be rechristened; applications for "adjustment" of claims became applications for "adjudication"; the "Supervising Referee" was retitled "Presiding Referee";[15] the state bar was requested to move jurisdiction over IAC problems from its Committee on Administrative Agencies to a Committee for the Administration of Justice. The extent to which this game was played is illustrated by the following report submitted in 1960 by a committee of referees charged with suggesting means of "creating a more judicial atmosphere" at the IAC:

> The Committee recommends . . . the following procedures which do not require any amendment or changes in either the Rules or the Labor Code.
>
> 1. That the referees' offices be referred to as "chambers" and not as offices.
>
> 2. . . . that the word "court" be used instead of the word "referee" in transcripts.
>
> 3. That the title "Referee in Charge" be changed to "District Office Presiding Referee."
>
> 4. That the word "Honorable" precede the referee's name in the first paragraph of all minutes of hearing.
>
> 5. That the word "Honorable" precede the referee's name in the first paragraph of all Findings and Awards and Orders.
>
> 6. That the title of "Report of Referee on Decision" be changed to "Opinion of Trial Referee on Decision."
>
> 7. That the title of "Report of Referee" be changed to "Trial Referee's Summary of the Evidence." . . .
>
> 8. That the word "claim" be stricken from all forms used in the future and the word "case" be substituted therefor.
>
> 9. That the general bulletin of information . . . include the statement that the Industrial Accident Commission is a Court in the State of California presided over by judicial officers called "referees."
>
> 10. That this same bulletin have a statement in it that the applicants will find it to their advantage to be represented by an attorney. . . .
>
> 11. That in offices with more than one hearing room, the hearing rooms be designated as "Departments A, B, C, etc." . . .
>
> 14. That a standard oath be adopted as follows: "Do you solemnly swear that the testimony you are about to give in this matter now pending before this Court shall be the truth, the whole truth, and nothing but the truth, so help you God?" The important addition here are the words "now pending before this Court."
>
> 15. The Committee is uncertain whether calling the hearing rooms "courtrooms" and substituting the word "trial" for "hearing" will be permissible. . . . The Committee, however, recommends that "the bull be taken by the horns" and that all rooms should be referred to as "court rooms" and that all hearings be referred to as trials. The Committee feels that if . . . these recommendations cannot be utilized without a change in the Labor Code, then these changes be adopted as part of the Association's legislative program.

> The following recommendations are recommendations requiring changes in the Labor Code. . . .
>
> 1. Labor Code Section 5708 . . . should be amended to read as follows: "All oral testimony . . . shall be taken down in shorthand by a competent stenographic reporter, who shall have the power to administer oaths to witnesses in proceedings pending before the Industrial Accident Commission." The Committee feels that the referee should not have to administer the oath and that it is more consistent with the judicial dignity of the Commission if the oath were administered by the reporter.
>
> 2. The Committee feels that the greatest drawback to the objectives in mind is the title "Referee." . . . The Committee recognizes that opposition will be encountered immediately should legislative support be sought to change the name to "Judge." . . . The Committee recommends the following addition to this Section (110 of the Labor Code): "(c) 'Referee' means a judicial officer of the Industrial Accident Commission." . . . This recommendation does not attempt to change the Labor Code. . . . It merely defines the title of a Referee, which has always been subject to misunderstanding. The advantage would be that the referees may then entitle themselves judicial officers of the Industrial Accident Commission, and within a very short while the title would be adopted by the Bar and we would find ourselves addressed as "Judges."

Many of those recommendations were carried out informally,[16] and it is not uncommon to see referees having themselves addressed "Your Honor," signing "The Honorable. . ." and referring to themselves as "this Court."

This agitation by referees for recognition of their judicial status has been quite contagious. The commission has made similar appeals to the legislature, demanding salaries equivalent to appellate court justices,[17] and insisting that every commissioner be given a research attorney to perform the same services as law clerks in appellate courts. The idea, embodied in the 1965 legislation, of an Appeals Board insulated from the staff offices of the former IAC, the new requirement that board members be lawyers, and that they receive salaries equal to those of Superior Court judges, were all in part products of the growing stress laid by the commission itself on its judicial character.[18]

There have, of course, been variations in the extent of this development. Compared to the judicial pomp of the Los Angeles office of the IAC, the style and atmosphere at San Francisco often seems quite informal. The difference reflects in part the less bitter and aggressive mode in which insurers and employees in San Francisco confront each other; more problems are settled by informal means.[19] Although this point cannot be documented, it would seem that carriers and employers in this area have learned to accommodate themselves to a labor movement that has established itself more comfortably and for a longer time on the political scene. But the difference is also due to differences in the character of IAC personnel at the two offices; as a result of an informal seniority privilege, San Francisco has been staffed with an older generation of referees who joined the agency at an earlier period of its history and under recruitment policies that were less concerned with the "judicial" nature of the office. The Los Angeles referees make up the "new breed." They are the more vocal and active in defending their judicial status, and their style has spread even to the commission panel that sits in the Los Angeles office; the latter has been known to have a penchant for holding formal sessions for the purpose of hearing oral arguments on reconsideration, a practice that was never condoned by the northern panel. And it has been observed that whereas "Panel Two (Los Angeles) often states its reasons in detailed judicial opinions, Panel One often announces its decisions on a mimeographed form." [20]

Whatever the variations, the trend has been clear everywhere in the agency. What is less clear is the actual significance it has had for the promotion of standards of procedure. The almost vulgar emphasis with which the agency has asserted its judicial character cannot mask the rather narrow and tenuous meaning of its commitment. The commitment has more often been *expressive* than substantive; it has also been characteristically *self-serving*, rather than grounded in a concern for meeting effectively the needs and demands of the parties. The judicial model served not only to enhance the status of agency staff members—an aim that by itself was attractive enough—at the same time it also served to protect the agency's own respectability; it provided the IAC with a symbolic warrant of impartiality, of immunity to those "political influences and class partisanship" of which it was continuously suspected. Neutrality practically exhausted the normative content of what the IAC meant in asserting its judicial nature; and even those standards had a primarily symbolic aim. The appearance of impartiality was more crucial than its actual achievement; the commission was reluctant to let its decision processes be brought under the control of rules, especially rules of justification, but it went to extremes in removing from its operations all visible features that could associate it with a partisan interest. It has been willing to do so even at potentially considerable cost in the quality of its adjudicative services, and sometimes indeed at the expense of their effective neutrality. It may have been compromising for the IAC to provide legal assistance to unrepresented claimants; but, by the restrictions it has placed on this service, it has allowed the outcome of its proceedings to depend upon the relative competence of the contending parties, thereby in effect offering a discriminatory advantage to employers and carriers. However much the competence of employees may have grown, it still is only a minority that enjoys the protection of active unionism, and only a portion of that minority has the benefit of competent legal representation. To the agency, judicialism has served primarily as a screen by which it could protect itself against threatening political assaults; it has enabled the IAC both to obviate the demands for a more committed defense of labor interests and to object to the criticisms of its "administrative" bias in favor of employees. For this purpose, the signs were more crucial than the substance, and the symbolism more relevant than the values it stood for.

This is not to say that the new look was devoid of significance for the parties; by formally adopting a judicial posture, the IAC inescapably bound itself to principles the parties would be able to invoke in their quest for standards of fairness. The agency would more easily be compelled to yield. However, the burdens of promoting those standards and of defending them once they were formally established were left in large part to the parties themselves; little leadership could be expected from the commission. In addition, as we shall see presently, the IAC has tended to give little weight to the values of judicial fairness when the latter came in conflict with other more pressing internal needs, and when they could be sacrificed at little visible cost.

The Factory

The limits of its judicial conscience are particularly apparent in the commission's handling of the administrative problems arising from the pressures of a growing caseload. The growth of litigation has made "production" an increasingly central problem for the IAC, and the temptation of expediency has become more pressing. When questioned about the "judicial" nature of commission proceedings, members of the staff emphatically profess their faith in due process and the adversary system. But if they are asked about caseload problems, they are eager to detail the variety of ways in which the IAC seeks to dissuade, if not prevent, the parties from asserting their rights.

Reduction of Procedural Opportunities. The most obvious way the legal process is undermined is by efforts to restrict opportunities for proof and argument. Demands for hearings come to be evaluated in terms of their costs for the agency in time lost and budgetary resources expended, and these costs become appropriate ground for denying the request. In its early days also, the IAC was intensely concerned with the problem of delay, but the value behind this concern was the welfare of the claimant—to the needy disabled employee, "Justice delayed is justice denied." Demands for prolonged hearings usually came from defendants and were easily interpreted as dilatory tactics designed to frustrate applicants' claims. In recent years, especially since the early 1950's, the character of the agency's concern with delay has profoundly changed; delay has become a problem of *internal* relevance, rather than of relevance to the claimants' interests. Although the idea that "Justice delayed is justice denied" is still invoked, the effective principle, as stated in a report of the Legal Bureau in 1959, has become that "No continuances should be granted except for the convenience of the Commission." An IAC rule, adopted in 1958, states that "requests for continuance are inconsistent with the [constitutional] requirement that Commission proceedings be expeditious." [21] But applicants' attorneys have had to protest against the manner of its enforcement, and remind the agency that the constitutional requirement was intended for the benefit of claimants and should not work to their detriment, and that at any rate it would be an abuse of power to deny additional hearing time when jointly requested by both parties.

Requests for cross-examination of reporting physicians and IAC disability rating specialists were a particularly troublesome source of delay, since they involved a well-established constitutional right of due process. The commission's approach to this problem is well illustrated in a report prepared by the Legal Bureau in 1959. Under the title "Red Tape Approach"—a more descriptive title might have been "How to Evade Due Process without Getting in Trouble with the Courts"—the report offered the following recommendations:

> I believe if we made it more difficult to cross-examine the [rating] specialists that the number of requests would decrease considerably. Needless to say, the wails of agony would be heard across the land. . . .
>
> For instance, in San Francisco and Los Angeles we can insist that every rating specialist be personally served with a subpoena if he is to testify. . . . We can require that he be served at least three working days before the hearing. . . . We can demand that a witness fee be paid. . . . We might insist that it be paid at the accounting office or some such place prior to service of the subpoena.
>
> We can insist that the demand for cross-examination not only be in writing but that it be accompanied by an affidavit in which the litigant demanding the cross-examination will be required to specify in detail his purpose in asking for the cross-examination and state what he hopes to accomplish. We can refuse to continue any of these hearings *except for the convenience of the Commission regardless of the argument of the parties.*
>
> We can be more ready to assess the 10 percent penalty against the carriers if, after making this affidavit, the attorney does not show that he had reasonable ground for thinking there was an error in the disability rating. . . .

A possibility, too, would be to assign one referee to hear all P.D.R. cross-examination. . . . He would not have to look at anything but the factors of disability and the resultant rating. It would be futile to argue to him that the factors selected are erroneous. He would not know anything about it. . . .

We should refuse to accept any demand for cross-examination made more than, for example, five days after the rating has been mailed out. . . .

The question of whether it would be wise to adopt these changes is not my concern. I believe that it would result in a considerable decrease in the demands to cross-examine. . . . In my opinion the protests would be fierce. We would catch it from all sides. The attorneys feel that they have a "right" to all the conveniences they now have. Unless we are willing to ride out the storm it would be foolish to start. [Emphasis supplied.]

The same report had some suggestions concerning the cross-examination of physicians:

Some referees refuse to send the applicant to an IME [Independent Medical Examiner] or to a Commission doctor unless both parties waive the right to cross-examine in advance. It is effective. A party is apt to think that if he refuses to waive this right that the referee will assume that he is afraid of the result of the examination. . . .

As far as the Commission doctors are concerned we can demand a subpoena, a payment of a witness fee, etc. . . .

If we raised the fee payable to an IME on cross-examination it might cut the demands somewhat. . . .

On these cross-examinations there should be no continuances except for the convenience of the Commission or the doctors. A more liberal use of the 10 percent penalty might help.

Rules were then drafted for the purpose of discouraging cross-examination of medical experts. One suggestion was that the right of cross-examination would be deemed waived when the report of the doctor has been filed and served on the parties twenty days or more prior to the hearing, unless the physician is produced at the hearing or good cause has been shown for not producing him. In its opinion on the legality of the rule, the Legal Bureau wrote:

As a practical matter, it might work a hardship on the applicant under certain situations. Occasionally, an applicant arrives at a hearing unrepresented and all the medical reports are unfavorable to him. The referee may suggest that the hearing be postponed so that he can obtain counsel. In such a case, the counsel would be barred from cross-examining the insurer's doctors. . . . This would not affect the legality of the rule; it is a matter of policy.

The rule was adopted in 1961, but in a milder version, and its impact on practice has been considerably mitigated by the parties.[22]

Routinization. More common and more effective abridgements of the legal process arise from the growth and enforcement of administrative routines. Routines are needed to organize the processing and disposition of the masses of cases that pass through the IAC. The agency has little time for analyzing issues, debating procedural strategy, or condoning a subtle casuistry. Cases must be fitted into readily identifiable categories, the path to be followed must be quickly pointed, alternative outcomes must be easily specified and promptly weighed. That is where time is saved at the least visible cost. In a couple of minutes before the hearing, a referee can, by a glance at the case file, get an idea of the story, of the issues that will be raised, and of what he is going to hear in the next hour. The questioning of witnesses follows well-established lines that operate almost as prescribed check lists; the referee will come back to the points omitted by the attorneys, and vice versa. Not infrequently the award can issue on the spot at the term of the hearing; for many cases, the referee will be able to use one of the mimeographed or printed blank forms of "Findings and Award" he or the commission has prepared.

Routine is, of course, most debilitating when it goes unquestioned. This is a particularly serious problem in workmen's compensation, in which the structure of legal practice tends to make the representatives of the parties almost as dependent upon administrative routines as the IAC. Given the relatively low level of fees, a compensation practice does not become viable unless it develops on a large scale. The compensation bar on both sides is dominated by large firms or legal departments, which can count on a steady and sizable supply of cases. Routines are quite conspicuous in the operations of these firms; it is not unusual in the halls of the IAC to see an attorney who is called away by an emergency hand over one of his files to an associate and ask him on the spot to appear at a hearing on the case; after a glance at the file, the "unprepared" colleague will be ready to proceed. Some firms often send one of their members to a pretrial session with a set of case files that he opens for the first time when the cases are called; for many regular hearings, an attorney needs no more preparation than a ten-minute review of the file.

Adversariness can be a powerful solvent of routines. If an attorney has overlooked some potential issue, there is always a good chance his opponent will raise it. The more active and competent firms seek to remain alert to the stifling effects of mass processing; incoming cases are more or less carefully screened; the more common are assigned to junior associates, and senior members are freed to devote their energy to those that offer special difficulties or opportunities.

But the IAC does not have this vested interest in overcoming routine. To the agency, routines are needed and must be enforced. If a referee seeks to obtain from the Rating Bureau specially detailed information on the process and reasoning through which a rating is determined in a particular case, or seeks to question the validity of standard assumptions that are built into the rating process, he is likely to be rebuffed as disrupting the smooth operation of agency procedure. A referee who attempted to test the issue met the resistance of the Rating and Medical Bureau and was ordered by the chairman not to depart from the routine form of rating instructions used by other referees:

> The Rating Bureau has estimated that the furnishing of this specialized information, desired by this Referee, would take one and a half to two times the time required for the normal handling of a rating, and from six to eight times the time required to pass on a compromise and release.

The referee objected to this infringement of his "judicial independence":

> Under the rules of practice we are forced to accept the advisement of the rating specialist. Are we forced to accept this advisement without an intelligent question? Must we accept this opinion blindly and give full weight to the conclusion without any effort to understand the basis of the rating, the weight that the specialist gave to the factors indicated by the statute? . . .
>
> I am of the frank opinion that the office of the Chairman has no power to control, either directly or indirectly, the judgment of a Commissioner or of a referee, or to force upon him practices and procedures which tend to interfere or to obstruct the exercise of the Commission's judicial power. . . .

To no avail.

Few referees would actually take such a principled posture. The nearly unanimous insistence of the staff on preserving the routine has in fact tended to modify the nature of the Rating Schedule, on the basis of which permanent disability ratings are made. In principle, the law treats the schedule as merely "prima facie evidence" of the percentage of disability to be attributed to injuries, and it offers independent standards by which percentages of disability should be determined:

> [A]ccount shall be taken of the nature of the physical injury or disfigurement, the occupation of the injured employee, and his age at the time of such injury, consideration being given to the diminished ability of such injured employee to compete in an open labor market.[23]

Thus, in theory, the opinion of the rater and the specifications of the schedule are only "evidence" and may be rebutted by other competent evidence that, given the injury, age, and occupation of a claimant, his ability to compete is impaired to an extent that differs from that provided by the schedule. In practice, this "evidence" has taken the character of a set of rules that are determinative of the amount of benefits.[24] The burden of proof that is required to demonstrate errors in the schedule is almost insuperable. Although the raters are subject to cross-examination, a rule of the commission limits the scope of questioning to checking whether the rater has correctly applied the rates of the schedule. The commission has repeatedly been accused of preventing the production of rebuttal evidence against schedule rates; such evidence has actually sometimes been openly ruled inadmissible, and when it has been admitted it has extremely rarely had any impact. The commission itself unwittingly concedes the point, when it shows that cross-examinations almost never result in changing the official rate, and uses that argument to discourage lawyers from cross-examining raters. The IAC has repeatedly sought in this way to "draw their [the parties'] attention . . . to the innate futility of the whole process of cross-examination," as the Legal Bureau put it in the 1959 report from which we quoted earlier.

In fact, the cross-examination of raters is often quite effective, as the persistence of the parties in using it indicates. It is a means of convincing the referee that, since the rating obtained is too low or too high, he should change his instructions to the rater, that is, his statement of the evidence of disability to which the rater applies the schedule. The rating is then changed, but through a hidden, unarticulated process; not by reasoned departure from the schedule rates, but by an *ad hoc* manipulation of the "factors" of disability to which the schedule is applied. The strategy is well known in compensation circles; IAC raters point out, in support of their criticisms of the "abuses of cross-examination," that their ratings are changed only seldom because of their own errors or of inadequacies in the schedule, and that alleged errors in ratings are typically the result of "inadequate or incomplete instructions" from the referees or of "misunderstandings" between them and the referee. Thus not only is the routine preserved, but a door is open for *ad hoc* accommodations that escape scrutiny and prevent the criticism and elaboration of policy. These difficulties account in large part for the persistent and seemingly contradictory criticisms the parties have addressed to the rating system—they find it both too rigid, unresponsive to change and to special individual needs, and too uncertain, often unpredictable in its application.

Routine has similarly affected the quality of the justifications the IAC offers in its decisions. The "findings of facts and conclusions of law" the agency is required to produce in support of its awards have often become standardized formulas, devoid of any reference to the concrete issues of the case. The referees have objected to the use of printed forms of findings and award on the ground this would undermine their "judicial" image. But they all avail themselves of such conveniences as mimeographed blank forms, or collections of instant formulas that can readily be copied by their secretaries. Since the early 1950's, the IAC has periodically requested legislation that would permit the parties to waive the writing and service of findings and referee reports on the ground it would thereby be saved much useless "paper work." When a lawyer wants to know the reasons behind an award, he hardly looks at the findings, but tries to gather them from the referee's reports of hearing and decision.

"Litigation Avoidance." Perhaps the most important consequence of the growing concern of the IAC with "production" problems has been an increasing tendency on the part of the agency to avoid its adjudicative responsibilities. A striking feature of the commission today is the amount of concern and energy it devotes to "litigation avoidance," a phrase recently coined to designate a variety of means by which the agency seeks to divert as many cases as it can from the process of trial and adjudication. The theory that warrants those efforts is that large numbers of cases do not "need" to be tried, either because they were filed "before a dispute has developed," or because they "should never have been controverted" and therefore have "no real litigable controversy." In support of such claims, the IAC offers abundant statistical evidence to the effect that (1) many cases are filed only to be taken off calendar, often on request of the applicant himself, and (2) many cases that are initially contested end up in a voluntary compromise.[25]

The "litigation avoidance" program began in the early 1950's when the commission decided to experiment with various methods of "preprocessing" applications, soon to be officially called "pretrial" and instituted in all agency offices. Incoming cases are screened and those that do not appear "ready" for trial are sorted out and set for a pretrial conference; the hope is that an amicable discussion will help to clear "misunderstandings," or to work out a settlement, or to bring the parties to stipulate to some potentially disputed facts and thus reduce the scope of the controversy.

In addition to pretrial, two other means of "avoiding litigation" at the screening stage have been developed in recent years. One of these consists in systematically taking off calendar all cases in which there is "no issue" or where there is only some "minor issue" that can await trial at a later date as an incident of some expected future controversy. This practice may be used in appropriate cases even when the parties have requested an immediate hearing. A second and still more recent innovation is a "summary procedure," by which, in selected cases, an award is made without hearing and on the sole basis of the application, the defendant's answer, and the medical reports filed by both parties following service of the application; the award is served with a "notice of intention to issue summary decision" in the absence of objection within ten days, and a mimeographed "report of referee," which concludes that "it is my opinion that the award accomplishes substantial justice to all parties expeditiously, inexpensively and without incumbrance"; in case of objection from any party, the matter is set for regular hearing or pretrial. Finally, the efforts at litigation avoidance have led to a resurgence of the legal information service of the agency. As a result of a conference between the IAC and representatives of insurance carriers and self-insurers in 1964, the information attorney was instructed to take a more active role in "litigation avoidance" and to transform his office into a conciliation service; his responsibility would be to dispel the "misunderstandings" between claimants and insurance adjusters that prevent the informal resolution of cases. Insurance companies would similarly instruct their adjusters to provide full cooperation toward the realization of this aim.

Those new programs may at first seem like a return to the old "informal" adjustment services the IAC had earlier renounced in professing its new judicial faith. In fact, many ideals of the past have been revived to support the acceptance of "litigation avoidance"; the faith in amicable problem-solving, and the emphasis on encouragement and education toward self-administration have seemingly been called back to the prominent place they used to hold in commission doctrine. Adversariness has again emerged as the prime enemy; one hears continuous complaints in the agency about "bloody applications," "trigger-happy" attorneys, and the "vicious animosity" in which the parties conduct their relations. These views were forcefully restated by the study commission that investigated the IAC in 1964–1965, and they made up the basic rationale of the reforms it recommended to the legislature. As a member of the group suggested in an interview, the target of the proposed reforms was to "get rid of adversariness." The report of the study commission was sharply critical of applicants' attorneys who file applications "at a time when no real dispute has developed between the parties";[26] ironically, the main reason it offered for the criticism was that this practice "starts many claims on the road to ultimate litigation and thereby diminishes the likelihood of amicable settlement."[27] It was equally critical of the slowness of payment by insurance companies, which causes suspicious workers and union representatives "in too many cases" to contact "an attorney as a source of guidance and information without waiting for a dispute to develop. Claims adjusters come to expect a controversy from the start and adopt methods of handling cases which assume a controversial attitude on the part of the injured workmen."[28] Therefore it concluded "that steps be taken to assure more communication and more prompt payment of benefits at the outset of disability," so that there be "less litigation".[29] It recommended that carriers be required to inform injured men regularly of the status of their claims, and that their compliance with this duty and their promptness in paying indemnities be regularly controlled by audits of their records.[30] Concerning the IAC, it recommended that the information services "be so directed that the filing of application for hearing becomes a last resort when litigation cannot otherwise be averted" and that they be entrusted to personnel "versed in the techniques of negotiation and amicable settlement and with amiable personal traits to facilitate undisputatious transactions"; in this way "all the disputes that derive from uncertainty and failure of communication could be materially reduced."[31] It also recommended that the use of informal ratings be expanded on the ground that they "should reduce the number of filings" before the agency.[32]

Yet, in spite of verbal similarities between the old doctrine of self-administration and the new "litigation avoidance," there are profound divergences in spirit and objective. The early idea of self-administration went along with a firm commitment to the social purposes of the workmen's compensation system; however deficient it may have been, it was thought of and used as a means of establishing the new law and realizing the rights and benefits that had been created. Since then this commitment has been greatly attenuated; the new "litigation avoidance" program has grown in response to internal needs of the agency, and not as a means of serving the constituency, even less as a means of promoting the law. It is aggressive in its tone; it scorns the "litigious," "inflexible" lawyer who abuses the services of the agency "for the sole purpose of making a big fee and showing his client he deserves it"; it has no patience with the "unreasonable" claimant who is unwilling to accept a "fair" compromise. The "convenience of the commission" is the primary aim, irrespective of consequences for the rights at stake.[33]

Of course, there may be abuses of litigiousness, but "litigation avoidance" cannot be explained as merely a response to abuse. There is little appreciation in the commission of the positive functions the sheer filing of an application performs for the implementation of the law. Not only does the application compel the defendant to disclose the medical reports he has gathered and will thereafter receive; it also routinely has two consequences that are crucial for the claimant. First, the carrier will usually raise his assessment of the "value" of the case and offer a higher settlement; second, and perhaps most important, the application transforms the claim into a legal case, with the result that the handling of the matter will usually be transferred from the carrier's claims department to his legal department or law firm. Decisions will henceforth be made by lawyers who are professionally more aware of the full extent of statutory obligations and more sensitive to the limits of lawfulness; by anyone's account, including insurance counsels and representatives, this makes a considerable difference for the injured man's interests. There is equally little appreciation in the IAC that its authority, and the determination to invoke it, are critically needed in the bargaining strategy of claimants who have no other weapon to advance their interests. The commission resents the fact that so much of its hearing time is "wasted" by parties who ultimately settle their case among themselves. There is even less appreciation that, beyond those immediate interests of the claimant in each particular case, the development of the law and the fulfillment of the rights it has conferred are dependent upon this partisan advocacy and upon the opportunities there are for the self-serving pursuit of legal interests. The IAC sees no place in its work for the too many claims that have "no validity whatsoever" and have "obviously no chance of getting anywhere"; such cases should be "cooled off" at the Information Desk or by the private attorneys who receive them. The commission is upset by "those attorneys who would try almost any case in the hope of forcing some sort of settlement out of it." It has little taste for the close or complex case that results in "endless litigation"; in its view, this is "the kind of case in which nobody can possibly benefit from litigation: these cases should be compromised; settlement is the only real solution."

Underlying those attitudes of the commission, there is a more general and basic unwillingness to recognize the profound extent to which conflict has been built into the very structure of the compensation system. To the IAC, litigation is a product of bad attitudes and suspect motivations—and not a rational response to the way in which compensation rights are defined and the conditions in which they have to be implemented. Adversariness is an outgrowth of "lack of communication," of "vicious animosity," "neurotic claimants," "suspicious adjusters," and "lawyers who are after their fees." The remedy is to remove the "misunderstandings" that are at the root of bad attitudes, and to control the motives, that is, the fees, that prevent amicable adjustment. As evidence for those claims, the commission points to the growing number of settlements and cases taken off calendar; but those statistics reflect more than free decisions by parties who have "needlessly" entered controversy. They are also indicative of the work the *agency* performs on the cases that are submitted to it. Therefore, instead of simply showing the extent of pointless controversies, they also reflect the extent to which the commission effectively discourages the litigation of controverted claims. Thus, although in many cases the parties themselves request that their cases be ordered off calendar, the order is often made by the IAC itself against the expressed desire of the parties. Similarly, the growing incidence of settlements must in part be a reflection of the mounting pressures the agency has put on the parties in order to obtain compromises. Those pressures are profoundly resented by compensation lawyers, especially when they come from referees in the course of contested hearings.[34] The commission appears indeed so penetrated with this concern for "amicable compromise" that there are widespread suspicions among the parties as to its willingness to decide even those cases it purports to decide. As one of our attorney informants put it in an interview:

> The Commission no longer decides its cases, it compromises them for us; it's too much work for them to look at the evidence and really judge it; they are too lazy to really make a choice as to who is right and who is wrong in the case. So, they take a figure in between and that's what they send you as their Findings and Award. Well, if they are to compromise it anyhow, I might as well settle the case myself, if it's possible at all.

The line is very thin, indeed, between "litigation avoidance" and "adjudication avoidance," between "needless" filings and controversy by the parties—which, to be sure, do occur—and evasions by the IAC of its responsibilities for decision.

That such evasions should occur in an agency that otherwise prizes its "judicial" character should not be surprising, given the kind of pressures under which its "judges" operate. The agency keeps detailed "performance records" of its referee staff. Each month a referee is required to submit a statement of the number of decisions he has issued, of the delayed cases that are still pending before him, and of the reasons for the delay in those cases. The data that are gathered in this process do not differentiate between decisions of different kind or difficulty. Whatever way a case has been terminated, it is worth the same credit to the referee who disposed of it. The fifteen minutes' review of a C&R file earns the same efficiency credit as a decision thought over a whole week-end after a series of long and difficult hearings. Maximum output is the aim, no matter what the quality of the product may be.[35] A referee who had been reprimanded for his lack of efficiency addressed an answer to the Chairman, which reads in part:

> I, personally, have observed on many occasions during my service with the Commission an approach to a case where the concern was directed more specifically to a desired statistical result rather than to the attainment of substantial justice to the parties. However appealing this may appear to others, to this I will not subscribe.

But the referee usually shares the perspectives of the commission. Thus a report on "simplification of procedure" prepared by a committee of referees in 1952 asserted that referees should be "relieved of non-judicial duties" and given recognition as judges, but procedures should be "streamlined to the optimum of efficiency" so as to avoid "slowing the output" in any "part of the machinery"; and, indeed, that the more the referee will be confined to his "judicial" duties, "the faster and better he can do his basic work." Thus judicial aspirations were made to converge with the necessities of production.

Average Justice

Together with a renewed emphasis on avoiding adversariness, the pressures of production have brought the revival of another old IAC doctrine—that the true aim of workmen's compensation is not "justice," but "average justice." In the report of the commission for 1913–1914, we read that:

> It is better for the state and for the people of the state that what may be termed "average justice" shall be speedily and inexpensively administered than that exact justice shall be striven for at a cost that, in many cases, would consume the entire amount involved and leave the applicant indebted for costs and expenses besides.[36]

And the head of the Rating Department made a similar point in 1929:

> Compensation acts attempt to give average justice to the average case, with such modifications as may be reasonably and fairly measured, without introducing too much refinement, and without leaving too much to human judgment, which would tend to argument and litigation.[37]

The justification for the doctrine of average justice was that standards applicable to the "average" case could be safely applied to all cases, in view of the fact that over a large number of cases injustices done in one direction would be balanced by injustices done in the other direction. This idea permitted the abandonment of the legal concept of "damages" assessed on the basis of the losses incurred in each particular case, and the establishment instead of a uniform schedule of benefits applicable to all cases. The IAC Permanent Disability Rating Schedule was the major embodiment of the idea of "average justice." As explained by one of the authors of the schedule in a report to the commission:

> There are other factors than those of age and occupation [the only factors besides physical injury taken into account by the California Schedule] entering into the matter, such as the makeup of the man, his desire to recover, his inherent adaptability, his general health, his nervous temperament, his surroundings,

> his opportunitites, his education, the attitude of his employer and his intelligence. All of these affect the individual only and are not capable of physical measurement or determination. Any schedule to be practicable must be based on conditions applying to the average man and must be designed to deal out average justice.

The major aim of the rating schedule and the doctrine of average justice was to remove the possibility of controversy over the assessment of cases. This aim in turn was closely related to the conception of a self-administered system based on consensus and cooperation among interested parties, and to the concern of the early IAC with keeping workmen's compensation free from "legalistic" influences. As a member of the staff reported to the IAC in 1947:

> The use of a binding schedule reduces the number of disputes on rating questions. . . . Extensive litigation would probably lead us away from the concept of compensation as social insurance back to the old common law concept of "damages."

Since the aim of compensation was "to cure and not to blame," the schedule would help avoid legal controversies and allow employers and administrators to set themselves to the real task—treatment and rehabilitation.

Later, the idea of average justice was considerably undermined by the strenuous attempts of unions and lawyers to enlarge compensation benefits and to make the law more responsive to the demands of claimants. The growth of ratings for such "subjective" factors as pain or psychic traumas was particularly significant in this respect. New rationales, such as "equal treatment," were sought for the rating schedule; justice, rather than "average justice," required uniform handling of like injuries.

But in recent years, internal agency problems have given new relevance to the old doctrine; the pressures of production made average justice particularly appealing as a definition of the work of the IAC. As now understood, the idea suggests that the agency should be relieved from the burdens of detailed analysis and deliberation of each particular case. Uniform treatment designed for the handling of the "average" case is what everyone is entitled to; no party should expect any special consideration. "Complex" cases, those that upset the routines, can then be shown to be unfit for decision by the commission, on the ground that, as stated by one of our informants from the IAC:

> Workmen's compensation has not been set up to provide this kind of exact justice. It's written in the Constitution: it says there that we are supposed to give "*substantial* justice in all cases without incumbrance of any character." It says

substantial, not exact. The whole system of workmen's compensation, and the Rating Schedule, are made for the average man.

The idea of average justice does another service for the IAC—avoiding adversariness. In the early commission also, the doctrine was intended to reduce litigiousness. But the purpose differed significantly; adversariness was to be overcome in order to free energies for practical action. Today, average justice has the very opposite aim of providing a defense for the agency against the growing burdens of decision that controversy has created. Thus, in a recent administrative communication discussing possible legislation on the quite thorny legal problem of how to determine the "earnings" on the basis of which benefits are computed, the author suggests that "we ought to find a good average justice solution to this issue." From the agenda of a commission meeting in 1962, we read about a legislative amendment bearing on the same question, that would have made the determination of earnings "mathematical" and no longer "a subject for tortuous litigation," "so simple that an average worker will readily understand." An "average justice solution" is one that specifies a clear-cut rule, to which the agency can stick without having to face controversial issues of interpretation and policy. It is "average," in the sense that the rule is rationalized with reference to the "average," or "common," or "simple" case, and then generalized in such a way as to exclude from consideration the special issues that might arise in cases deviating from the "average."

Adjudication and the Flight from Policy

We have dwelt in the last few pages on the tendency of the IAC to slight its adjudicative responsibilities. This point needs some further analysis in the light of other characteristic features of the agency. The tendency may have been set in motion by the growing problems of production and efficiency the commission has met; but it had more profound roots in the perspectives of the agency, which made it a particularly attractive course of action.

Those roots can be found in the administrative doctrine the agency evolved in the process of its retreat from social action. Up to a point, administrative withdrawal entailed positive contributions to the development of a judicial posture in the IAC. It did, indeed, convert the commission into an agency that saw its primary mandate as responding to individual demands and lending them the protection of its authority. When an agency becomes primarily oriented to the *recognition of claims*, when it develops this dominant concern with the impact of public policy on individual interests, it begins taking on the attributes of a court. Administration gives precedence to the accomplishment of the social objectives defined in public policy; in this perspective, individual claims appear as incidental to this pursuit. They may provide opportunities for the furtherance of public objectives, or conversely they may raise obstacles to it; they are treated accordingly. In adjudication the perspective is reversed; in a court, public policy is tested in view of the interests of the persons affected. This may indeed be the special competence of adjudication, that it can recognize such interests and lend them protection. This does not mean adjudication will necessarily involve, on the part of the decider, a weaker commitment to state policy; nor that it will of necessity be subversive of public action. Rather its concern will be to define such limits on opportunism and expediency in the pursuit of policy objectives as will give security to recognized interests. In so doing, it may extend as well as restrict the policies involved; it may take them as sources of rights, as well as limit them in view of rights they threaten; it may facilitate, enhance, or indeed compel the pursuit of their aims, as well as restrain or impede this pursuit.

Thus, although the adjudicator does tend to adopt a more detached and critical posture toward policy, it does not follow that his fidelity to policy and public aims is thereby attenuated. For, as we have argued earlier, another and indeed essential characteristic of adjudiction is that it holds the decider *accountable to rules and principles.* Adjudication has unique potentials for recognizing the claims of persons affected by public policy. But those potentials are linked to a special manner of reaching decisions by making and applying rules. The task of a court is not merely to work out compromises or accommodations between particular claims and governmental desires. And, indeed, the claims it handles are not simply blunt assertions of will or wishes that it then would confront with public aspirations. Rather they are demands that claim for themselves a justification in principle. The court is asked to subject those claims to a process of reasoned assessment on the basis of authoritative standards. Thus, whether they challenge a policy or appeal to it, claims of right always involve an attempt to test the authority of that policy; they request the court to define the extent and limits of that authority, to weigh it against competing standards, and assess it in view of established principles.

Policy can thus be a central concern of the adjudicator, even though he views it from the point of view of the person affected. His approach to policy issues is of course characteristically different from that of the administrator. To the latter, policy is an expedient for the accomplishment of certain objectives; administration tends to underscore the *instrumental* character of standards. Policies have weight only insofar as they are capable of reaching their expected outcome. In the early IAC, compensation was taken as a means of reducing poverty, of rehabilitating the disabled; benefits could always be withdrawn if they were not shown to contribute to that end. Being responsible for results, the administrator insists on preserving the freedom to respond to concrete problems on their own terms; he cannot afford to let policies become binding upon him and sources of entitlement to the constituents. But those are precisely the issues with which adjudication is concerned—to what extent does a policy carry binding authority and establish rights? To what extent should it be restricted in view of other binding standards and vested rights? The adjudicator emphasizes the *normative* aspect of standards; he looks at policies as moral commitments to the citizenry that the latter can invoke in support of its demands. That is not to say that he is unconcerned with the actual consequences of policies and their effectiveness in accomplishing public aims. He will indeed be compelled to examine consequences insofar as they have a bearing upon the authoritativeness of the policies under scrutiny. It is, however, typical of adjudication that the decider is not free to manipulate applicable standards in view of the outcome he desires in particular cases. He is expected to "let the chips fall where they may," in accordance with binding norms; he is not free to extend or restrict a policy for the sole reason his decisoin will produce some "good" or "bad" result. Results become salient only when and insofar as they warrant the making or application of some authoritative standard that is or will be binding on the decider. Therefore, the difference between administration and adjudication is not that one involves discretion whereas the other does not. The judge may, indeed, have considerable leeway in choosing and interpreting the standards he applies; his distinctiveness lies in the special perspective in which he exercises his discretion—the concern for affected persons—and in the special burden of justification that is thrown upon him in view of this responsibility for the protection of rights. Accountability to rules does not necessarily reduce discretion; rather it disciplines its exercise by imposing on the decider a duty to establish a reasoned relation between his judgment and recognized authoritative standards.

In spite of these differences in perspectives and modes of accountability, it remains that both administration and adjudication share in the task of making and applying social policies. For certain purposes, the similarity may actually be as critical as the difference. An administrative agency needs energy and commitment in developing and implementing its policies. But it may take as much, if not more, strength for an adjudicator to announce a new rule; for the policy thus announced is not one that remains open to *ad hoc* accommodations; it has binding authority, it vests rights that will have to be recognized. And it takes as much, if not more, fidelity to established policy for an adjudicator to stick to the rule "without respect for consequences"—a position the administrator can avoid, if need be, by the prudent defense that "of course there is nothing inflexible to this policy."[38]

This is the point at which the withdrawal of the IAC from its administrative responsibilities becomes salient to the assessment of its "judicial" character. The retreat of the agency meant more than renouncing the active pursuit of the injured men's welfare; it meant more than abandoning a commitment to the partisan interests of a private group. It was a *flight from policy.* The loss of authority it entailed had significant consequences for the competence of the commission as a court.

In the setting of organized group conflict that characterizes workmen's compensation, political consensus is hard to create and remains always precarious. Policy-making is a controversial enterprise, in which the legitimacy of authority is exposed to continuing assault. That is what the IAC sought to avoid when it retreated from administration to the determination of claims. To the agency, the focus on individual claims was a way of depoliticizing the compensation controversy, a means of avoiding policy issues and the necessity of making political choices that would expose it to challenge. This point is crucial; it accounts both for the growing acceptance by the commission of a judicial concept of its role and for the particularly selective character of this acceptance. In the eyes of the commission, a judicial posture would offer a refuge from the responsibilities and hazards of policy-making.

In practice, the refuge has tended to become more and more elusive. As organized groups on both sides took over the task of promoting and sponsoring the presentation of claims before the agency, even those seemingly narrow individual disputes began assuming a political character. The focus of controversies was displaced from the particular claims at hand to the policy issues and class interests for which they stood. The agency was again being pressed to take sides and to expose itself. Actually, the more the commission was made subject to those judicial standards of procedure its doctrine called for, the greater the pressure became; the agency was urged to give reasons for its decisions, to account for particular results in terms of announced rules, and, indeed, to hold itself open to criticism at all stages of its processes. The politicalization of the legal debate was more than the IAC could take, given the precariousness of its authority. Therefore it is hardly surprising that the agency would resist the growth of procedural standards, at the same time as it professed its judicial faith. Before authority can respond to argument and criticism it must be secure enough to face challenge and appreciate its value.[39]

The whole pattern of "litigation avoidance" becomes clearer in the light of this flight from policy. A settled case does more than save time. Actually the time saved may be quite unworthy of the efforts invested in saving it.[40] But a case avoided is a decision avoided; it saves authority if not time. Thus much more efforts are made to reach a settlement in "close" or "complex" cases than in matters deemed "clear-cut." Although the latter would presumably be easier to terminate amicably, they do not raise any problem of authority; the rule is clear and undisputable. The former, on the contrary, may be quite troublesome; as a referee indicated in an interview:

> If I decide it, one side is bound to be dissatisfied. Whatever I find, it's going to go on reconsideration, and whatever happens with the panel [of Commissioners who will decide on reconsideration] the whole thing is going to end with bitter feelings on both sides. So, I try to get them to listen to a little good sense.

In a profound sense, the IAC has lost much of the ability, characteristic of a court, to decide "without respect for consequences"; not because it makes its awards in view of any specific result it favors, but because, in its eyes, only those outcomes are satisfactory that do not harm one party more than the other. To the commission the ideal decision is the one the parties would have reached had they compromised their difference.

In this perspective, the efforts to reduce and avoid controversy appear quite consistent with the obsessive concern of the IAC with its "judicial" purity. Both help the agency to avoid committing itself to policy. This accounts for the primarily symbolic character of the commission's emphasis on judicial impartiality. The focus is more on the signs of impartiality than on its substance; in this way, the IAC can avoid assisting incompetent injured men and evade responsibility for the integrity of the medical expertise upon which it relies, even though it may thereby allow its processes to become biased in favor of more powerful defendants.

That is not to say that the judicial doctrine has no other significance for the agency. In the many routine cases where the applicable policy is settled and well understood, judicial accountability has been quite effective in legitimizing IAC decisions. There the agency has found in rules a shield against pressures to exercise discretion and relax policy, and a defense against criticisms addressed to the consequences of its decisions. In such case a rule offers a means of denying authorship of one's decisions and referring issues to some other responsible policy-maker, for example, the courts or the legislature. The IAC has come to value this important advantage of sticking to the rules by which it is bound. Many political pressures can be averted in this way. More generally, the agency can avoid being held to account for the results of its actions; rules have relieved it of the burdens of administrative discretion. It is at ease and confident in its handling of "clear-cut" cases, and in them, at least, its claim to judicial status appears rather solid and warranted.

But a court need not be a slot machine; although the majority of IAC cases belong to that "clear-cut" class, the more important ones are the others. And if the main value of judicial accountability lies in the defensive advantage of sticking to the rules, there is a danger that the agency will be unwilling to respond even to the legally warranted challenges that may be addressed to seemingly "settled" rules. What looks like fidelity to rules may then become another way of evading adjudicative policy-making; it transforms into a kind of *legalism.* A rigid adherence to formal rules comes to prevent the decider from responding to claims and needs that the law would otherwise be competent to protect. Legalism is very much alive in the IAC; it is particularly evident in the almost compulsive manner in which the agency enforces its permanent disability rating schedule. At this point it makes little difference whether the IAC is asked to unsettle a "clear-cut" rule, or to settle an admittedly ambiguous issue; whether it blindly sticks to past policy or seeks to compromise differences. Both reactions respond to the same problem of a precarious authority that is unable to manage the fires of controversy.

Today, with the problems of authority that paralyze it, the commission would often seem to be more successful as a mediator than it is as adjudicator. Forty-five percent of its decisions are orders approving compromises, in spite of a law that is in principle restrictive of settlement.[41] Mediation is, indeed, the mode of conflict resolution that is best adapted to avoiding issues of principle and policy; it builds upon consensus and averts the escalation of controversies into radical challenges. There, fidelity to policy is at its lowest. But the mediator becomes resourceless when he is confronted with basic distrust and morally unyielding claimants on all sides, and is asked to account for the ground of his actions. If it is to be trusted, the commission needs those warrants of integrity and accountability the model of a court offers. Those are the constraints that have put the IAC on the path of its judicial development. However, they have not solved the critical problem of authority that has plagued the agency ever since the 1930's. Before the commission acquires the ability to confront political conflict with ease and security, before it can authoritatively announce its choices and lay down its reasons, before it can face the ambiguous, unsettle the obvious, and see to the integrity of established policies and processes—before it can achieve the judicial status it has set as its goal—much will have to be done to free it from the captivity in which its constituents have placed it, and to give it the kind of institutional security that will protect it against political assault.

If we compare the IAC with other institutions we routinely designate as "courts," that is, agencies of the formal judicial system, it is true of course that the commission is very much like other courts. Most "courts" in that sense do not care, or are only beginning to concern themselves, for the rights of the unrepresented; most courts seek to promote amicable settlements and to avoid delay and "needless" litigation; most courts are at ease only with the more routine tasks of adjudication; most courts shy away from issues of policy, and prefer to leave them up to the appellate bodies. But those tendencies appear less significant in tribunals whose main job is to settle a disparate array of individual disputes, of little apparent import beyond the parties immediately involved. Most courts do not usually confront the kind of legal controversy the IAC faces.

First, the IAC is a specialized court. It has special jurisdiction over problems arising under a determinate set of legal principles; hence the cases that come before the agency raise continuously and systematically the same kinds of issues between the same parties. This specialization entails a more sharply defined responsibility for maintaining the integrity of legal principles; at the same time it provides a ground for claiming a special expertise and authority.

Second, and more important, in workmen's compensation the basis of adversariness has shifted from individual to group conflict. Under such conditions, the political character of legal controversy acquires a greater salience. What matters in this context is less the resolution of particular disputes than the authoritative determination of policy and the fulfillment of purpose. A court may then be asked to make full use of the resources of adjudication for making and interpreting policy.

Judicialization opened new opportunities for the IAC to assume a positive role in the realization of legal purposes. The failure to seize those opportunities reflects an impoverished understanding of the potentials of adjudication, and points to the limitations of the agency's competence as a court.

Notes to Chapter VIII

1. Such was the argument made in 1915 by a referee and legal counsel for the Industrial Accident Commission. See Warren H. Pillsbury, "An Experiment in Simplified Procedures," *California Law Review*, Vol. III, No. 3 (March, 1915), pp. 181–194.

2. See, for instance: "Report of the Northern Section of the Committee on Practice and Procedure before the Industrial Accident Commission," *Journal of the State Bar of California*, Vol. VIII, No. 9 (1933), pp. 45–56; and Delger Trowbridge, "Functions and Status of Judicial Officers of the Industrial Accident Commission," *Journal of the State Bar of California*, XI (1936), 205–211.

3. *Investigation of Procedure of the Industrial Accident Commission* (Sacramento: California Legislature, Assembly, Subcommittee of the Interim Committee on Governmental Efficiency and Economy, 1945). Hereafter cited as *Investigation of IAC Procedure, 1945*, p. 83.

4. See, for instance, *ibid.*, pp. 48, 82.

5. *Ibid.*, p. 11.

6. *Ibid.*, p. 7.

7. *Ibid.*, p. 92.

8. California Statutes of 1951, Chap. 778. See also Chap. VII, pp. 184–187, and references cited.

9. California Statutes of 1951, Chap. 1613, Sec. 54; California Labor Code, Sec. 123.

10. Objections to this policy were first voiced in 1944, when the referees petitioned the State Personnel Board for a reclassification of their position as "judicial." Parts of the record of those proceedings are quoted in *Investigation of IAC Procedure, 1945*, pp. 124–125.

11. The qualifications required were graduation from a law school and 5 years of legal practice or "some other equivalent combination" of education and experience. The referees insisted that the requirement of 5 years of legal practice should be made absolute. In 1955, they obtained partial satisfaction under new rules that required 5 years of practice or 3 years as a full-time hearing officer in an agency or court conducting judicial or quasi-judicial proceedings.

12. Quoted from an unpublished text of the referees' argument submitted at a legislative hearing in 1962. See *Report of the Assembly Interim Committee on the Judiciary* (Sacramento: California Legislature, 1963), pp. 34–44. The salaries of commission members were determined in amount by statute (California Government Code, Sec. 11550 ff; California Labor Code, Sec. 112). The referees' demands for a salary at a judicial level would have placed them above their superiors in salary.

13. *Report of the Workmen's Compensation Study Commission* (Sacramento: State of California, April, 1965), p. 108; California Administrative Code, Title 8, Chap. 4.5, *Rules of Practice and Procedure of the Industrial Accident Commission*, Sec. 10820.

14. California Administrative Code, Title 8, Chap. 4.5, *Rules of Practice and Procedure*, Sec. 10850 (c).

15. California Administrative Code, Title 8, Chap. 4.5, *Rules of Practice and Procedure*, Sec. 9752.

16. In spite of a recommendation of the recent study commission, that referees be called "hearing officers," their formal title has not been changed (*Report of the Workmen's Compensation Study Commission*, p. 71).

17. See, for example, *Final Report of the Assembly Interim Committee on the Judiciary* (Sacramento: California Legislature, 1963), pp. 40–43.

18. See Chap. VII, p. 193, and references cited.

19. Unpublished statistics for the year 1962 indicate that, whereas applications filed in Los Angeles amount to 31.5 percent of the reported injuries for that area, the corresponding amount for San Francisco is only 23.5 percent.

20. *Report of the Workmen's Compensation Study Commission*, p. 64.

21. California Administrative Code, Title 8, Chap. 4.5, *Rules of Practice and Procedure*, Sec. 10773.

22. California Administrative Code, Title 8, Chap. 4.5, *Rules of Practice and Procedure*, Sec. 10794.5.

23. California Labor Code, Sec. 4660.

24. The law itself has recognized that the rating schedule amounts to more than "evidence" and is practically a set of rules determining the level of benefits. This has indeed been the main rationale for holding that changes in the schedule must be applied prospectively, just as all changes in "substantive" provisions, and in contrast to rules of evidence and procedure that can be applied immediately to all pending cases. See California Labor Code, Sec. 4660, and the discussion and references cited in Chap. VII, p. 197.

25. A discussion of this evidence, very much in line with IAC interpretations, can be found in *Report of the Workmen's Compensation Study Commission*, pp. 81–89.

26. *Ibid.*, p. 86.

27. *Ibid.*, p. 87.

28. *Ibid.*, p. 186.

29. *Ibid.*

30. *Ibid.*, pp. 186–193.

31. *Ibid.*, p. 73.

32. *Ibid.*, pp. 78–81.

33. Summary decisions are issued even though important issues may be overlooked. As a member of the staff puts it, "We assume that temporary disability has been paid; if it has not, the party can always protest." The Industrial Accident Commission implicitly recognizes the potential damage involved; it has a policy not to issue summary decisions in cases where the applicant is unrepresented. In a recent issue of a newsletter published for the insurance industry, one reads that, at a discussion among carriers' representatives, it was reported that "about half of the [summary] judgments met with objections and half did not. [The report] continued that applicants' attorneys were the objectors four times as often as defense attorneys." But in an interview a member of the staff of the commission asserted that "most of the objections are for the sheer purpose of getting an increased fee." Only through a decision of the commission either by award or by approval of C&R can the attorney's fee be determined "reasonable" and a lien for its payment be granted on the benefits payable by the insurer.

34. Continuing complaints are heard among them that one can hardly appear before a referee without being asked whether the possibilities of compromise have been fully explored; that too many referees refuse to hear a case before having been shown that "reasonable" efforts to settle have been made; that referees often recess the hearing for the best part of the time allowed to the case, for the purpose of "giving" the attorneys a chance to discuss settlement, and then force a continuance of the case on the ground there is not enough time left to hear it; that the parties are often compelled to fake a settlement discussion in order to convince the referee that they have a *bona fide* controversy.

35. *Report of the Workmen's Compensation Study Commission*, p. 71.

36. *Report of the Industrial Accident Commission, 1913–1914* (Sacramento: California Legislature, 41st Sess., 1915) Appendix to the *Journals of the Senate and Assembly*, Vol. I, No. 14, p. 8. See also *Proceedings of the Conference on Social Insurance* (Washington, D.C.: U.S. Department of Labor, Bureau of Labor Statistics, December, 1916), Bull. No. 212, p. 203.

37. *Proceedings of the Annual Safety Convention of the Lumbermen's Accident Prevention Association*, San Francisco, June 1929, n.p., n.d., p. 37.

38. Moreover, a court may well need the same kind of "administrative" resources as an agency needs for the implementation of its policies. It may, for instance, need appropriate means of investigation if it is to preserve its competence to recognize interests that warrant legal protection and evolve remedies that adequately meet those claims. It may need the ability to provide counsel to its claimants if it is to preserve the integrity of its proceedings.

39. The precariousness of the IAC authority is deeply felt by the members of the commission. Although some of them sit on the board at least informally as representatives of interested groups, they are all quite careful to avoid conveying any impression of dissent among themselves. One commissioner stated in an interview: "I would hate to expose any of my colleagues to criticism that would harm him and embarrass the commission." It practically never happens that a decision issues with a dissenting opinion.

40. It is widely believed that a large proportion of pretrials are virtually a waste of time; that settlements often come when the case has almost completely been fought out; that most orders taking off calendar only delay the time when the case will be litigated. This is not to say that the problems of mass production are not real and that agency efforts are not genuine. The parties themselves often remind the agency of its duty to avoid delay. The point is that, in confronting those problems, the agency has laid special emphasis on a set of means that had political value for it, irrespective of their effectiveness in meeting production problems.

41. See Chap. VII, p. 173, and references there cited.

IX Legal Development and Institutional Change

LEGALIZATION HAS BEEN A central theme of this study. We have traced the emergence of legal perspectives in a contested area of social policy. We have explored the conditions that foster a competent use of and participation in the legal process. And we have seen the impact of these changes on the role of government, especially the drift from administrative to judicial discretion. In this chapter we consider some of the larger issues that arise from the interplay of legalization, administration, and politics.

From Policy to Law

As the IAC drifted from administration to adjudication, workmen's compensation evolved from a piece of welfare legislation into a part of the law of employment. The story of the IAC offers an opportunity to explore the meaning and significance of a broader question: When and how does a set of official policies, statutory or administrative, become "Law"?

As we have pointed out at the beginning of this study, a principal concern of the early commission was to keep workmen's compensation insulated from the law; the agency wanted to preserve its program not only from the impact of adverse legal doctrines, but more generally from contamination by the techniques and perspectives of the legal process. Even otherwise "good" policies would be distorted if they were transformed into legally binding rules; they would lose their adaptiveness to concrete experience. Had the commission had its way, workmen's compensation would have been built into the framework of public welfare and social insurance programs; its standards would have been those of professional expertise and political prudence.

A mere glance at a modern treatise on workmen's compensation shows how deeply this ideal has been frustrated. Workmen's compensation legislation has become vitally imbedded in the corpus of legal doctrines. Of course, abstract connections have always been made between its concepts of liability and parallel concepts in other branches of the law. But today the roots that workmen's compensation has thrust into the law have become much more profound and significant for practical problem-solving; there is hardly a compensation question that does not involve some consideration of legal concepts and principles beyond the specific provisions of the statute. Workmen's compensation has become intimately tied to the law of employment. Was there an employment contract? Was the injury related to employment? What is the impact of collective contract benefits on the right to compensation? It is also tied to the law of contract. What was the remuneration of the employee? Was the employer insured? Did insurance coverage extend to the injury or occupational classification involved? Workmen's compensation has become tied to the law of torts. When is there a causal relationship between injury and employment? What is an act of God? Is there a third party liable? Does the employer have a right of subrogation? It is tied to the law of persons. What members of the family or household qualify as dependents? What is the impact of the status of prisoner or parolee on compensation rights? And, of course, it is tied to the many branches of the law, constitutional, administrative, civil procedure, and evidence, that make up the law of the judicial process. The modern setting of workmen's compensation is thoroughly legal; also, quite characteristically, it is a setting from which the ideals, policies, and perspectives of public welfare are conspicuously absent. To be sure, there is a literature that treats workmen's compensation from the parties and administrators alike, who operate within the system; and it holds fare. But it has come mainly from outside critics and scholars, not from those, parties and administrators alike, who operate within the system; and it holds very little place on the office shelves or in the minds of those actors. Compensation has been incorporated into the law, and in this process withdrawn from the realm of administrative problem-solving.

Although in an obvious sense statutes are law, it takes a long work of legal analysis to transform a discrete piece of legislation into developed law, in the sense of law embedded in and informed by a larger matrix of legal thought. Ideas and policies must be scrutinized in their potential relations to known legal concepts and principles; in this process arguments come to be framed for new lines of development in policy, new interpretations, and new discriminations; those arguments must then be pressed for recognition as authoritative. Although the energies for this work may come from many varied sources, including legal scholarship and various legal authorities acting on their own, adversariness may, as we have seen, provide special impetus for legal development. It does so when conflict is transformed from a blunt confrontation of adverse interests into a vehicle of legal criticism and controversy.

Reliance on partisan criticism, as a source of legal development, is, of course, nothing new to the law; indeed, it has been a fundamental premise of the Anglo-American legal system. But representative groups and organized advocacy impart to it a more concerted and systematic character. What has qualified legal criticism as a tool for concerted social action is its special competence to gear the law to the demands and experience of affected persons. It confers on legal institutions a sensitivity to problems and opportunities that they might never acquire if they were to depend on legal scholarship or on pronouncements from hierarchical authority as their main source of development. Law then becomes a politically effective instrument. It permeates the practical world, is used in day-to-day problem-solving, and constitutes both resource and target for a continuing process of change. Legal institutions are thereby rooted in society, not only in the theoretical ways that sociological inquiry would postulate or uncover, but through an institutionalized process of dialogue and interaction. Although, as we shall see, this political use of legal criticism may create special strains for the legal order, it also fosters the growth of a deeper commitment on the part of the citizen to the institutions and the special mode of government that law offers; to those, at least, who can participate in the legal process, law becomes a social instrument the value of which is continuously demonstrated in day-to-day action. This can be seen in the massive involvement of employees and employers in the process of compensation adjudication and their growing use of legal advocacy as a preferred strategy in the promotion of their interests.

Thus, the fact that legalization has removed workmen's compensation from the ambit of welfare does not mean that the law has lost its effectiveness in meeting the demands of injured workers and industry; quite the contrary. What has changed rather is the way problems are defined and resolved.

Law and Authority. With legalization, policies are transformed into rules that bind the decider. Law is a source of restraints on authority; this is particularly striking in the case of the adjudicator, who must not only decide within the *limits* imposed by rules on his discretion, but is required to justify the outcome of his judgment *by* authoritative principles. By contrast, although the administrator is always subject to a variety of limitations set by rules on his powers, he is also allowed a range of discretion within such limits. He is thereby permitted to respond to concrete situations in view of his expert assessment of problems, alternatives, and expected results. Within this range of discretion, he takes policies only as guides, the authority of which remains always conditional upon his experience and open to reassessment in the light of his expertise. Should a rule come in his way, the effective administrator will typically seek to reconstrue it as just a policy directive.

This conception of policy, just as the idea of a binding rule, is of course always more a model toward which the administrator strives, than an established reality. In practice, it continuously tends to be frustrated; internal pressure for consistency, appeals to precedent by the constituency, routinization and bureaucratization, all work to confer on administrative policies a more rigid and binding character than would ideally be recognized. Legalization is a natural pathology of administration. It takes energy to preserve and exercise discretion; deciding by rules is generally easier and safer, more conservative.

The contrasting conceptions of policy that characterize administration and adjudication correspond to different definitions of the issues to be resolved. As has been suggested,

> The administrator . . . looks to an end-in-view, the refashioning of human or other resources so that a particular outcome will be achieved. A judge becomes an administrator when his objective is to reform a criminal, avert a strike, or abate a nuisance. For then his aim is not justice but accomplishment, not fairness but therapy.
>
> Administration may be controlled by law, but its special place in the division of labor is to get the work of society done, not to realize the ideals of legality. Adjudication also gets work done, in settling disputes, but this is secondary and not primary. The primary function of adjudication is to discover the legal coordinates of a particular situation. That is a far cry from manipulating the situation to achieve a desired outcome.[1]

To the administrator, as we have shown before, issues are defined as social problems that call for action with a view to the accomplishment of some determinate result. The emphasis on expertise and discretion in the implementation of policy is an outcome of this orientation toward concrete action. To the adjudicator, on the contrary, issues are structured as competing moral claims, involving an appeal to principle, and which call for a determination of authoritativeness.

We have already pointed to some of those differences as they were relevant to procedural standards and rules of accountability. They also have important substantive consequences. One of the most interesting instances of administrative reasoning in the early IAC is its handling of "neurosis" cases. In a report written by the head of the Rating Department in 1923, one finds the following account of the origin and rationale of agency policies concerning those cases:

> The proper basis for awarding compensation in cases of traumatic neurosis is one of the most difficult in compensation. . . . Frequently the medical reports from neurologists in such cases advised that the best method of disposing of the cases was by settlement, the reason being that the condition was a mental one, and the employee knowing that a final settlement had been made would forget his trouble

and soon return to work. In order to have a settlement made it was necessary to agree to a proper amount and in many cases this was found to be impossible. It was felt that some method must be taken to force the employee to return to work and forget his trouble, yet the medical reports acknowledged that he was disabled by reason of the neurotic condition directly traceable to his injury, and was not malingering. The man, therefore, under the law was entitled to disability indemnity.

A policy was adopted, for that reason, of issuing an award in such a case cutting the man's disability indemnity in half in the hope of forcing him to work, and that by work his condition would be remedied. At the same time that the award was made for disability indemnity, an order was issued for medical treatment in a hospital for a period of thirty days, the employee being cut off if he failed to cooperate. This was done in the hope that by a course of treatment, including work, he might be cured.

In a memorandum of the Compensation Department in 1931, it was acknowledged that the "neurotic" claimant "theoretically should be entitled to total disability, where the neurosis is in fact disabling"; but this did not impress the IAC in view of the "difficulty . . . that if we give total disability the neurosis would continue and the man would never get better." The policy apparently encouraged some abuses; insurance physicians were too prone to report as "neurotic" symptoms that could have been signs of serious physical injury. The 1923 report from which we have quoted explains how the IAC responded to this problem:

In cases arising particularly from injuries to the head and back, it has frequently been found that while the physicians in their examinations made a diagnosis of neurosis and found no pathological conditions to account for the condition, yet later developments have shown that there was a pathological condition and that it was merely a case where modern medical methods could not discover a pathological condition. It has been felt, therefore, that where an employee suffered a severe injury, particularly in head cases, an injustice might be done him by entirely closing the case even though the doctors at the time could not find pathological symptoms.

In many such cases, for that reason, a settlement agreement between the parties has been approved by the Commission. The insurance company, however, has entered into a gentlemen's agreement in writing with the Commission that if within a definite time, varying from a year to four and one-half years in time [four and one-half years from the date of the injury was the continuing jurisdiction of the Commission] they would consent to reopen the case where the condition of the injured party became such as to justify such proceedings in the opinion of the Commission. . . .

> It will be seen from the above that no fixed policy has been developed to apply to all traumatic neurosis cases.

The so-called "gentlemen's agreement" amounted to a waiver by the employer or carrier of his defense of lack of good cause against potential petitions to reopen the case under the continuing jurisdiction of the IAC. It was progressively detached from the specific problems of "neurosis" cases for which it had been originally designed, and was used in a variety of cases where the specific consequences of the injury were hard to determine, but potentially serious and likely to develop over the course of time. In such cases, should the claimant have to wait for clear symptoms to develop, he would have been barred by the statute of limitations; should he simply settle for a meager compromise, his case would have been in effect removed from the continuing jurisdiction of the commission and later remedies would have been barred. The "gentlemen's agreements" purported to resolve this dilemma. In addition, they included a curious provision to the effect that "It is understood that the fact that this agreement has been entered into will not be communicated to the employee, his friends, or representative." The rationale for this provision was explained in a memorandum from the Compensation Department in 1931:

> The whole theory of a gentlemen's agreement is that it should be kept absolutely secret from the man himself and his attorney. If it is known that there is a gentlemen's agreement in a case it will affect the employee's state of mind and he will never get well, and it will counteract the intended effect of the settlement agreement.

Thus, what was originally a means of keeping open the possibility of future remedies for claimants whose present rights were "doubtful" tended to become in practice a means of denying the possibility of future redress in cases in which the commission found such final settlement of "therapeutic" value. Whichever way they worked, "gentlemen's agreements" were meant to free the agency from otherwise authoritative policies and to give it discretion in the provision of relief and rehabilitation.

A similar impatience with legal restraints underlies the "exacerbation awards" the IAC issued in hernia cases. In those cases it was often difficult to distinguish between the parts played by employment and by prior disease in causing the disabling hernia. The commission was irritated at the idea of having to give a yes-or-no answer to the question of compensability; few cases would warrant finding the hernia industrially caused, and therefore many deserving applicants would be left without a remedy. From a 1928 report of the Compensation Department, we learn how the commission found "that it was advisable to put as many employees back in as an efficient working status as possible" and decided to grant benefits to a maximum number of claimants, but in reduced amounts:

> With the idea of returning as many men as possible to an efficient working status, it developed that the exacerbation award was given in nearly all cases and unless there were extreme conditions at either end of the line, the award would be an exacerbation award, giving him operation and no indemnity except after a ten weeks period, the ten weeks period being put in with the idea that if the disability lasted for a very long time it was unfair not to allow him compensation.
>
> The bulk of the cases, therefore, at the present time, come under the exacerbation award. We have fewer denials of award and fewer full awards.

The report was followed by an official restatement of the "hernia policy," which specified that "The policy here outlined is *intended to serve as a guide and can not be considered as binding in all hernia cases.*"[2]

In the framework of administrative discretion, the range of relevant factors that may affect decisions is kept very broad and indeterminate. To the early IAC, such factors included not only the "needs" of injured workers but also the capacities of industry as a resource for meeting those needs. Thus, it was important to take account, if possible, of the necessity of maintaining smooth relations with insurance carriers. The IAC had a special word for decisions that were made in that perspective—they were "euphonious awards." This meant, for example, that if a carrier's agent had made some "honest" mistake, either way, or manifested "good will" in his handling of a case, he should not be rebuffed by a too harshly adverse decision. We read, for instance, from a memorandum addressed by the head of the Compensation Department to a commissioner in 1932, that a referee was reprimanded for having found

> . . . that the hernias were not caused or exacerbated by the employment or the injury in a case where the adjuster voluntarily furnished the operation. He [the adjuster] naturally does not look forward to the criticism that he is bound to receive from the home office.
>
> The writer has often had occasion to refer to such problems, using the term "euphonious awards." It has always seemed unnecessary cruelty to deliberately make findings that may bring criticism on an insurance carrier, or its representatives. . . .
>
> It is hard to even touch on the various angles of this problem within the scope of a letter, as such decisions followed by the reprimand that is bound to follow will simply cause an adjuster to be exceedingly strict rather than liberal as the law intends. This will increase the number of cases brought to the Commission,

in addition to causing unnecessary delay and inconvenience to the injured parties.

By the late 1930's, all those practices had acquired the stigma of illegitimacy. A formal commission resolution in 1939 abolished the "gentlemen's agreement" and hernia policies. Having progressively been incorporated into a framework of legal doctrine, workmen's compensation policies had increasingly taken on the character and authority of binding law. This formal incorporation reflected a social transformation, in that the parties themselves had come to perceive their interests in compensation as consisting of rights and duties governed by rules. The law mainly provided the tools for the effectuation of this change and the fulfillment of the moral aspirations involved.

The transformation of policies into rules operates as a source of restraints on the administrator; his freedom of judgment is restricted by the necessity of justifying decisions by reasons founded in law. The emergence of rules points to the *restrictive* side of law; rules restrain discretion in problem-solving. But law is not only a limit on discretion; it also provides a *manner* of exercising discretion, a method of solving problems. Law does not consist only of rules; it also has special resources for making rules. One of the peculiar characteristics of the legal order is that it provides it own built-in principles of criticism, and through those its own sources of elaboration and change. It is for this reason that law is competent at the same time to affirm the authority of policies, and yet to expose this authority to challenge and open policies to change. Policies become more binding, but also less settled; concepts are sharpened, but their contours become more ambiguous. H. L. A. Hart has drawn attention to the "open texture of law."[3] By this he referred, rather narrowly, to the necessary indeterminacy of abstract formulations and the problems of meaning that arise at the margins of legal categories, when they are applied to concrete situations. This ambiguity arises initially from problems of classification that inhere in all language. But the "openness" of legal discourse has another, more specific source. In the legal process, meanings and classifications are subject to systematic scrutiny, especially when there is strong reliance on partisan criticism. In this effort, ambiguities are generated as new issues are raised. In the search for authoritative interpretations, there is a strain toward the formulation of larger principles, that help assess the meaning of concepts and policies. But those principles in turn open new avenues of argument and lay foundations for legal change. In this process, a built-in mechanism of evolution is created.

This paradox—that rules are unsettled as their authority is more strongly affirmed—can be better understood if we remain aware of the social foundations of authority, including legal authority. One critical condition of legitimacy is that government be useful and effective in meeting the problems and aspirations of society. If law is to keep the authority it affirms, it must ideally be responsive to the changing demands of those it governs. This it does by subjecting its own rules to a built-in process of analysis and elaboration. Indeed, the very act of taking rules seriously and recognizing their authority tends to make them the object of a more attentive scrutiny on the part of both government and the governed; more sophistication is required in interpreting and applying them. Rationales are explored, inconsistencies are tested, concepts are defined; in this process, principles emerge, connections appear and are made with other previously unrelated sets of rules, which in turn supply new standards and concepts and provide tests and guidance for future elaboration. The more self-consciously this process is cultivated, the livelier are the institutions through which it is effectuated, the richer the sources of rules and the available principles of evaluation, the more one can speak of a developed law.

Thus the restraint law imposes lies finally less in the specific rules it provides than in the more general requirement that government exercise its authority through rules—existing, interpreted, amended, or new.[4] Accordingly, adjudication does not require the decider to "stick to the rules" or judge "by the rules" but it does require him to account for his decision through a process of justification *by rules and principles.* Law is thus responsive to problems, but in a special manner; it resolves new issues by refashioning old rules, making new rules out of old principles, and constructing new principles from new sets of settled rules.

Of course different legal systems vary in the extent to which they emphasize law as a set of rules, and a restriction on authority, or law as a process of generating rules, and an instrument of problem-solving. Such variations are closely related to differences in the character of the institutions through which the work of legal analysis is performed, especially in the degree to which those institutions are rooted in or severed from society.

Therefore, while law confers more authority on rules, it can also make them more unsettled, more open to refashioning and change by criticism in the light of a broader corpus of law. The legalization of workmen's compensation has not meant that statutory policies have become more rigid and restrictive. Indeed, the reverse has actually happened. The early commission's concern with administrative discretion and its impatience toward legal issues actually went along with an excessively strict conception of the restraints imposed by rules. The low respect the IAC had for law was associated with a rather overdrawn view of legal authority; it is in part because the law appeared so compelling and restrictive that the agency sought to free itself from legal rules. Both attitudes grew from a basically unsophisticated view of law; concerned as it was with practical and concrete action, the agency found legal issues unworthy of attention and sought to prevent them from arising. The commission paid a price for this neglect. Although it used considerable discretion in administering benefits, it did so within a framework of undeveloped statutory policies that remained unexamined; thereby it allowed statutory rules to preserve precisely the kind of narrowness and inflexibility that the agency was concerned to avoid.

With legalization, compensation policies became the object of a systematic process of scrutiny and elaboration. The incorporation of the statute into law supplied rich sources of concepts and principles by which policies could be tested and refashioned. In this process, the ideas and policies of the statute were profoundly transformed. As used by the early IAC, such concepts as "injury," "employment," "causation," "earnings," "disability," were common-sense ideas, the meaning of which was largely taken for granted. The commission had a rather mechanical conception of "injury"; some visible strain, blow, or precipitation of suffering had to be shown in order to prove the occurrence of an injury; psychic harms were taken into account only as incidents of more palpable physical injuries. "Employment," although conceived more broadly than in the common law contract doctrine, still encompassed almost only the activities that went on at the place of and during work; it did not include injuries arising on the way to work, at company parties, in private activities surrounding actual work. Those ideas of employment and injury were related to a rather crude notion of "causation," which required an almost visible link between events of work and an event of injury. As to "earnings," we read from a memorandum of a referee in 1939 that "the writer wishes to point out that we have been too blindly following payroll statements, and that we should start making inquiry in order that the working man may not be penalized"; income other than wages were not routinely considered, nor was inquiry made into possible differences between the earnings normally due, and the wages actually paid, which were often affected by layoffs, vacations, sickness, and other accidental leaves from work; the same earnings were used in the computation of both temporary and permanent disability benefits, even though the first compensate for short-term wage losses, while the second indemnify for long-term expected loss of ability to work. "Disability," especially in its permanent consequences, was rather strictly seen as a palpable impairment of function; feelings and pain without a medically demonstrated basis were not seen as compensable disability. The statutes of limitation were rather mechanically interpreted, without much discrimination as to when they began running in different kinds of injuries.[5]

Legalization has loosened those restrictions and has extended the benefits of the law to many classes of situations and claimants, that the commission had formerly and more or less inadvertently excluded. The trend is well documented in the legal literature.[6] Its practical significance is demonstrated by a study of changes in the amounts of compensation benefits disbursed over the past decade; more important than the aggregate increase of paid benefits is the finding that the nature of the benefits has been materially transformed: there has been a disproportionate increase in permanent disability benefit payments, as opposed to temporary disability and medical care costs. This suggests that in a growing number of cases that formerly involved only temporary disability benefits, the claimants are now found entitled to some permanent disability indemnity; this change only reflects the broadening of the concept of compensable disability.[7]

This work of expansion and elaboration of workmen's compensation law has proceeded largely without any support from the IAC, and indeed often against the desires of the agency. It was the product of committed legal advocacy carried up to the appellate courts. The latter bore the main burden of judicial discretion and legal policy-making, the "judicialized" IAC serving mainly as a forum for the confrontation of arguments and as a place where case records were built for the higher courts later to examine and evaluate. The IAC has typically responded to legal challenges, either by avoiding the issues or by deciding them on a conservative, "sticking to the rule" basis, and then being reversed by the appellate courts.[8] The attitude of the commission is illustrated by the following account of IAC policy on the compensability of heart diseases, written in 1952 by the chief counsel of the agency. The commission had previously followed a rather strict rule, under which heart diseases were compensable only if they were shown to be related to some "unusual work or exertion"; otherwise they were presumed to be the result of previous disease, rather than of employment. But the IAC had been overruled in several cases. The document states:

> . . . it became uncertain as to which line of decisions might be followed in any given case—*the tendency of the Commission to follow a more or less strict interpretation* of the McNamara rule, or *the more liberal view of the courts* as seen in the Knock, Fogarty, Nielsen and Mark cases. At this time the Calabresi case came before the Commission.
>
> . . . the Calabresi case, *Liberty Mutual Ins. Co.* v. *Ind. Acc. Com.*, 73 Cal. App. 2d. 555, 11 C.C.C. 66 (1946) . . . is well beyond the rule in the McNamara case, because there was nothing unusual or exceptional in the work he [the employee] was doing. It was hard work although normal to the employment. *The parties requested the Commission to make a decision which could be taken*

> *to the courts with a clear cut issue* so that doubt arising from the McNamara decision could be resolved. *Ordinarily in a case with the facts similar* to those in the Calabresi case *a denial award would have issued.* However for the purpose of establishing a test case *in accordance with the wishes of the parties,* a compensable award issued and was affirmed by the District Court. . . .
>
> The court pointed out that decided heart cases fall into three classes:
>
> 1. Those in which the Commission denied an award and the courts affirmed the denial. . . .
>
> 2. Cases in which the Commission awarded compensation and the courts affirmed the award. . . .
>
> 3. Cases in which the Commission denied an award and the courts annulled the denial. . . .
>
> The court then states, "The astonishing thing about the state of the decided cases is that *counsel have not cited nor have we found a California Appellate or Supreme Court case where the Commission has made an award of benefits in a heart case and such award has been annulled.*"[9] [Emphasis supplied.]

The point is that the courts did not prevent the IAC from extending the scope of compensation principles; indeed they served mainly to reverse overly restrictive agency interpretations.

Thus, far from restricting the exercise of discretion, legalization has rather facilitated it; the farther the movement has proceeded, the more issues, choices, and controversies have been engendered, the more the agency has been called upon to adapt, change, and make policies. But the discretion the commission has been offered in this process is of a special kind, one for which the agency has had little taste. Judicial discretion is discretion exercised by the making and interpretation of rules. In adjudication, the decider is compelled to *commit himself,* beyond the particular case at hand, to a general policy applicable to the *class* of all similar cases. This follows from the special burden of justification the adjudicator must bear. Given this feature of judicial discretion, we can understand better the reasons why the agency has, at different stages of its history, remained so reluctant to accept law and judicial accountability as the foundations of its authority. Those reasons were mainly two: (1) In view of his duty to justify decisions by rules, the adjudicator is brought to *see particular problems as instances of a class of problems.* (2) He *cannot decide without committing himself to some policy* by which the case and other problems of the same class will be decided. It is this latter burden, the burden of policy-making, that accounts for the reluctance of the "judicial" IAC to assume the full responsibilities of its role as adjudicator; the commission has preferred to "pass the buck" to the appellate courts. But this would not account for the attitude of the early IAC, which in spite of its weaknesses did have considerable political energy. At that time it was mainly the first reason that was operative; concerned with practical problems of social action, the old commission was particularly sensitive to the discrepancies between abstract formulations and concrete situations. It insisted on not being compelled to extend rulings made in particular cases to more general classes of problems. Expertise, rather than acknowledged rules, was to provide authority for its determinations.

Law and the Person. The larger aim behind the early commission's emphasis on administrative discretion was to keep policy responsive to the full variety of needs that injured employees might have. The common law had treated industrial accident cases as narrow claims of right, detached from their concrete social and human context; it had treated employees as strangers to their masters, judging their demands by the highly abstract and general principles of the law of negligence. In this way, the law had cut itself off from the special problems of industrial life. The IAC proposed a new approach; its concern would be not for the abstract individual, but for the whole human being; not for the plaintiff as a legal entity, but for the injured man and the full range of his problems, income, safety, physical and mental health, rehabilitation, and family adaptation.

For all its humane purposes, the welfare approach to compensation entailed some important costs for the injured man. First, by assuming a need for personal help, it effectively denied the injured man's competence to handle his own problems. The commission was thus called upon to manage the employee's life rather than to provide him opportunities to fulfill his wants and needs on his own. For instance, rehabilitation, medical care, and the expenditure of money awards had to be controlled by the agency rather than organized by the beneficiary himself. In 1921, to an employee who protested this treatment, the head of the Rating Department answered:

> You also state that you resent the imputations trusting your competency in handling the amount judiciously. That may be the case as far as you are concerned, but the Commission does not know that until after they have made an investigation and have gotten sufficient evidence to that effect. Not all men are able to handle an amount of money judiciously. Many of them in fact cannot be trusted to do so. Until such time it is proven otherwise the Commission must assume that any one man is no better than any one else.

A second and perhaps more important drawback of the welfare approach was that the demands of the employee were no longer taken at face value, but rather were treated as manifestations of, and opportunities to delve into, some more real, underlying problem. The injured man not only needed expert help in handling his problems; he also needed the agency to define what the problems were. It was up to the experts to identify true needs, just as it was their responsibility to prescribe and control treatment. The victims were in effect denied the competence to assert grievances and make criticisms. Indeed, the claimant who insisted on his demands was exposed to treatment as an "unreasonable." Thus, around 1914, the head of the Rating Department wrote a detailed paper on "How best to deal with the unreasonable claimant." In it he argued:

> The injured person who is *unreasonable* (*many are of the opinion that they are not receiving what is justly due them*), not dissatisfied, is either consciously or unconsciously simulating or exaggerating an injury. [Emphasis supplied.]

He suggested a number of means of preventing "unreasonable" claims: for example, long waiting periods, a low scale of benefits, forbidding the injured to supplement compensation with personal insurance, giving the selection of doctors to the employer and not allowing evidentiary value to the reports of the applicant's doctor, making all awards subject to reopening in case of change of conditions. "Unreasonableness" sometimes came to mean "dishonesty." In another paper of 1917, a referee argued:

> There is no doubt that as time passes, compensation benefits will tempt the unscrupulous.
>
> Claims resting upon the testimony of the employee alone should be regarded with increasing suspicion. In these cases the *history or career of the applicant for a respectable period before his injury will be instructive.* If he shows a *clean and industrious record his character will be in his favor.* If on the other hand he shows only a short period of employment by his present employer, and *frequent idle periods,* or *former compensated injuries, his career is open to suspicion.*
>
> Even an attending physician supporting such a claim by his testimony may become a proper subject for close investigation. In short, every fair device should be employed to uncover and entrap a faker or malingerer. Employers are entitled to the fullest protection against these classes, the benevolence of compensation laws is too valuable an asset of the community to be impaired by fraud, and the referee is the natural guardian against such attacks. [Emphasis supplied.]

And a report of the head of the Compensation Department in 1919 states:

> In many cases the disabled man, knowing that he will still receive his indemnity, does not try to return to work at the earliest date he can return to work and, therefore, the time when he returned to work could not be taken as the time of termination of temporary disability.

In other cases, as we have shown before, the "unreasonable" claimant exposed himself to being found "neurotic." His benefits were then adjusted for treatment by hospitalization, reduction of the award, and a forced return to work. Whether the claimant was "consciously or unconsciously exaggerating," whether he was "unscrupulous" or "neurotic," the issue was always one of doubt as to his competence and trustworthiness as a plaintiff. Did he have the "clean and industrious record" that would warrant recognizing him a reliable character?

That the commission gave little weight to the claimants' own wishes and grievances is indicated by its policy of discouraging legal representation of applicants and by the meager role it gave to injured workers in the proceedings on their claims. The commission knew best what was good for them; it would take up their side of the case. The results are illustrated in the following appellate case of 1932:

> Each insurance company and party in interest was represented by at least one attorney, while Black [the claimant] who appeared to have no knowledge as to the law or procedure, and who was most in need of an attorney to protect rights involved in a technical branch of the law, was without the aid of counsel. It is very apparent from an inspection of the record that he suffered for the want of advice and assistance of counsel, both in the preparation and presentation of his case. He sat mute during the proceeding, except when called as a witness by his adversaries.[10]

Those tendencies were of course partly fostered by the ideology of control that often colored the welfare perspective of the commission. In addition, when the authority of the IAC began declining in the 1920's, its notions of the "good" of injured workers were undoubtedly very much affected by the viewpoint of industry. In 1935, a member of the staff criticized the agency on the ground that too often "we give industry the benefit of the doubt upon the theory that we are perhaps punishing an unsatisfactory applicant."

It is arguable that the very purpose of assuming care of the claimant as a whole human being tended to divest him of his dignity as a person. This objective legitimated unrestrained inquiry into the character of the injured employee, and lent the inquiry the warrant and authority of expertise. The consequences were that (1) the disabled worker was subjected to extensive control over many spheres of his life; (2) discretion in the exercise of this control was maximized; and (3) agency judgments, having the weight of expertise, were placed above criticism. The victim's integrity as a person and citizen was thus always exposed to challenge. The assistance he received was accompanied by controls that made benefits quite precarious; they were liable to be withdrawn or adjusted whenever information about the man seemed to warrant some new treatment or, indeed, punishment; idleness, irregular work history, uncooperative behavior, or even previous compensation awards—a sign of what a member of the staff called "compensationitis"—were all proper grounds for some form of sanction. In effect, the recipient could be made to shape his life in accordance with norms imposed by the agency at its discretion. It was no hazard that injured employees were more vulnerable to this kind of treatment than employers and insurers. Given their higher status and their greater political and legal resources, the latter made up an effective constituency; they were more likely to be taken as competent critics. Before them, the claim to expertise stood more tenuous.

By its tendency to discount the grievances of injured claimants, the IAC was unexpectedly depriving itself of a source of information and impetus in the pursuit of the very aims of welfare it sought to realize. This loss was not so significant as long as the agency kept its own dynamism. It became critical when, after 1920, the commission began to lose many of the administrative resources upon which its expertise and authority depended. The discounting of claimants, coupled with the broad discretion and the attendant lack of determinate standards governing decisions, made the IAC extremely vulnerable to the influence of the perspectives and standards promoted by employers and insurers. In addition, the latter were allowed to exercise the same discretion in the same manner in their own relations with claimants; they had primary control over the adjustment of claims, and the surveillance of the commission was weak and of limited effectiveness. The aims and processes of the IAC became therefore seriously exposed to corruption by the interests of industry.

With legalization, the injured employee was transformed from a passive recipient into a demanding applicant, from an object of public action into a person with a status and rights of its own. The change was, of course, facilitated by other transformations in the character of the parties and of the agency itself. The loss of instruments of control compelled the agency to rely more on help and encouragement than on direction and surveillance; the erosion of administrative expertise made it increasingly necessary to take the injured man's complaints at face value. The growing political and social competence of labor brought added weight to the workers' demands. But legalization itself made a critical contribution to the change, owing to the restraints it placed on administrative discretion.

Here again, legal restraint had both a restrictive and a liberating influence. It was restrictive in the sense that the scope of inquiry into and control over the injured man's life was sharply reduced to what appeared relevant and permissible under determinate rules. What moved the IAC was no longer a concern for the *whole man*; its mission was now confined to the definition of a *specific social and legal status.*

But law was also liberating. Specifically, it freed the injured employee from his dependence upon agency and industry notions of what was good for him; it compelled the commission and employers to respond to demands and problems they had formerly kept outside the compass of their concerns. The major reason for this change was that legalization prevented the IAC from discounting the claimants' demands. The incompetence of the injured *man* did not matter any longer; the only issue was: Did his *argument* have any validity? Law gave the injured employee the right to demand and criticize, as well as authoritative instruments by which this right could be effectuated. From an *object* of government, the legal process made him an *actor* in government.

This transition from fulfillment of needs to recognition of rights and status is described in the following letter written in 1935 by a deputy commissioner to the head of the Rating Department. The IAC resented the change quite bitterly:

> . . . . the applicant seeks to get as much as possible, and the carrier seeks to pay as little as possible. Both sides may be and frequently are badly mistaken as to the facts. . . . These facts in turn are highly colored by the viewpoint the parties may hold as to the purpose of compensation legislation.
>
> . . . . Labor's viewpoint, for the most part, has been that all compensation, in its final analysis, is damages, and their sole goal for many years has been to push up the amount of recovery and to enlarge the field of those entitled to recovery. Any fair analysis of the industrial set-up must convince you that the rights of the few who have a bona fide claim for recovery have been minimized or reduced in order to give benefits to a large number who, except for compensation, would have no possible recovery. In other words, what I term "chicken feed" recoveries have been at the expense of that element of our industrial workers who have sustained a real disability.

Thus, the commission was losing its ability to do good, but rights were more broadly recognized; concepts of "real" and "bona fide" needs were being subverted, but the parties' aims and demands were acquiring more weight.

Today, the injured worker no longer appears before the commission as a recipient of rehabilitative care; he is a citizen having his day in court. The IAC is a place where he challenges his employer and affirms his rights as citizen and employee. He stands there with his own lawyer, as does his employer. His claims are what moves the agency to act and his word counts; his testimony, most often unsupported, has in almost all cases determinative evidentiary value. The sole work of the commission is to assess his claims and lend them the protection of legal authority.

Law and Politics

Perhaps the most striking feature of this pattern of legal development is its dependence upon a close relation of law and politics. This is apparent from the crucial role that interest groups and political controversy have played in the evolution of the IAC. We have discussed earlier the significance of political resources in the growth of legal competence; we have also seen how the sponsorship of representative groups gives impetus to legal advocacy, by gearing it to the needs and aspirations of a constituency. This link of advocacy to class interests made law politically effective and meaningful, and provided a source of dynamic legal development.

It is worth noting at this point how much the administrative philosophy of the early IAC contributed to the emergence of this pattern. Those features of the commission that made for its weakness as an administrator of public policy also helped to transform the agency into a site of flourishing legalization. The emphasis on self-help and voluntarism tended to tie administration to political interests and to blur the distinction between public ends and the private aims of the parties. The agency had thus placed itself in a position where it would be inclined, and indeed compelled, to be responsive to the demands of affected persons and groups. Furthermore, the adversary structure of the compensation system underscored the necessity for the parties to have effective means of pressing their claims. As the agency retreated from its active role, labor was continuously reminded that workers could not count on much protection from the commission and would eventually have to rely upon their own strength. Finally, the weaker the competence of the agency became, the less authority its administrative judgments were able to carry. The agency had lost its qualifications for prescribing what were the best interests of employer and employee. The parties themselves had become the judges of that question. It was therefore easier for them to press the IAC to renounce administrative discretion, and easier for the IAC to settle for the role of an adjudicator. Thus, although the agency had expressly sought to avoid the intrusion of law and adversary contentions in its program, its own strategy of administration helped lay the foundations for a quite different institutional outcome.

The Privatization of Public Policy. This institutional link between judicialization and the growing political initiative of interested groups had important implications for the character of compensation policies. Briefly, one might say that the legalization of workmen's compensation went along with a privatization of its public welfare aims.

Initially, as we have seen, workmen's compensation was seen as entirely divorced from the employment relation and the concerns of the private law of employer and employee. Its purpose was to remove industrial accident problems from the realm of free contract, and to make them a responsibility of society. The new legislation was interested in the injured man as a poor man, rather than as an employee; it was a welfare program, a War on Poverty, and not a regulation of employment. Compensation was a matter of public concern; injured men's claims were demands to the state, not to the employer. In practice, of course, this idea received important qualifications. Compensation was based on a liability, and responsibility for payment was in effect vested in the employer. But liability was considered only a means of financing the program, one that did not detract from its public character; and the "direct payment" system was conceived of as a kind of delegation of state authority to the employers, who were thus entrusted with a public mandate, always liable to be revoked. Those views fitted nicely in the ideology of welfare capitalism, which envisioned that industry would, out of good will and a sense of civic responsibility, provide for the welfare of its employees beyond and apart from its strict legal contractual obligations to them. That welfare was not seen as an ingredient of the law of employment is indicated by the policy, continued well into the 1930's, of avoiding the incorporation of private benefit plans in collective agreements or individual contracts of services.[11] Welfare was a matter of public or civic responsibility, not a duty between employer and employee.

However, this purported segregation of welfare and the contract of employment could not long be maintained. By assuming control over the administration of workmen's compensation, industry inevitably committed itself to the program. Operationally, if not in theory, liability and "direct payment" established a bridge between public welfare and the relation of employer and employee. Workmen's compensation became, for most practical purposes, a responsibility of the employer, independent of the aims and control of the state. Public welfare therefore tended to be "privatized." It implicitly became a duty of the employer *qua* employer. Labor's own emphasis on self-help and voluntarism would further contribute to remove welfare from the ambit of the state. When workers acquired independent means of promoting their interests through unions, welfare matters increasingly became a bargaining issue between them and employers, with the state confined to a role of support and arbitration. Just as private and formerly unilateral welfare plans have been made objects of bargaining between unions and industry, so have public welfare programs, including workmen's compensation, been supplemented, adapted, and refashioned through collective agreements.[12] Thus, legally and institutionally, workmen's compensation has been absorbed into the private setting of the employment relation. This outcome was accomplished in two ways: (1) First, by assuming control over the program, industry implicitly accepted it as a responsibility of its own. (2) Later, through collective bargaining, the compensation legislation was woven into the contractual law of employment. Today, each policy issue is a controversy between industry and organized labor, and each particular claim is a challenge by the worker against his employer.

This does not mean that the welfare ideals of early workmen's compensation have been entirely lost. The incorporation of public policy into the law of employment has fostered important changes in legal ideas governing the relations of employer and employee. Welfare made the concrete human problems of the employee relevant again to the conduct of work relations. The worker would no longer be regarded as a mere object on the market and otherwise a stranger. The focus of attention was displaced from contract, the mere exchange of services for wages, to the broader set of social conditions created by the employment relation. This paved the way toward an enlargement of the legal concept of employment and a recognition of the employee as a person with a status and rights to be legally protected.

By itself, however, welfare was unable to accomplish this evolution. It treated the worker as a human being, but not as a person. The effort to help the "whole man" tended to divest him of his rights. It took a return to the law and its impersonal system of governance by rules to transform the values evolved through welfare into a secure set of rights. This return was facilitated by the privatization of public welfare. Welfare was redefined as a set of definable interests to be aggressively and self-servingly pursued by the parties. From a provider of care, the employer became a debtor. The needs the worker had as a man, dependent upon the understanding and generosity of his master, were transformed into specific claims he asserted as an employee. The resources of private law, including the law of employment, were made relevant as tools for vesting benefits as legally protected rights. From a stranger, and later a human being, the disabled employee became a person, with rights that took account of his condition and needs, which protected his autonomy and dignity by a web of impersonal rules.[13]

But the attenuation of public aims and governmental responsibility that went along with this evolution has entailed important costs. This is quite apparent in the declining significance of rehabilitation and public health as goals of workmen's compensation. More important, privatization has profoundly weakened the idea that government is responsible for bringing assistance to the more incompetent and helpless members of its constituency. It has promoted a view of the injured claimant as a full-fledged citizen, equal under law, and to be treated accordingly. While this evolution made law more responsive to his demands, more ready to recognize him as a carrier of rights, it also left many needs unfulfilled: to the many workers who have no connection with a union, and no way of getting to a lawyer, to the many whose union is tame or resourceless, or who fall in the hands of incompetent attorneys, to all those who have no opportunity to learn their rights, and no support in asserting their claims, the attenuation of public responsibility has been a considerable loss.

This dependence of the legal process on self-help and self-serving advocacy can give impetus and direction to legal change. But for the very reason that it makes law more responsive to political demands, it also tends to distort the balance of interests in the legal order. The recognition of legal interests becomes dependent upon those interests as they are defined by affected groups, and upon what resources those groups are able to muster for political and legal action. Even where representative groups are powerful and articulate, the citizen tends to be captive of their special commitments and perspectives. It is no unmitigated blessing for employers and injured workers that insurance and unions have provided for their representation. Among workers, there are many for whom organized labor has had little concern, and whom it has sacrificed to the narrower interests of its active membership. The increased richness and vitality of the law is therefore purchased at the price of added obstacles to the realization of legal ideals. Justice develops greater potentials, but equality becomes more problematic.

Political Tensions in the Legal Order. This problem is all the more significant as political tensions tend to strain the capacity of legal institutions to define and affirm the values and policies of the legal order. The reduction of public responsibilities we have observed in the IAC is but one aspect of a larger phenomenon. When legal advocacy acquires greater political significance and the legal process becomes an arena of political controversy, the authority of legal institutions becomes more vulnerable. One characteristic response that is illustrated by the IAC is to evade the responsibility for making and affirming legal policies. Therefore, those very features of the legal process that enhance its potentials also make the realization of those potentials more difficult.

One traditional source of strength and security for legal institutions was relative insulation from political controversy. The making of policy and the creation of rights have always been central tasks of the judicial system; but the system was sparingly used and its work had little visibility, being viewed as focused on particular cases of narrowly confined import. As long as the claims dealt with remain isolated individual disputes, as long as decisions appear bound to the case at hand, as long as precedents are made almost without knowing it, it is comparatively easy for the courts to assert their authority in defining the values and standards of the legal order. These conditions change when the pursuit of legal interests is organized under the sponsorship of groups. The aggregation of legal demands underscores their political import and authority is then exposed to more serious challenges. This tendency to politicize legal debate is by no means confined to the narrow setting of workmen's compensation. It corresponds to a characteristic trend of the modern social and legal order. The increasing demands on government to solve the problems of society, the growth of representative organizations, the extension of citizenship, all contribute to make law and legal institutions the target of more active and more deliberately concerted appeals.

It is about this process, and the kinds of strains and responses it arouses in the administration of justice, that we can learn from the experience of the IAC. When a court enjoys a well-guarded political immunity it may be capable of withstanding a high exposure to political controversy. The blurring of law and politics serves then to create opportunities for extending the role of law in society, and legal institutions can assume leadership in defining and affirming the moral commitments of the political community.

But when judicial authority lacks political immunity, the response is more likely to resemble that of the IAC—a defensive retreat from politics and a flight from policy. It is through the appellate courts, not through the IAC, that the legal development of workmen's compensation has proceeded. In the commission, the impoverishment of the legal process was particularly visible in the efforts of the agency to avert legal controversies. In a more subtle form, it was apparent in the growth of legalistic modes of adjudication. We speak of "legalism" when insistence on legal rules or modes of reasoning tends to frustrate the purposes of public policy. Law is then presented as abstract, rigid, and unable to respond to actual needs; those who invoke it are made to appear irrational, or indeed irresponsible. Legalism tends to weaken the authority of the law in the eyes of those whose needs and aspirations are frustrated; legal institutions come to seem ineffective and arbitrary, and tend to lose their claim to reasoned obedience.

Basically, legalism is an issue about the competence of the law as an instrument of problem-solving. That is not to say that whenever the law frustrates certain aspirations or grows costly to certain interests it thereby becomes legalistic. The legal process, like any other mode of social ordering, affects and can expressly be used to alter the balance of interests. The law also tends to promote certain values, such as accountability and respect for the person, at the expense of other social aims. The idea of legalism suggests more than merely the range of costs attendant on the normal functioning of legal institutions. What it points to is a pathology of the legal order, an impoverishment of its competence, rather than any cost flowing from the use or development of the law. Legalism develops when emphasis on specific rules and technicalities of the law prevents a response to problems and demands that the legal order would otherwise be competent and inclined to meet by a creative use of its own principles.

Symptoms of legalism in the IAC were its rigid and myopic interpretations of rules pertaining to the assessment of disability, even when the very rationale of those rules called for greater openness and flexibility. Even more significant was its appeal to the standards of judicial office as requiring that it renounce its authority over matters, such as medical expertise and counseling of unrepresented claimants, in which the integrity of its judicial processes was directly at stake. It has never occurred to the commission that, as a judicial guardian of the principles of workmen's compensation, it might have to assume responsibility for promoting the legal competence of its constituents. This failure occurred in spite of a long tradition of administrative concern and, indeed, at a time when the courts and government, in other domains of the law, were recognizing new responsibilities for making citizens equal and effective participants in the legal order.

Today, the agency seems to cling to those very conceptions of law that in its administrative role it once abhorred; and yet, as a court, its responsibilities call for a kind of affirmative authority that has much in common with what it formerly aspired to. The concessions that the early IAC made to the values of self-help, and that reduced its power as an administrator, also laid the foundations for those patterns of legal advocacy which today would require that the agency return to a more assertive use of its authority.

One may conceive of this historical dilemma of the IAC as a quest for a new conception of the mission of state and law in society, one that would reconcile the concerns of the liberal state for the demands and interests of the person with the efforts of the welfare state to play a more active role in the pursuit of social aspirations. The IAC has not succeeded in resolving this problem; it remains, now as before, torn between an overly ambitious notion of government action and an overly restrictive view of the limits of law. In more positive terms, the problems of the commission point to a basic dilemma of government: How can authority respond to demands for participation without impairing its ability to preserve the integrity of policy? This dilemma cannot be resolved until agencies of government find means to overcome the contradictory requirements of authority and participation, and learn to keep their self-confidence while being responsive. What is needed is a more humble and realistic conception of authority, that would acknowledge the dependence of power on criticism and free government from a too severe test of acceptance and respect; and a more positive view of the value of participation, as enhancing the competence of authority to define and realize public aims.

The ideals and experience of the legal process have much to contribute to this reconstruction of authority, and there are signs that this may come about. The attempt to construct a "welfare law," under which the purposes of social action would be related to the development of citizenship and the rights of persons, is a characteristic concern of the contemporary legal order. The IAC may eventually find in those efforts an answer to its own institutional problems.

Notes to Chapter IX

1. Philip Selznick in collaboration with Philippe Nonet and Howard Vollmer, *Law, Society and Industrial Justice* (New York: Harper and Row, in press), Chap. I.

2. An earlier version of this policy statement is published in *Proceedings of the 5th Annual Meeting of the International Association of Industrial Accident Boards and Commissions* (I.A.I.A.B.C.), *September 1918* (Washington, D.C.: U.S. Department of Labor, Bureau of Labor Statistics, 1919), Bulletin No. 264, p. 175.

3. H. L. A. Hart, *The Concept of Law* (Oxford: Clarendon Press, 1961), pp. 121–150.

4. This point is related to the view expressed by Lon L. Fuller that law is "the enterprise of subjecting human conduct to the governance of rules." Lon L. Fuller, *The Morality of Law* (New Haven: Yale University Press, 1964), p. 96.

5. The Industrial Accident Commission was equally indiscriminate in its interpretation of the limits of its continuing jurisdiction. In a letter written to a referee in 1939, the chief of the Compensation Department remembered that "prior to some six or eight years ago, this commission did not realize that it had any authority to award medical treatment beyond a period of 240 weeks" even though the law set no time limit on the right to medical treatment.

6. See, for instance, from the point of view of an applicant's lawyer, Samuel B. Horowitz, "Current Trends in Workmen's Compensation," *The Law Society Journal*, XII (1947), 465–538, 611–682, 765–790; from the standpoint of a defense lawyer, Warren L. Hanna, *The Law of Employee Injuries and Workmen's Compensation*, II, *Principles* (Albany, Calif.; Hanna Legal Publications, 1953), 136–156; and from a legal scholar's point of view; Stefan Riesenfeld, "Forty Years of American Workmen's Compensation," *Minnesota Law Review*, XXXV (1951), 525–548.

7. *Report of the Workmen's Compensation Study Commission* (Sacramento: State of California, April, 1965), pp. 13–58, especially pp. 45–46.

8. Of course, the Industrial Accident Commission has much more often been upheld than reversed in appellate proceedings, as all its statistics indicate. But this test is not relevant. The majority of appellate cases do not involve significant issues of policy. What matters here is the respective positions taken by the IAC and the courts in the few but critical cases where definite challenges are made to prevailing policies. This is admittedly hard to measure in any precise way. Our argument relies mainly on documentary evidence.

9. *Partial Report of the Senate Committee on Labor on Workmen's Compensation Benefits* (Sacramento: California Legislature, 1955), pp. 160–161. The primary role of the courts in liberalizing workmen's compensation is further emphasized in the same report, pp. 264 ff. It must be noted that the commission is not apologetic about this fact at all; indeed, it insists that it has had no part in expanding the principles of compensation.

10. *Black* v. *IAC* (Johnston), 18 IAC 206, 215 Cal. 639, 12 P. 2d. 640 (1932).

11. See Abraham Weiss, "Union Welfare Plans," in J. B. S. Hardman and Maurice F. Neufeld (eds.), *The House of Labor* (New York: Prentice-Hall, 1951), pp. 276–289.

12. On private welfare plans and workmen's compensation, see Duncan McIntyre "Workmen's Compensation and Private Benefit Programs," *Industrial and Labor Relations Review,* VII (October, 1955) 63–72; Harland Fox, "Company Supplements to Workmen's Compensation," *Management Record* (National Industrial Conference Board, January, 1955), XVII, 19–22.

13. A similar point is made in connection with the "human relations" ideology in industry, in Philip Selznick in collaboration with Philippe Nonet and Howard Vollmer, *op. cit.,* Chap. III.

Index